Key Terms in Semiotics

Key Terms in Semiotics

Bronwen Martin and Felizitas Ringham

continuum

Continuum
The Tower Building, 11 York Road, London SE1 7NX
80 Maiden Lane, Suite 704, New York, NY 10038

www.continuumbooks.com

British Library Cataloguing-in-Publication Data
A catalogue record for this book is available from the British Library.

ISBN 0-8264-8455-7 (hardback)
0-8264-8456-5 (paperback)

Typeset by BookEns Ltd, Royston, Herts
Printed and bound in Great Britain by
MPG Books Ltd, Bodmin, Cornwall

Contents

Introduction

As a critical theory, semiotics has increasingly gained ground in the last two or three decades. It is now included in many secondary education literature programmes as well as in academic surveys. The approach was also quick to establish itself within the fields of media, film, and advertising and in recent years has widened its field of investigation to include, for example, law, architecture, psychology, music and the natural sciences. Yet whereas research into the discipline has advanced – particularly in France – to many the very term 'semiotics' has remained an enigma and its appeal restricted. This book proposes to familiarize students – or indeed anyone interested in language and meaning – with the semiotic approach. There will be a brief outline of the aims of semiotic theory, its history and working method. This will be followed by a reference section providing definitions of terms used in semiotic metalanguage, by twelve short essays on key thinkers and finally by an example of semiotic analysis applied to a text.

Whilst focusing primarily on the Paris School of Semiotics, the dictionary recognizes the contribution of other schools: indeed we note an increasing cross-fertilization and a growing convergence between the European and American branches of semiotics. A number of critical terms and theories have also been included, which, though not strictly semiotic, nevertheless afford the student a wider perspective and background to the subject. As the borderline between linguistics and semiotics is extremely fluid, we also feel that the explanation of some more general linguistic and narratological terms could be helpful to anyone undertaking a semiotic/textual analysis.

What is semiotics? What does semiotics mean?

The term semiotics is derived from the Greek word *sèmeion*, denoting 'sign'. Already, in the seventeenth century, the philosopher John Locke referred to *semiotika*, which he defined as '*the Doctrine of Signs*, [. . .]; the business whereof, is to consider the Nature of Signs, the Mind makes use of for the understanding of Things, or conveying its Knowledge to others'.[1]

In modern usage the concept semiotics refers to a theory of signification. There are different branches of semiotics under this heading. There is an American branch, for instance, strongly influenced by Charles Sanders Peirce, which focuses on logic and meaning and has become central in linguistics linked to philosophy. Much of Peirce's work is devoted to the development of sign categories such as making a distinction between icon, index and symbol.[2] This approach differs considerably from European semiotics represented by the *Ecole de Paris* [Paris School] and founded by Algirdas Julien Greimas. The Paris School is concerned primarily with the relationship between signs and with the manner in which they produce meaning within a given text or discourse. Importance is attached not only to the elaboration of theories but also to their application as methodological tools for textual analysis. Compared to Peirce, the Paris School thus takes a more wide-reaching approach and, in the final analysis, is of greater practical use.

Semiotics according to the Paris School posits the existence of universal structures that underlie and give rise to meaning. These structures are susceptible to representation in the shape of models which – conversely – can also be applied to any signifying object to decode and interpret its effects of meaning. A concern with structures, however, does not mean that semiotics is synonymous with structuralism, a theory concerned solely with the perception and description of structures. Neither is it simply a sign system, and should not be confused with semiology. Nor is it confined to the theories of Roland Barthes. Semiotics, in fact, has a much wider aim: the theory purports to explore the generation of signification in all its forms. Semiotics thus covers all disciplines and signifying systems as well as all social practices. And as the leading semiotician Jacques Fontanille has pointed out, its ultimate aim is *une critique des valeurs,* that is, a critique of the values underlying all signifying practices, a mission that becomes all the more urgent in an age of rapid technological and socioeconomic change. Semiotic practice can thus become a tool of personal empowerment and an expression of social commitment, leading not only to a deconstruction but also to a reinvention of the fundamental values underlying our societies. It is the expression of human freedom and creativity in the face of dominant ideologies and dominant power groups. In the words of Greimas himself, it is a new humanism.

Semiotics and the *Ecole de Paris*: a brief history

In 1985, when speaking about the development of semiotic theory, Algirdas Julien Greimas, the founder of the *Ecole de Paris*, said: 'My theoretical genius, if I can so call it, was a form of ''bricolage''. I took a little Lévi-Strauss and added some Propp . . .'. He also said that, as a linguist, he was more inspired by Dumézil and Lévi-Strauss than by other linguists, 'with the exception of Saussure and Hjelmslev of course'.[3]

It all started at the beginning of the twentieth century with the Swiss linguist Ferdinand de Saussure, who was the first to apply scientific theory to the study of language and to relate this science to social psychology. It was he who introduced the term *sémiologie*, which he defined as forming a link between linguistics and psychology.

Saussure viewed language as a social phenomenon. His great contribution to its study was the discovery that meaning does not reside in individual words but in a complex system of relationships or structures. His motto was: 'Il n'y a de sens que dans la différence' [There can be no meaning without difference]. He pointed out that language structures could be explored by describing them in their current form (synchronically) or historically (diachronically). Saussure is perhaps best known for having divided the language phenomenon into *langue* (abstract language system, language as a structured system of signs) and *parole* (the individual utterances, or speech, making use of the abstract system). In his study of language, however, Saussure went even further. He applied the structure principle to the individual sign or word. The linguistic sign, according to him, is characterized by the relationship of its two components: the 'sound-image' or material substance which he named *signifiant* (signifier) and its 'concept' or *signifié* (signified).

If Saussure and his revolutionary findings[4] paved the way for structuralism and semiotics, the same can be said for the Dane Louis Hjelmslev and the Linguistic Circle of Copenhagen. Even without any immediate link to the Swiss linguist, Hjelmslev's theoretical approach was very close to that of Saussure, whose work he can be said to have continued. In his *Prolegomena to a Theory of Language* (1943) he formalized language, dividing the phenomenon into 'system' and 'process'. Hjelmslev also refined the Saussurean definition of the two aspects of the language-sign by recognizing two fundamental levels or planes of language, one of 'expression' and one of 'content'. Each one of these, he believed, was possessed of a 'substance' and a 'form'. Hjelmslev's contribution to linguistics included his theory of the semiotic function which he defined as existing between the twin aspects of the signifying act – between signifier and signified (according to Saussure) or between expression and content (according to Hjelmslev). Finally, Hjelmslev extended his semiological studies to incorporate non-verbal language systems such as traffic lights or the chimes of Big Ben.

Like Hjelmslev, the anthropologist Claude Lévi-Strauss found a new territory to which he applied a linguistic-structuralist approach. Lévi-Strauss set out to identify the constituent parts of cultural behaviour which he studied as if it were a language phenomenon. Searching for the semantic structure (the 'language system' or *langue*) that underpins culture, his concern focused on 'myths'. He analysed myths from different cultures and discovered a number of recurrent elements – which he called 'mythemes' (as compared to 'phonemes' or 'morphemes' in linguistics) – and functions that seemed to operate like the components of universal signifying structures.[5]

At the same time an earlier study by the Russian folklorist Vladimir Propp appeared in English translation.[6] Close analysis of 100 fairy-tales had led Propp to establish an analogy between language structure and the organization of narrative. He identified 31 functions or fundamental components that formed the basis of any tale. A function in this sense is a unit of 'narrative language', such as 'a difficult task is proposed to the hero' (25), or 'the villain is punished' (30). The 31 functions, moreover, were distributed amongst seven spheres of action including those of villain, donor and helper. The narrative taxonomy developed by Propp as well as his model are still held to be valid by researchers today.

Such was the groundbase that inspired Algirdas Julien Greimas to compose the founding work of what was to become semiotics: *Sémantique structurale*, 1966 [Structural Semantics]. This seminal text contained the axiomatic base of a scientific theory, anticipated hypotheses for subsequent research and provided samples of semiotic practice, demonstrating its value as a tool for discovery. It marked the starting point of a scientific project which is still today in the process of developing. Over many years, Greimas and a group of researchers dedicated themselves in weekly meetings to elaborating, testing, changing and refining a theory of signification. The meetings took place at the *Ecole des Hautes Etudes* in Paris to which Greimas had been appointed. It was there that the Paris School of Semiotics originated.

The development of semiotic theory took place in several phases. The first stage focused, within the context of structuralist thought, on the problematics of semantics as demonstrated by the very title of Greimas' *Sémantique structurale*. Saussure's notion of meaning resulting from relationships had inspired Greimas to analyse and define specific kinds of difference. He first identified the distinctive traits of oppositions and produced a typology. Oppositive properties were then categorized to be used as working concepts in the elaboration of a rudimentary signifying structure. At the same time, the encounter with Propp's work encouraged Greimas to apply linguistic models to narrative. In an attempt to reformulate the elements of narrativity, he discovered that what Propp had called 'function' was in fact a verb plus actants (someone or something executing or undergoing an act), that is, a complete sentence. He also found that it was possible to reduce Propp's seven spheres of action to three pairs of binary opposition (subject/object; sender/receiver; helper/opponent) that would describe any narrative structure.

The theoretical advances made during this first stage of development concerned two apparently heterogeneous areas: on the one hand the search for an elementary structure of meaning comprising the logical classification of paradigmatic differences; and on the other, the formulation of a theory of narrativity which streamlined Propp's syntagmatic model into the components of a narrative grammar. During the second phase of semiotic research, in the 1970s, attempts were made to find a synthesis between these different fields in order to define a consistent general theory of the generation of meaning.

Concentrating on the surface structures of narrative, semioticians discovered that function, as represented by an action verb, was over-determined by modalities: two virtualizing (wanting, having to) and two actualizing (knowing how to, being able to). When this discovery was pushed to its extremes, it emerged that the entire narrative grammar was in fact composed merely of modalities plus content, that is, semantics. This allowed for powerful models to be constructed. Moreover, these models could also be applied to social practices and behaviour patterns. Narrativity was no longer seen to be the exclusive property of the written text. From then on it was perceived as underlying all discourse and accounting for the organization of the social world.

Research during this period also showed that Propp's formula of the tale could be broken down into important sequences which together reflected the stages of all human action. The sequences – manipulation, action, sanction – were condensed into what came to be known as the canonical narrative schema. This was found to be applicable not only to stories but to a great variety of texts (e.g. legal, culinary, journalistic, etc.) and, in the end, to something as basic as man's quest for the meaning of life.

While work on the surface level of narrative structures progressed, essential findings on the abstract or deep level of signification yielded the link needed to perfect semiotic theory. Greimas proposed a visual representation of the elementary structure of meaning: the semiotic square. This is the logical expression of any semantic category showing all possible relationships that define it, that is, opposition, contradiction and implication. It was discovered, moreover, that apart from illustrating opposing relationships, this square also portrays the operations they generate. In fact, it allows us to retrace a process or the trajectory of a subject performing acts of transformation. In other words, the semiotic square not only represents underlying categories of opposition but also gives account of surface structures of narrative syntax. At the end of the 1970s, all the semiotic findings of the last two decades were published in an authoritative dictionary by Algirdas Julien Greimas and Joseph Courtés: *Sémiotique, dictionnaire raisonné de la théorie du langage* (Paris: Hachette, 1979).

In the *Dictionnaire* semiotic theory appeared to have found its ultimate expression: its working concepts were defined seemingly once and for all, its models ready to be applied. This was, however, not the case. Research continued. The major preoccupation during the years following the publication of the *Dictionnaire* concerned the discursive level of meaning. This level relates to the figurative and enunciative surface of an utterance which gives expression to, and is supported by, the underlying semio-narrative structures. During the 1980s and 1990s, efforts concentrated in particular on aspectualities, that is, the spatial, temporal and actorial organization of texts. Concern with aspectual problematics also led to renewed investigation of systems of valuation. How does a being, an object, a time or a place assume value? And to whom? The last few semiotic seminars at the *Ecole des Hautes Etudes* in Paris were devoted to the study of 'Truth', 'Beauty', 'Good and Evil' and how these classic values function in language. It was discovered that the system of valuation for each one of them operated along different aspectual lines. Morality, for instance, seemed to fall within the categories of 'excess' and 'insufficiency', while the study of aesthetics revealed the aspects of being accomplished (perfect) or unfinished (imperfect) as determining factors. This discovery was all the more important as the aspectual categories concerned were not oppositive or binary but gradual. It was not a question of 'either or' but of 'more or less'.

While the new findings contributed to semiotic knowledge, they also challenged earlier notions, including the logical bases of the elementary structure of signification. In 1983, Greimas wrote an article, *Le Savoir et le croire: un seul univers cognitif* [Knowing and believing: a single universe of cognition], in which he presented for the first time a semiotic square based on gradual transformation and not on contradiction and oppositive stages.[7] In 1986, the second volume of *Sémiotique, dictionnaire raisonné de la théorie du langage* was published. It reflects both the large number of contributors now engaged in research and a science still in the process of being defined.

In the final years before his death in 1992, Greimas focused his attention on 'passions' and the thymic sphere. Passions were no longer described in terms of modal structures but were reinterpreted in aspectual terms and specific discursive sequences. Simultaneously, attempts were made to define deep-level aspectualities which concern specific valorizations.

Looking back over this period, it would seem that the mid and late 1980s marked a turning point in the evolution of semiotics, heralding what came to be known as the 'new semiotics'. A resurgence of interest in Merleau-Ponty as well as in the philosopher Antonio R. Damasio contributed to a move away from narrative, from an 'objective semiotics', towards a concentration on the figurative level and on the role of the body in the construction of meaning. The focus is now on *le discours en acte*, that is, on the process whereby meaning emerges from sensations and emotions.

The increased importance accorded the subject led to a reformulation of what is known as the semiotic function, that is, the relationship between the two levels of language (Hjelmslev), the level of expression or signifier and the level of content or signified. Instead of this relationship being purely formal or fixed, it is now seen to be determined uniquely by the position of the perceiving subject. The imaginary body or *corps propre* takes up a position between the perception of the outer world of sensations and the inner world of feelings and affects. As a result significance is no longer considered only as stable, conceptual and cognitive, but also as a process of an emotional, emotive or passionate nature.

The switch of emphasis towards 'the inner self' led to the further development of a semiotics of passion. The year 1991 saw the publication of the seminal text *Sémiotique des passions* [The Semiotics of Passions] in which A. J. Greimas and Jacques Fontanille elaborate a canonical schema of passion, that is, they present a trajectory divided into four sequences: predisposition, sensitization, emotion and moralization – a model that has since been successfully applied to music as well as to literature. This book was followed in 1995 by Anne Hénault's *Le Pouvoir comme passion* [Power as Passion] and in 1997 by Jean-Claude Coquet's *La Quête du sens* [The Quest for Meaning], in which the contribution of Merleau-Ponty to the change of direction is also examined. Studies of jealousy in Proust, as well as those of avarice and of anger, were produced.

At the same time a semiotics of the senses was beginning to emerge. Attention was initially paid to the position of the observer in the text. Examples include Denis Bertrand's study of Emile Zola's *Germinal* in *L'Espace et le sens* [Space and Meaning] published in 1985 and Jacques Fontanille's *Les Espaces subjectifs: introduction à la sémiotique de l'observateur*, 1989 [Subjective Spaces: Introduction to the Semiotics of the Observer], in which he also examines film and painting.

This movement away from narrative and fixed structure was heralded by Greimas himself in his seminal text published in 1987, *De l'imperfection* [On Imperfection], a landmark in the history of semiotics. Here he introduces into semiotics the concept of the aesthetic, that is, beauty apprehended as sensory bodily presence. For Greimas, the aesthetic defines the mode of appearing of things, the unique way they reveal themselves to us before any preliminary codification. He links the experience of beauty with the aspectual moment of the finished or perfect: it is the moment at which subject and object fuse in a state of ecstatic indifferentiation. The experience is frequently marked by a process of synaesthesia. The book contains studies of writers such as Michel Tournier, Rainer Maria Rilke and Italo Calvino, and examines not only vision but also smell, taste and touch.

From the late 1980s onwards research continued to flourish in the fields of the senses. Significant studies were produced by Jean-François Bordron, Anne Hénault, Eric Landowski, Jacques Fontanille and Claude Zilberberg, amongst others. For instance, Claude Zilberberg has examined the smells of good and evil in the works of Baudelaire and Anne Hénault has studied smell in relationship to Freud's writings on hysteria. Areas of investigation also included the activities of drinking wine and smoking cigarettes. The 1990s saw the publication of studies on light and colour, again in relationship to literature, film and painting. For instance, a very stimulating analysis of a picture of Mark Rothko appeared in *Nouveaux Actes sémiotiques* in 1994.

This widening of the parameters of semiotic investigation has produced an enriched metalanguage and led to the development of new concepts and models, many of which are outlined in this dictionary. These concepts include those of *presence, intensity, intentional drive* and *spatial apprehension.* They relate to the process of continuing signification or tension (*tensivité*), a concept introduced by Greimas and Fontanille in their *Sémiotique des passions* in 1991 and further elaborated during the 1990s. An *elementary structure of tension* was produced and presented with great clarity in works such as the seminal text *Tension et signification* [Tension and Meaning] written by Jacques Fontanille and Claude Zilberberg and published in 1998. Unlike the semiotic square concerned with fixed categories, the elementary structure of tension attempts to account for the actual process whereby meaning emerges from the senses/perceptions. In his book *Sémiotique du discours* [The Semiotics of Discourse] published in 1998, for example, Jacques Fontanille examines the treatment of smell in Louis-Ferdinand Céline's *Voyage au bout de la nuit* [Journey to the End of Night] in the light of this model. He notes, for instance, how an increase in intensity of smell can be correlated with a decrease in the volume of air. These figurative patterns then carry abstract or symbolic meanings: the increase in intensity of smell is an increase in moral corruption and in evil. In the elaboration of these models we may note the influence of Charles Peirce and of his triadic model of the sign.

The new semiotics is a movement that has not superseded earlier research but rather developed alongside more traditional elements. Greimas' narrative models are still widely applied not only in the field of literature but in areas such as law, politics, architecture and the natural sciences. It is increasingly recognized that we – human and non-human alike – are all, in A. S. Byatt's words, 'caught in a story': the very condition not only of meaning but of life itself.

At the same time, from an original interest in the folk-tale, semiotics has widened its domain of study to include areas such as psychosemiotics, biosemiotics and zoosemiotics. Sociosemiotics in particular is a rapidly expanding field represented by Eric Landowski amongst others. In 1989 Eric Landowski published his highly influential book *La Société réfléchie* [Society Reflected] which contains, for instance, studies of political and legal discourse as well as an analysis of the concepts of public opinion and of everydayness. His more recent works such as *Présences de l'autre* [Presences of the Other], 1997, and *Passions sans nom* [Passions without a Name], 2004, include an examination of the role of sensory perception in human interaction.

During the period in question semiotics has revitalized itself by drawing on the thought not only of Merleau-Ponty but also more recently of Noam Chomsky, Charles Peirce, Thomas S. Sebeok and René Thom. Far from being a movement confined to the 1960s or 1970s – a common misunderstanding in England at least – semiotics is a discipline in a constant process of evolution and of dialogue with a rapidly changing sociopolitical and cultural environment.

Semiotics as a tool for analysis: the Greimassian method

What, then, is the semiotic approach? How does it work? Semiotics takes as its fundamental premise that there can be no meaning without difference. There can be no 'up' without 'down', no 'hot' without 'cold', no 'good' without 'evil'. As Greimas says,

> We perceive differences and thanks to that perception, the world 'takes shape' in front of us, and for our purposes.

There are four basic principles on which the semiotic analysis of texts is based:

1) Meaning is not inherent in objects, objects do not signify by themselves. Meaning, rather, is constructed by what is known as a competent observer, that is, by a subject capable of 'giving form' to objects. To give an example: confronted with an implement from a different culture, say African or Asian, we would probably be incapable of grasping its significance. However, left alone with it, we will give it a meaning that is based on what knowledge we have and what will suit our purpose.
2) Semiotics views the text, any text, as an autonomous unit, that is, one that is internally coherent. Rather than starting with ideas/meanings

external to the text and showing how they are reflected within it, an approach that is still widely adopted in the academic world, semiotic analysis begins with a study of the actual language and structures of the text, showing how meanings are constructed and, of course, at the same time what these meanings are. Semiotic analysis becomes, then, a discovery method and is clearly an invaluable tool for all those engaged in original research.

3) Semiotics posits that story structure or narrativity underlies all discourse, not just what is commonly known as a story. For instance, it underlies political, sociological and legal discourse. One can even go as far as to say that narrativity underlies our very concept of truth: recent studies in the field of legal discourse, for example, have shown that those witnesses in a law court whose account conforms most closely to archetypal story patterns are those whose version is most likely to be believed.
4) Semiotics posits the notion of levels of meaning: it is, for instance, the deep abstract level that generates the narrative and discursive levels. A text must, therefore, be studied at these different levels of depth and not just at the surface level, as is the case with traditional linguistics.

Keeping in mind these principles, semiotic analysis is aided further by **schemas** or **models** whose application contributes to decoding the meaning of texts. We will give a brief survey of the most important of these and explain how they relate to different textual levels.

The discursive level

The discursive level is a surface level of meaning or level of manifestation. Here we examine the specific words – or grammatical items/structures that are visible on the surface of the text. Most grammar teaching – and indeed textual analysis – has hitherto been concerned exclusively with this level. Key elements on this level are:

The **figurative** component: by this we mean all the elements in the text that refer to the external physical world. They are known as figures. Figurative reality, then, is that reality that can be apprehended by the five senses – vision, smell, hearing, taste and touch. It can be contrasted with the inner world of the conceptual abstract, that is the third and deep level of meaning.

To explore the figurative component we start with examining the vocabulary. We try to extract the most important lexical (semantic) fields. This is done by grouping together words that have a meaning in common or a common denominator. These groupings are called 'isotopies' (*isotopies* in French). The lists of isotopies can then be interpreted: How are they distributed in the text? Which is/are the dominant one/s? Can we extract oppositions at this level? This kind of interpretation will already give us an indication of what will be the significant themes.

Grammatical/syntactic features: the use of the active or passive voice, for example, or procedures like nominalization or cohesive markers throw light on the organization of a text and thus reveal textual strategies of manipulation.

The **enunciative** component: this relates to traces of the speaker/author and the listener/reader in the text. What image does the utterance construct of either of them? Investigation of pronouns, of the narrative voice (personalized or depersonalized), of forms of speech (direct/indirect), for instance, indicate intentionality. Most important in this respect is also the modality of a statement: categorical, for example, in the case of news reporting or tentative on the part of a pupil, etc.

The narrative level

This level is more general and more abstract than the discursive level. It is the level of story grammar or surface narrative syntax, a structure that, according to the Paris School, underpins all discourse, be it scientific, sociological, artistic, etc.

Semiotic analysis of this level of meaning makes use of two fundamental narrative models: 1) the actantial narrative schema and 2) the canonical narrative schema. These models jointly articulate the structure of the quest or, to be more precise, the global narrative programme of the quest. They can be applied to an extract, for example a single paragraph, or to a whole text.

We will first look at the actantial narrative schema. This schema presents six key narrative functions (actantial roles) which together account for all possible relationships within a story and indeed within the sphere of human action in general:

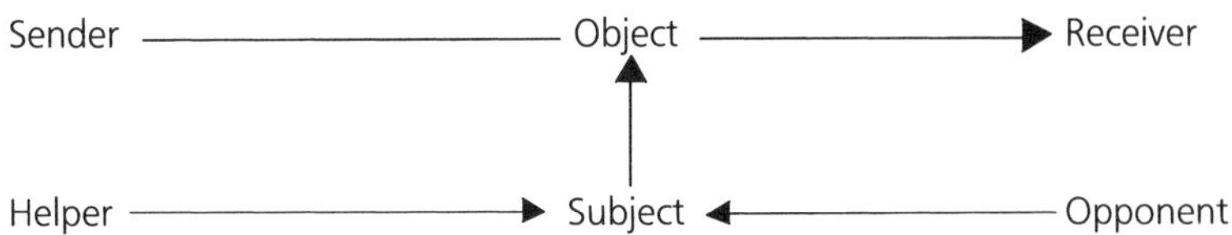

The schema is a simplification of Propp's seven 'spheres of action' or roles elaborated from a study of the Russian folk-tale – roles such as those of hero, villain, helper, etc. The diagram depicts the following relationships:

1) Subject/object

This is the most fundamental relationship: there can be no subject without an object and vice versa. A subject goes in quest of an object. The object of the quest could be concrete – a person or thing – or abstract, such as knowledge, truth or love.

There is usually more than one subject and more than one quest in, for example, a novel or a newspaper article.

2) Helper/opponent

The subject could be helped or hindered in its quest. Again these actantial positions could be held by objects or internal qualities as well as by people. Money or courage could be my helper and laziness my opponent.

A variant of the opponent is the anti-subject. An anti-subject is a subject who, to achieve its goal, obstructs the quest of another subject. The subject/anti-subject relationship characterizes all fiction and most newspaper articles or TV broadcasts: it is, of course, the hero/villain scenario.

3) Sender/receiver

The sender is an actant (person/idea) that motivates an act or causes something to happen. In other words, the sender provokes action, causes someone to act. The sender transmits to the receiver the desire to act (*vouloir-faire*) or the necessity to act (*devoir-faire*). We call the desire or obligation to act 'modalities'. What is known as a contract is established between sender and receiver. The receiver, when in possession of one (or both) of the relevant modalities, is transformed into a subject ready to embark on a quest.

We will now look at the canonical narrative schema. This presents in detail the different stages of any quest.

Contract/ Manipulation	Competence	Performance	Sanction
	Qualifying test	Decisive test	Glorifying test
Acquisition of a wanting-to-do or having-to-do	Strengthening of desire Acquisition of a being-able-to-do and/or knowing-how-to-do	The primary event where the object of value is at stake	Subject is recognized (praise/blame, success/failure)

The contract

The sender motivates the action, communicating the modalities of desire or obligation to the receiver. A contract is established, the receiver becomes a subject and embarks on the quest. The contract is followed by three tests:

1) The qualifying test

The subject must acquire the necessary competence to perform the planned action or mission. The desire or obligation to act is in itself not sufficient. The subject must also possess the ability to act (*pouvoir-faire*) and/or the knowledge/skills (*savoir-faire*) to carry it out. For example, if your intention is to shoot somebody, you first need to acquire a gun. The gun functions as your helper providing you with the necessary ability to act. However, you must also know how to shoot otherwise the gun is useless. The *being-able-to-do* and the *knowing-how-to-do* are also known as modalities.

2) The decisive test

This represents the principal event or action for which the subject has been preparing, where the object of the quest is at stake. In adventure stories or newspaper articles, the decisive test frequently takes the form of a confrontation or conflict between a subject and an anti-subject.

3) The glorifying test

This is the stage at which the outcome of the event is revealed. The decisive test has either succeeded or failed, the subject is acclaimed or punished. In other words, it is the point at which the performance of the subject is interpreted and evaluated by what is known as the sender-adjudicator. The sender-adjudicator judges whether the performance is in accordance with the original set of values (ideology or mandate) instituted by the initial sender. To distinguish the two senders we call the first one mandating sender and the second the sender-adjudicator. These roles are not necessarily played by the same actor or person.

When applying these fundamental narrative models to texts, it is important to be aware of several points:

- Each individual text exploits these schemas in its own way. It is highly significant which stages of the quest are explicit, or manifested in the text, and which are implicit. The media, for instance, tend to foreground the stage of performance (decisive test) and the stage of sanction (glorifying test).
- Correlations can be made with the discursive level: figurative elements that have emerged as dominant isotopies or determining oppositions may, on the narrative level, take the positions of object or subject of a quest.
- Not all stories or quests are completed. A quest may be aborted through the successful intervention of an anti-subject: if you set out to sail around the world and your boat capsizes, your quest is rather abruptly terminated.

The deep or abstract level

After analysing the narrative level of meaning, the next stage is to examine the deep level, sometimes also known as the thematic level. This is the level of abstract or conceptual syntax where the fundamental values which generate a text are articulated. These values can be presented in the form of a semiotic square.

The semiotic square is a visual presentation of the elementary structure of meaning. Articulating the relationships of contrariety (opposition), contradiction and implication, it is the logical expression of any semantic category.

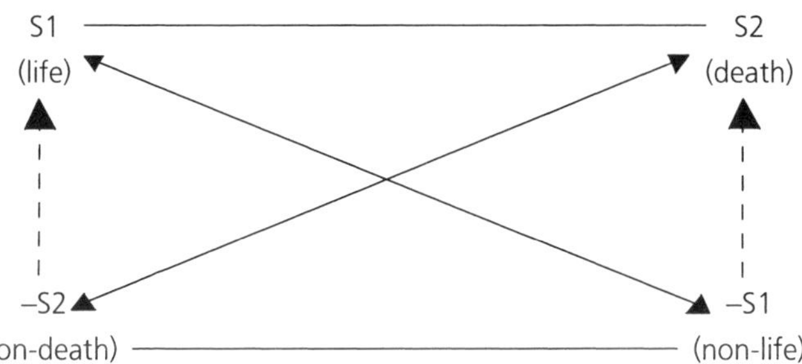

1) S1 and S2 are in a relation of opposition or contrariety (one term presupposes the other).
2) S1 and –S1 are in a relation of contradiction: –S1 negates S1. S2 and –S2 are also in a relation of contradiction: –S2 negates S2.
3) –S1 and S2 are in a relation of implication: –S1 implies S2. Similarly, –S2 implies S1.

The semiotic square is a useful tool to illustrate the basic semantic or thematic oppositions underpinning a text. It also allows, however, a demonstration of textual dynamics by plotting essential stages or transformations in a story and following the narrative trajectory of the subject.

At the end of this book we give an example of a semiotic analysis. The approach is applied to a well-known fairy-tale.

Notes

1. *An Essay Concerning Human Understanding*, ed. Peter H. Nidditch (Oxford: Clarendon Press, 1975/79), Book IV, ch. XXI, p. 720.
2. Peirce's ideas have influenced the work of U. Eco, who both developed and contested Peirce's categories.
3. 'On Meaning', *New Literary History*, 20 (1989), 539–50 (p. 541).
4. They are recorded in his *Cours de linguistique générale* which was put together from notes, taken by his students, of lectures delivered at the University of Geneva between 1906 and 1911 and published posthumously in 1915.
5. See also Claude Lévi-Strauss, *Anthropologie structurale* (Paris: Plon, 1958).
6. Vladimir Propp, *Morphology of the Folktale* (Bloomington: Indiana University Press, 1958).
7. The article is reproduced in *Du Sens II* (Paris: Seuil, 1983), pp. 115–33.

Key Terms in Semiotics

Absence

The notion absence is defined by the opposite term **presence**. In semiotic terms, absence often denotes existence *in absentia*, that is, virtual existence. For example, the term 'death' implies the absence of life. The concept of life would therefore be present *in absentia* when 'death' is mentioned. Or a text about trains might signify in conjunction with or in opposition to other means of transport which, though not necessarily mentioned, would nonetheless be 'virtually' present in the text.

Abstract

A term is abstract if it refers to a *conceptual*, non-physical universe, i.e. an inner, mental world. An abstract reality is one which cannot be perceived by the five senses: good and evil, love and hate are abstract concepts. Generally accepted abstract values are known as universals.

Abstract notions can be contrasted with the concrete, physical universe: kissing or beating someone with a stick belongs to the concrete world. They are the specific manifestation in time and space of underlying abstract values. The distinction between concrete and abstract, therefore, is expressed in the two levels of meaning: in the figurative (superficial) level of manifestation and on the deep level. Crying, for example, could be an indication of sorrow, or killing one of evil.

See also *conceptual* and *concrete*.

Achrony

The term achrony affirms the atemporal nature of logico-semantic structures. Semiotic structures on a deep level are achronic whereas discursive structures (e.g. those of the figurative level) exist 'in time' and call for temporalization. In Robert Louis Stevenson's story of *Treasure Island*, for example, events are arranged and signify in temporal sequence. Moreover, the hero, Jim Hawkins, sets a temporal framework for the story from its very beginning by telling us that he is old yet writing about himself as a young boy. The deep-level structures of the tale, on the other hand, involving social and moral order and disorder, being and not-being, are achronic, their logical relationships and dynamics not being subject to time.

See also *diachrony* and *synchrony*.

Acquisition

Acquisition belongs to the discursive level of discourse. Paradigmatically opposed to deprivation or lack, the term designates the act or transformation that brings about the conjunction of a subject and an object of value. Acquisition can be brought about in two ways:

1. In a transitive manner through a process of **attribution**: the subject acquires an object of value through the action of another object. For example, your mother may give you £5,000.
2. In a reflexive manner through a process of **appropriation**: the subject acquires the object of value through its own action. For example, you may go exploring to find the hidden treasure.

In terms of the actantial narrative schema, acquisition represents the successful outcome of a quest.

See also *lack*.

Actant

An actant is someone or something who or which accomplishes or undergoes an act. It may be a person, anthropomorphic or zoomorphic agent, a thing or an abstract entity.

Situated on the level of narrative syntax, the term describes a narrative function such as that of subject or object. In the sentence 'Prison officers vote for work to rule which could bring jails to a standstill', 'work to rule' in the first part of the sentence functions as actant/object of the prison officers' quest while 'which' (referring to the same 'work to rule') in the second part of the sentence functions as actant/subject capable of bringing about a transformation. In the fairy-tale *Sleeping Beauty*, the prince functions as actant/subject in his own quest to marry the beautiful princess and as actant/helper in the quest to break the spell of the nasty fairy godmother.

Actant has to be distinguished from actor, a term used when describing the discursive organization.

See also *actor*.

Actantial narrative schema

This is a fundamental universal narrative structure that underlies all texts. There are six key actantial roles or functions arranged in three sets of binary opposition: subject/object; sender/receiver; helper/opponent. Together the six actants and their organization account for all possible relationships within a story and indeed within the sphere of human action in general:

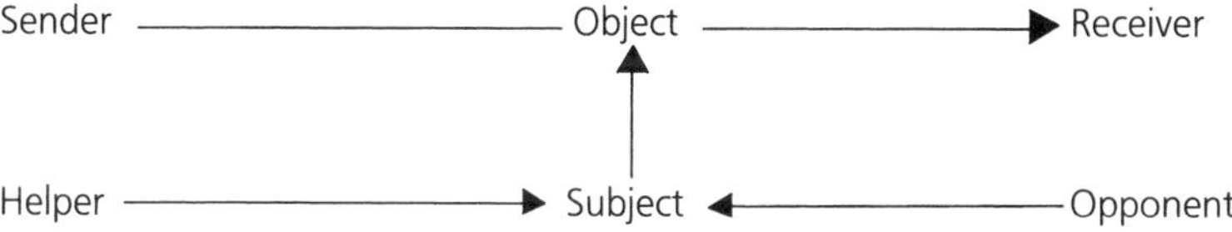

The role of anti-subject, a variant of the opponent, may also be included within this diagram. These narrative positions may be held by people, places, objects or abstract ideas.

The diagram illustrates in the first place the necessary relationship between a sender and a receiver. This is based on the desire for an object or on an obligation which the sender transmits to the receiver, inducing the latter to pursue it. The function of the sender therefore is to make the receiver do something (*faire faire*), thereby turning the receiver into a subject.

The relationship between the subject and the object, on the other hand, also based on desire or obligation, is geared to change a state of being (*faire être*): its function is to transform a state of deficiency or wanting into one of sufficiency through conjunction with or disjunction from an object. Helper and opponent entertain a subsidiary relationship to the subject, their function being to intervene positively or negatively in the pursuit of the goal. Thus the desire for an object becomes the focal point of the whole scheme. Examples illustrating the different functions are to be found under separate headings for each particular actant.

Action

In semiotics, the term action designates a series of acts or transformations organized in a logical sequence (narrative trajectory). Accordingly, an action is a narrative programme in which an actor is engaged in concrete acts at a specific time and in a specific place. In other words, action describes the stages of competence and performance of the canonical narrative schema. The action in *Treasure Island* consists of the voyage to the island (stage of competence) and the search for the treasure (stage of performance).

The analysis of narrated actions enables us to recognize stereotypes of human activities and to construct typological and syntagmatic models which take account of them. These models form the basis of a semiotics of action.

See also *canonical narrative schema* and *narrative trajectory*.

Actor

Semiotics uses the term actor to refer to any individual, anthropomorphic or zoomorphic agent, to a group (e.g. a crowd) or to an abstract entity such as fate that is perceptible on the *discursive* level of an utterance and plays a part in a story. In semiotic analysis, actor has replaced the traditional terms of 'character' or 'protagonist'. Actors are individualized and represent concrete figurative elements. In the fairy-tale *Cinderella*, the main actors are Cinderella herself, her sisters, the fairy godmother and the prince.

The term should be distinguished from **actant**, which is more abstract and refers to a narrative function.

See also *actant*.

Actorialization

The term actorialization refers to the process whereby actors are established in discourse. Like spatialization and temporalization, it is a necessary ingredient in the production of a referential illusion or reality effect. To be an actor you must possess at least one thematic role (a socially defined 'theme' or function) and one narrative function (such as subject or object of a quest). Example: A poor fisherman (thematic role) wants to marry (designating the fisherman as subject of a quest) the beautiful princess (thematic role plus object of the quest).

See also *spatialization*, *temporalization* and *thematic role*.

Actualization

The term actualization designates one of two basic modes of semiotic existence: virtual and actual. Actualizing modalities are knowing (*savoir*) and being able to do or to be (*pouvoir*). With regard to language, actualization denotes the operation by which any given language unit is rendered 'present' within a particular linguistic context. Resulting actual existence (*in praesentia*) characterizes the syntagmatic axis of language, that is, the sentence in the speech flow (*parole*) as opposed to the language system (*langue*) from which individual units are selected. Any lexeme, for example, has only virtual existence until it becomes actualized in the context that turns it into a sememe.

Narrative semiotics replaces the couple virtualization/actualization with the ternary virtualization/actualization/realization in order to describe accurately all possible kinds of junction between a subject and an object. Before any junction has been specified, subjects and objects are in *virtual* positions. Their position is *realized* once subject and object are conjoined. When, however, they are in a state of disjunction, they are termed *actualized*. This kind of actualization relates to two possible moments in a quest:

1. It applies when the subject of a quest has acquired competence but has not yet reached the stage of performance and is therefore still disjoined from its object of value. Example: When Bluebeard's wife has obtained the key to the rooms she is not allowed to open, her quest can be described as actualized. Once she has transgressed the taboo, opened the door and seen the horrible truth, she is conjoined with the object of value (knowledge) and the positions are thus realized.

2. Actualization also relates to a state of disjunction that succeeds a quest which has been realized. Example: When Cinderella wishes for a dress to go to the ball, the dress has only virtual existence (*in absentia*) for her. Once her fairy godmother has produced the garment and given it to Cinderella, subject and object are conjoined and are therefore realized. After the ball, the garment has been returned, subject and object are again disjoined and in the event are merely actualized. In other words, actualization here corresponds with a transformation which amounts to an operation of disjunction. This, on the discursive level, is often tantamount to deprivation.

See also *lexeme*, *realization*, *sememe* and *virtualization*.

Adjudicator

The term adjudicator denotes the actor who judges the success or failure of a subject's performance in a quest. A teacher takes the role of an adjudicator when s/he judges a pupil's performance by giving him/her a good (or bad) mark. The little boy judges his own action when saying 'I did a brave thing'. In this case we talk of auto-adjudication.

Judging a subject's performance is the last stage in the structure of a narrative. It is called the glorifying test or sanction. The judge here is normally called sender-adjudicator since this instance often, though not always, also functions in establishing the initial contract with the subject pursuing a quest.

See also *canonical narrative schema* and *sender-adjudicator*.

Advertising – Semiotics of

The semiotics of advertising has its roots in the work of Roland Barthes who in 1964 published his seminal article 'Rhétorique de l'image' [Rhetoric of the Image], an analysis of an advertisement for Panzani noodles. However, although his rhetorical and semiological approach was particularly influential during the 1970s, it came increasingly under fire from adherents of the Paris School, notably from Jean-Marie Floch. In 1985 Floch published his *Petites Mythologies de l'œil et de l'esprit. Pour une sémiotique plastique* [Eye on Mind: A Collection of Short Mythologies. Towards a Theory of Plastic Semiotics], a pivotal text in the development of this field of study. In the chapter 'Sémiotique plastique et communication publicitaire' [Plastic Semiotics and Communication in Advertising] he challenges Barthes' concepts of the sign, of communication and of connotation. Instead he argues for the Greimassian theory of the production of meaning. He applies to the advertisement the notion of levels of meaning as they relate to the generative trajectory, examining, for example, the discursive, narrative and deep levels as well as the semiotic square. Unlike Barthes, he brings together the visual and the verbal in this process of generation of meaning, stressing at the same time the importance of non-figurative elements in the visual, such as positioning, form and colour.

With the publication in 1990 of *Sémiotique, marketing et communication* [Semiotics, Marketing and Communication] and in 1995 of *Identités visuelles* [Visual Identities], Floch opens up new areas of research to include the field of sociosemiotics. He focuses here on the relationship between sender and receiver and on the construction of social identity in, for example, the advertising campaigns of Habitat or Chanel. He argues that there are different strategies or ideologies behind advertising which can be outlined in a semiotic square. Floch also develops the notion of the aesthetic, that is, the construction of concepts of beauty from a semiotic perspective.

Other notable researchers in this field include Andrea Semprini, Erik Bertin, Jean-Jacques Boutard and Jean-Paul Petitimbert. For instance, Semprini has analysed adverts for McDonald's using Greimas' generative trajectory. His perspective is sociosemiotic, stressing the different relationships (contractual, etc.) with the receiver/consumer. Nicole Everaert-Desmedt has also analysed several advertisements adopting the Greimassian approach.

Recent developments mirror many of the preoccupations of the 'new semiotics'. Attention has been paid to the role of the senses in advertising. Researchers in this area include Denis Bertrand, Eric Landowski and Juan Alonso.

See also *visual semiotics*.

Aesthesis/*esthésie*

Taken from the Greek language, the term aesthesis generally denotes feeling or sensitivity resulting from sensory perception, as, for example, with a flower, whose beauty is experienced through sight, touch and smell.

In semiotic theory, *esthésie* or the aesthetic experience relates more precisely to the perception of the external world as it appears to us through the senses in their organizing capacity. Aesthetic in this context is defined as the mode of appearing of things, the unique way in which they reveal themselves to us, independent of all preliminary codification. Semiotics here makes a difference between the appearance and the appearing of things: appearance is referential and informative. The appearance of a rose tells us by sight and smell that it is a rose. It is codified by a pre-existing knowledge. Appearing, on the other hand, catches the thing at a moment of its actual being as a process or in evolution. Part of its apprehension is therefore virtual. To take the rose once more as an example, the momentary aesthetic experience perceives it in full bloom or already wilting, its smell anticipating its decline and death.

Finally, aesthesis or the aesthetic experience in general is, of course, closely linked to aesthetics, that is, the theory of the experience of beauty or the philosophy of taste and art. In his seminal book, *De l'imperfection* [On Imperfection], A. J. Greimas attaches the aesthetic experience to the notion of perfection.

See also *aesthetics* and *mode of existence*.

Aesthetics

The term aesthetics designates the theory of the experience of beauty or the philosophy of taste and art. Normally, aesthetic perception is a mixture of appreciation and pleasure which we experience, for instance, when listening to music, admiring a painting or being faced with a spectacular sunset.

The semiotician A. J. Greimas attaches aesthetics to the notion of perfection. He believes the aesthetic experience to reside in a momentary glimpse of a wholeness of life which goes beyond rational explanation. Semiotically, the event could be described as subject and object, for a brief instant, blending into one. The positive joy produced by this event links it to the thymic category. An example of such an aesthetic experience in literature would be Proust's tasting of the *madeleine* which gave rise to his famous work *A la recherche du temps perdu*.

See also *thymic*.

Agent

Semiotics employs the term agent (or operating agent) to designate the narrative role of a **subject of doing**, that is, of a subject engaged in the carrying out of a particular narrative programme. It contrasts with the term **patient** which designates a **subject of state**. In the sentence 'The knight slays the dragon', the knight is the operating agent. Equally, in the sentence 'The electorate opted for Labour', the body of electors is the agent carrying out its role in the narrative programme of the poll.

See also *patient, subject of doing* and *subject of state.*

Alethic modalities (*modalités aléthiques*)

In semiotic theory the modal structure known as alethic is produced when an utterance of state is governed by a modal utterance of obligation or possibility (having-to-be; being possible/impossible). For instance: 'She had to be very clever', 'They did not have to be in London for the event', 'It was impossible to be generous', 'It was possible to make the journey within the time given'.

The alethic modal structure can be projected onto the semiotic square as follows:

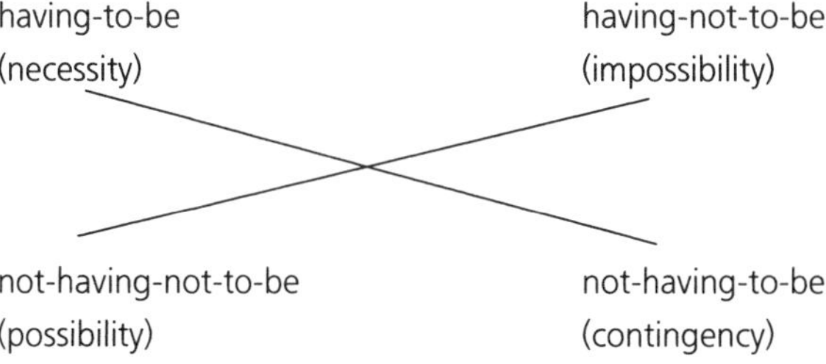

See also *having-to-do* and *modalities.*

Allegory

An allegory is a work such as a poem, novel or story that has a meaning beyond the apparent surface meaning. For instance, John Bunyan's *The Pilgrim's Progress* is not just an account of the experiences of a particular individual in a particular time and place. It has a general moral significance as an allegory of the Christian's journey through life. Similarly, George Orwell's *Animal Farm* can be regarded as an allegory of a totalitarian society and not simply as a story about animals.

Allegory differs from symbolism: in an allegorical text the deeper meanings are relatively fixed or stable whereas in a symbolic text there is a far greater degree of fluidity and ambiguity.

Anachronism

An anachronism is the setting of an event, scene, person or object in the wrong historical period. The most famous example is the clock in Shakespeare's *Julius Caesar*.

Anachrony

This term describes any discrepancy between the order or chronology of events in a story (story-time) and the order in which they are narrated or told (discourse-time). The term focuses on the extent to which time is manipulated and restructured in narrative discourse and was a central preoccupation of the French narratologist Gérard Genette. The analysis of anachronies can, for example, provide important indications about narratorial assumptions, intentions and reliability and may therefore feature in a semiotic decoding of a text.

There are two fundamental categories of anachrony: the *prolepsis*, or evocation of a future event, and *analepsis*, the description or evocation of a past event.

See also *analepsis* and *prolepsis.*

Analepsis

This term designates the description or evocation of an event that took place earlier in the story. In other words, it is a movement back in time so that a chronologically earlier event is related or evoked later in the narrative. The device is similar to that of the flashback. An analepsis could refer back to a single incident or to a whole section of a story. An *internal analepsis* refers back to events within the time-span of the story whereas an *external analepsis* refers back to events outside the story's temporal framework.

Analepsis is the most common type of anachrony, its most obvious function being to provide additional information relating to the background of a character or of an event. The opening pages of many texts incorporate analepsis in the form of summaries of a character's earlier life or of events preceding the main situation. For example, the introductory paragraphs of Angela Carter's short story *The Bloody Chamber* refer the reader back to events prior to the narrator's train journey to the castle. We are told of her past life and given key details about her mother and about her own feelings. Analepsis here is a means of introducing the key psychoanalytical themes of the book as well as of highlighting the unconventional nature of the relationships.

See also *prolepsis*.

Analysis

The term analysis designates procedures employed to describe a semiotic object. Considering any semiotic object as a signifying whole, these procedures aim to establish, on the one hand, relationships among the different components of the object and on the other, between its constituents and the whole.

Procedures, moreover, focus on different aspects. *Syntactic* analyses concentrate on narrative grammar. They investigate narrative functions and actorial roles such as those of the wolf and the grandmother in *Little Red Riding Hood* and how they relate to each other. *Semic* analyses, by contrast, compare units of meaning. What do units of meaning such as mother/child/wolf/grandmother have (or have not) in common? Are they related? What separates them?

See also *function*, *seme*, *sememe* and *syntax*.

Anaphora

An anaphora serves to link two utterances, two paragraphs, etc., by using a connecting term referring back to some concept already mentioned. In the example 'John came into the room. He was wearing a new coat', the pronoun 'he' functions as an anaphora.

Anaphorization is one of the main procedures that enable the enunciator (addresser) to establish and maintain interphrastic textual continuity/cohesion. It is one of the methods whereby internal networks of meaning are set up.

See also *cataphora.*

Anthropomorphic

The term anthropomorphic refers to the representation of animals or lifeless things as though endowed with human attributes such as feelings or speech.

'The mountain spewed its breath of death and exhaled its milky vapours' (Guy de Maupassant, *Two Friends*).

Anthroponym

An anthroponym is the designation of actors by their proper names such as 'Joanne' or 'Paul'. Like toponyms, they contribute to the creation of an illusion or simulacrum of the real. They are, therefore, a key component of the process of figurativization.

See also *chrononym*, *simulacrum* and *toponym.*

Antiphrasis

The term antiphrasis describes a figure of speech whereby one word in a sentence is used in a sense directly opposite to its literal or usual meaning. As a result, an effect of irony is produced. Drenched by rain and shivering with cold, one might, for example, talk of the 'beautiful sunny' weather or refer to an exceptionally ugly person as 'Mr Handsome'.

Anti-sender

The anti-sender represents an actantial instance (person or idea) in conflict with the principal sender and its programme. As a result the anti-sender not only institutes a system of values that opposes the original quest but also attempts to manipulate the receiver/subject to act in a way contrary to the desires of the first sender. In the case of a strike, the sender of the employees' quest may be a trade union leader (as well as a sense of social justice) whose aim is to persuade them to stop work. The anti-sender here is the employer whose goal is to persuade the employees (by means of threats, etc.) to continue work or return to it.

See also *sender*.

Anti-subject

A story may contain two or more subjects whose quests are in conflict. An anti-subject is a subject who, to achieve its goal, obstructs the quest of another subject. The wolf in *Little Red Riding Hood* is the anti-subject who obstructs the little girl's quest to see her grandmother in order to pursue his own goal of eating her. In the fight for a territory two opposing armies may each take up the positions of subject or anti-subject, depending on the point of view from which events are reported.

See also *opponent*.

Antonym

The term antonym designates a particular type of oppositeness. 'Boy' and 'girl' are antonyms because they oppose each other while sharing a semantic feature, that is, they possess the common denominator, children. Similarly, the antonyms 'hot' and 'cold' possess temperature in common, 'high' and 'low' verticality, etc.

When pairs of opposites occur in proximity to each other in a text, they exert a marked cohesive effect. To give an example: 'At least 125 people died of AIDS in Bulawayo between April and June this year, according to City Health authorities . . . Out of the 125, 71 were males while 54 were females.'

In semiotic theory the word antonym can be replaced by the term seme. The semes 'high' and 'low', for example, articulate the semantic category of verticality.

See also *lexical cohesion*, *semantic category* and *synonym*.

Aphoria

Aphoria is the neutral term of the thymic category euphoria versus dysphoria. Examples: 'The death of the cat did not make her feel particularly happy or sad'; 'He was indifferent to the loss of his money'.

See also *thymic.*

Appropriation

The term appropriation designates the transformation whereby a subject of state acquires an object of value through its own efforts, i.e. through a reflexive act. For example, I (subject of state) buy (doing of which 'I' am the subject) two tickets for the play (object of value). In abstract terms, this is represented in the following way:

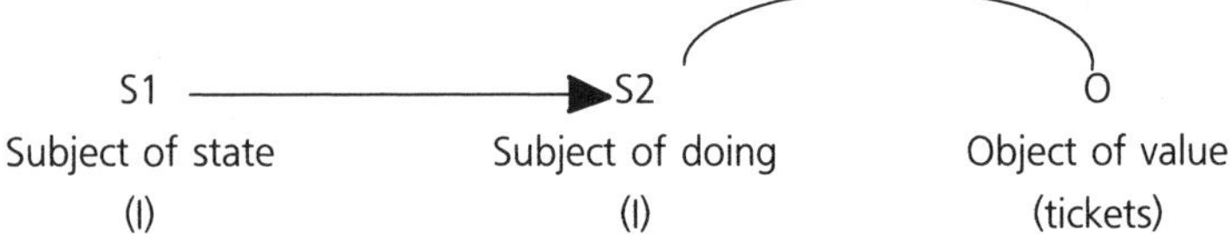

Appropriation can be contrasted with attribution where the subject of state acquires an object of value thanks to a subject of doing other than itself, i.e. it represents a transitive act. For example, my mother gives me some apples.

See also *attribution*, *subject of doing* and *subject of state.*

Archetype

A central concept in the thought of the German psychologist Karl Gustav Jung, the term archetype designates a universal image, symbolic pattern or motif embedded in the collective unconscious or human psyche. Archetypes are, therefore, inherited and form part of a collective memory. Seen by Jung as evidence of the survival of earlier non-Western modes of thought, the archetype may manifest itself in dreams, art, religion and myth. An example of an archetype is the animus/anima figure where the animus represents the woman's archetypal image of man and the anima the man's archetypal image of woman. In a literary text archetypes can be found in the plot (e.g. the quest for the philosopher's stone), the setting (e.g. the garden or forest) and character (e.g. the villain or traitor). In his analysis of Russian folk-tales

V. Propp uncovered 31 archetypal patterns of behaviour which he termed functions. These were later reduced to six by the semiotician A. J. Greimas to produce his *actantial narrative schema*, a narrative model that was central to the emergence of semiotics in France.

The archetype plays a key role in the thought of the philosopher and scientist Gaston Bachelard as well as in the literary theory and myth criticism of Northrop Frye. Feminists have viewed particular archetypes as evidence of the universal oppression of women.

Architecture – Semiotics of

The semiotics of architecture comprises the study of buildings and of the values attached to them. It would include an analysis of the structures of space, of places and objects and of the human activities associated with them. The term architecture denotes, therefore, a collection of elements possessing a particular syntactic status and determining the relations between the people interacting with it. The application of the Greimassian narrative models in this field has been particularly illuminating. An example would be M. Hammad's analysis of the relationship between the Japanese ritual of the tea ceremony and the buildings and garden that were constructed for this purpose. This study presents a further development of a number of key spatial concepts as well as an elaboration of the notion of the aesthetic.

Aspectualization

The term aspectualization refers to the process whereby the implied presence of an observer is established in the discourse. It involves the spatial, temporal and actorial co-ordinates set up by the utterance which characterize and position the observation. In spatial terms for example, reference to objects placed on the left or on the right is only meaningful in relation to an implied point of observation. Temporal aspectualization makes itself felt in the stopping and starting of enunciative (or discursive) events; or in the duration of a process on the syntagmatic axis or the punctuality (lack of duration) of a process on the paradigmatic axis of the discourse. In *Treasure Island* the evocation of the length of the sea voyage as well as its punctuation by significant events are founded on aspectual techniques in the novel.

The procedures involved in aspectualization are closely linked to those of ***débrayage***.

See also *débrayage*.

Attribution

Attribution designates the transformation whereby a subject of state acquires an object of value thanks to a subject of doing other than itself, i.e. attribution represents a transitive act. I may, for example, acquire wealth – my object of value – when my rich uncle gives me a million pounds. In abstract terms, this is represented in the following way:

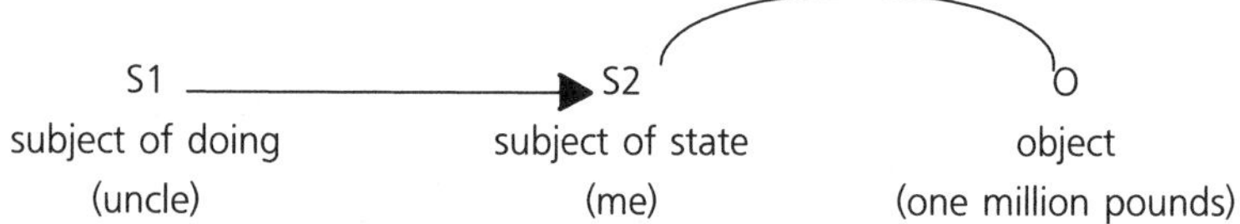

Attribution can be contrasted with appropriation, where the subject of state and the subject of doing are represented by the same actor, i.e. the act is reflexive. For example, I go out and buy a loaf of bread.

See also *appropriation*, *subject of doing* and *subject of state*.

Author

The term author describes the sender of a message or discourse. We speak of the author of a written text or of any sign system that emanates from a competent source intent on transmitting a message.

In semiotics, the term enunciator is used in preference to author.

See also *enunciator/enunciatee* and *reader*.

Axiology

In general terms, axiology relates to the theory and/or description of systems of value. In a semiotic perspective, the term axiology is used for value systems arranged on a *paradigmatic* axis. In other words, values in axiological structures, while occupying the same place within a narrative syntax, signify in systems of equivalence or opposition. For example, good or honesty (equivalent values) oppose evil (contrasting value); the thymic term euphoria is in opposition to dysphoria.

The term **ideology** is reserved for the *syntagmatic* arrangement of values, that is, their organization in an actantial perspective. Subjects (individual or collective) express or desire values which become objects of a quest. The values themselves are part of axiological systems which, for example, place 'virtue' opposite 'vice'; their selection and actual pursuit in particular instances, on the other hand, define an ideology. The stories of the Bible are an example of values arranged and displayed to form an ideology, in this case that of the Christian faith.

See also *ideology*.

Axiomatic

The term axiomatic relates to a body of non-definable and/or non-demonstrable propositions which are interdefined and demonstrated by means of an arbitrary decision. An axiomatic concept, therefore, permits the construction of a theory by deductive steps. This process contrasts with traditional scientific practice which proceeds from a set of hypotheses and aims at proving them with the data of experience.

Being

The term being possesses at least two meanings:

1. It serves as a copula (link word) in utterances of state. Example: 'Mary was ill'. Such utterances characterize descriptive passages. Together with utterances of doing they make up a narrative.

   In semiotic terms, being expresses a relation of conjunction or disjunction between a subject of state and an object. Examples: 'The sky is blue'; here 'the sky' (subject of state) is in conjunction with the object of value, i.e. blueness. In the utterance 'The man is not rich', on the other hand, the subject of state, 'man' is in disjunction with the object, 'wealth'.

2. The term being is also used to name the modal category of veridiction: being/seeming. This modal category is often brought into play in stories relating to acts of treachery or deception where the hero/heroine is not what s/he appears to be. In the story of *Aladdin*, for example, the exchange of Aladdin's old lamp for a new one appears to his wife to be an act of generosity (seeming) whereas we (the reader) know that it is theft and that the old lady is a villain in disguise (being).

   The opposition being versus seeming can also be paralleled with the dichotomy immanence versus manifestation. Being here relates to the plane of underlying structure (immanence) whereas seeming relates to the plane of outward manifestation.

See also *veridiction*.

Being-able

The modal structure of being-able governs utterances both of doing and of state.

1. Utterances of doing: being-able-to-do. Examples: 'He was unable to contain his anger'; 'You can refuse to come; there is nothing to stop you'; 'We could not decipher your handwriting'; 'The children were unable to swim in the lake'; 'I shall certainly be able to come to the party'.

   This modal structure can be mapped onto the following semiotic square:

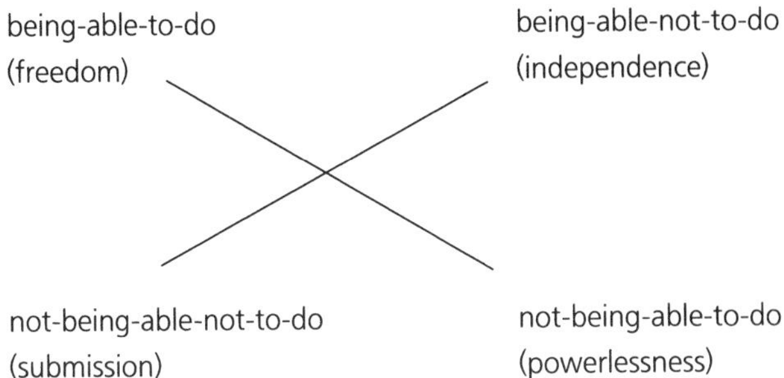

In the canonical narrative schema the acquisition of a being-able-to-do is a key component of the stage of competence: without possessing this modality of being-able-to-do, the subject cannot proceed to the next stage of the quest, that is, the decisive test or performance.

2. Utterances of state: being-able-to-be. Examples: 'He was sure that one day he could be happy'; 'The money could not have been there'; 'I might be wrong but I don't think so'; 'He must be poor'.

   This modal structure can be mapped onto the following semiotic square:

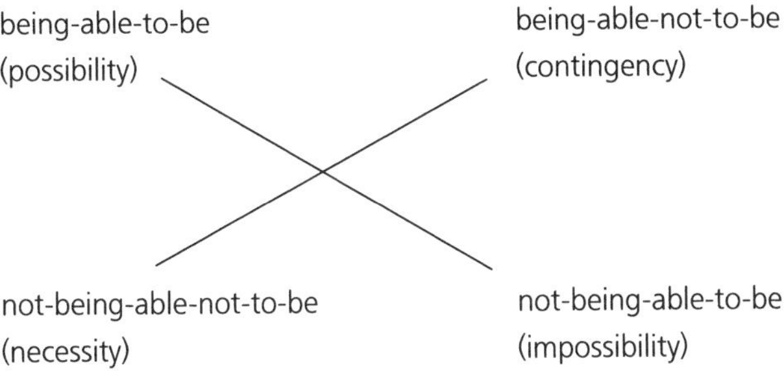

See also *canonical narrative schema* and *modalization*.

Believing-to-be

Believing-to-be is a synonym (i.e. the syntactic definition) of the notion of *certainty*. It constitutes the positive term of the epistemic modal category and can be mapped onto the semiotic square as follows:

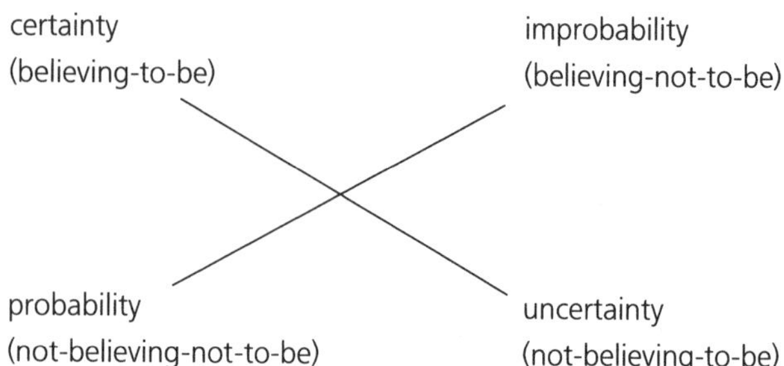

Example: Frank believes to be in love with Tina = he is certain he is in love. Tina, on the other hand, thinks that she is probably in love with Frank = she does not believe that she is not in love, while Max believes not to be in love = his feelings are at the opposite end of Frank's. The different (or changing) positions of certainty and uncertainty of the actors can thus be plotted on the semiotic square.

See also *uncertainty*.

Binarism

Binarism is an epistemological concept which holds that the structure of binary opposition is one of the characteristics of the human mind. The concept owes much to the work of Roman Jakobson.

Binary

A binary structure refers to a relationship between two terms that are mutually exclusive: up versus down; hot versus cold; good versus evil; etc.

There are two types of binary opposition: (a) that of **contradiction**: cold versus not cold; and (b) that of **contrariety**: cold versus hot. These two types of opposition were developed by Greimas in his formulation of the semiotic square which outlines the elementary structure of meaning.

See also *semiotic square*.

Biosemiotics

The term biosemiotics designates the study 'concerned with living semiotic systems' (Rudolf Jander, 1981) excluding, however, cultural semiotics considered as a domain of its own. Generally defined as the study of biological codes, biosemiotics was pioneered by the theoretical biologist Jakob von Uexküll who focused his research on the role of environmental (*Umwelt*) factors in human and animal semiosis. Believing that every organism has a specific mode of its outward and its inward life and that the anatomical structure of an animal gives us a clue as to the reconstruction of its outward and inward experience, Uexküll developed an *Umweltlehre* (a theory about phenomenal self-worlds) according to which organisms do not perceive an object in itself. They only perceive signs 'and from these signs, each according to its *Bauplan*, or blueprint, builds up mental models of the world' (Sebeok, 1979).

As a field of research, biosemiotics is considered a discipline covering three areas: anthroposemiotics (focusing on messages – verbal or otherwise – between human beings); zoosemiotics (animal information transfer) and phytosemiotics, that is, the study of plant semiosis. Later, the prokaryotic communication systems, that is, the exchange network between different bacterial cells, were added to the programme.

See also *zoosemiotics*.

Canon

In the context of literary theory the term canon designates generally accepted rules or criteria of particular genres, that is, the representation of their ideal; it also refers to literary works of a similar standard or to the genuine recognized works of any author. With regard to nineteenth-century novel writing, for example, the canon would be works obeying the general rules and setting the standard for the novel of the period.

These days, the term canon is sometimes used in a somewhat derogatory fashion to refer to the list of approved literary works in opposition to novel, more inventive writing.

Canonical narrative schema

This schema presents a universal prototype for the structure of narrative. It is composed of three tests: the qualifying test, the decisive test and the glorifying test, which unfold in a logical succession. These tests are preceded by the stage of manipulation or contract.

Contract/ Manipulation	Competence	Performance	Sanction
	Qualifying test	Decisive test	Glorifying test
Persuasive doing of sender Acquisition of a wanting-to-do or a having-to-do	Strengthening of desire Acquisition of a being-able-to-do and/or knowing-how-to-do	The primary event where the object of value is at stake	The subject's performance is recognized (praise/blame, success/failure)

This narrative macro-structure can be exploited by individual texts in a variety of different ways. Certain stages or tests may be foregrounded, others remain implicit: in adventure stories, for example, the emphasis is on the decisive test, whereas legal discourse is centred more on the stage of sanction.

Contract/manipulation: The sender transmits to the receiver the desire or obligation to act. What is known as a contract is established between the two and the subject embarks on a quest. The contract is followed by three tests. These tests mirror the fundamental logic of human action.

The qualifying test (or stage of competence): Here the subject acquires the necessary competence needed to carry out the planned action or mission. The desire or obligation to act is not in itself sufficient: the subject must also possess the ability to act (*pouvoir faire*) and/or the knowledge/skills to do so (*savoir faire*). For example, if your intention is to shoot someone, you first of all need to acquire a gun; the gun functions as your helper, providing you with the necessary ability to act.

The decisive test (*or stage of performance*): This represents the principal event or action for which the subject has been preparing, where the object of the quest is at stake. In adventure stories or newspaper articles, the decisive test frequently takes the form of a confrontation or conflict between a subject and an anti-subject.

The glorifying test (*or sanction*): The outcome of the event is now revealed, the decisive test has either succeeded or failed, the subject is acclaimed or punished. In other words, it is the point at which the performance of the subject is interpreted and evaluated by what is known as the sender-adjudicator.

For more details see under individual headings.

Cataphora

Like an anaphora, a cataphora serves to produce textual continuity or cohesion through a network of internal references. Unlike the anaphora, however, a cataphora marks a referral back that precedes mention of the term to which it refers. Put more simply, a cataphora refers forward whereas an anaphora refers back. In the sentence 'It was wonderful, that wedding', 'it' exemplifies a cataphora.

See also *anaphora*.

Categorization

The term categorization denotes the operation of ordering objects or assertions according to root-notions or classes possessing some common denominators. In linguistics, Emile Benveniste uses the term to designate the application of a natural language to the world around us – as perceived by the sum total of our senses. A child thus gives meaning to its world by categorizing its experiences. In this perspective, the terms categorization and classification are sometimes interchangeable.

In semiotic theory, categorization is also applied to designate the projection of a particular value onto the semiotic square. This projection, which articulates a semantic value, turns it into a category. For example, the semiotic square which opposes the term hot with the term cold, contradicting it with non-hot and non-cold, represents a visual demonstration of the semantic category 'temperature'.

See also *classification, semantic category* and *taxonomy.*

Category

See *semantic category.*

Certainty

The term certainty designates the positive pole of the epistemic modal category. Its syntactic definition is believing-to-be.

See also *believing-to-be, epistemic modalities* and *uncertainty.*

Chora

The term chora was borrowed by Julia Kristeva from Plato's *Timaeus* where it means receptacle and is synonymous with womb. In *Revolution in Poetic Language* Kristeva redefines the term as 'an essentially mobile and extremely provisional articulation constituted by movements and their ephemeral states'. The chora is a force or dynamic, a drive-determined locus that cannot be represented in language. It can be described only in terms of basic primal vocal or kinetic rhythms.

From a psychoanalytical point of view the chora exists at the level where the child's basic drives are directed towards the mother. It is the home of the signifying drives which serve to structure the semiotic. Although all language is based on the bodily rhythms of the chora, these are more or less repressed when the child enters the Symbolic Order of representation. The chora can only then be perceived as a pulsional pressure on language when discourse breaks down, emerging, for example, in contradictions, linguistic disruption, silences and absences. The chora is most evident in poetic texts such as those of Mallarmé and Lautréamont.

See also *semiotic/symbolic*.

Chrononym

The term chrononym designates a specific length of time such as 'day', 'spring' or 'coffee break'. Together with anthroponyms and toponyms, chrononyms help to create the referential illusion and are associated, therefore, with the figurative level of meaning.

See also *anthroponym* and *toponym*.

City – Semiotics of the

The semiotics of the city focuses on urban space as the projection of meaning and of human values. It concerns itself not only with uncovering underlying ideologies but with the elaboration of new urban projects. The field of research includes an examination of representations of the city as well as the production of methodologies for the implementation of urban policies. In recent years emphasis has been laid on the dynamic interaction between the self and the urban environment, in particular on the role of the individual in the transformation of the environment and of its meanings.

The semiotics of the city was developed by A. J. Greimas and the Paris School in the early 1970s where it emerged as a branch of the Semiotics of Space. It has been further developed by James Gibson, M. Certeau and Svend Erik Larson amongst others.

Classeme

A classeme is a generic seme such as human, animal, inanimate, concrete. In other words, it refers to a particular class of objects. Dog, cat, hamster and mouse all belong to the generic class of domestic animals.

See also *seme*.

Classification

In general terms, classification designates the ordering of a given total of elements in a certain number of groups and subgroups. For example, domestic animals could be divided into hamsters, cats, dogs, etc. Dogs could then again be subdivided into spaniels, terriers, and so forth. The results of such classifications are also referred to as taxonomies.

See also *categorization* and *taxonomy*.

Code

The term code designates one of the six elements that make up Jakobson's model of communication. In order to function properly, that is, in order for it to be effectively transmitted, a message must contain a code that is understood by both sender (addresser) and receiver (addressee). In other words, there must be some measure of agreement about the meanings of the words used (or of the gestures, movements, colours, sounds).

Shared assumptions on the figurative level, to offer an example, might be the use of the term 'night' to indicate darkness, or a time to sleep. On the symbolic level, on the other hand, 'light' and 'height' are commonly associated with 'spirituality', 'goodness' or 'truth' whereas 'darkness' and 'depth' might suggest 'error' and 'evil'. Likewise, the term 'Jupiter' evokes a Roman god, and so on.

It must be noted that some cultural codes vary according to their place of origin. A reference to 'Jupiter', for instance, might be incomprehensible to someone born in China.

See also *communication model.*

Cognitive

There are two fundamental dimensions of narrative, the pragmatic and the cognitive. The *pragmatic* dimension relates to external physical events such as killing a giant, or catching a thief. The *cognitive* dimension, on the other hand, relates to internal mental activities such as knowing, convincing, deceiving. The importance attached to each dimension varies according to the nature of the discourse. In adventure stories, for example, it is the pragmatic dimension that dominates, whereas in legal discourse, it is the cognitive.

In recent years attention has been focused on a third dimension of narrative known as the *thymic* dimension. This relates to the feelings of euphoria and dysphoria (i.e. pleasant or unpleasant) experienced by the actors. These feelings can be correlated with the stages of a narrative programme. They can, for example, describe a state of disjunction or conjunction with the object of value. In Flaubert's *Madame Bovary*, Emma's disjunction with money and status gives rise to feelings of dysphoria expressed in terms of grief and frustration.

See also *pragmatic* and *thymic.*

Coherence

In discourse analysis the term coherence designates the extent to which a discourse is perceived to 'hang together' rather than being a set of unrelated sentences or utterances. The linguist Michael Halliday distinguishes between the notions of cohesion and coherence. Whereas cohesion relates to the formal (i.e. *explicit*) links between parts of a text, coherence relates to all those links that are *implicit*, such as reference to cultural and historical context or reference to underlying models or schemata.

The implicit plays a key role in the construction of meaning: a text that relies solely on surface linguistic linking would not make sense.

See also *cohesion* and *connector.*

Cohesion

Cohesion describes the process whereby sentences or utterances are linked together to form a text. Cohesive devices (or ties) are those words or phrases which enable the writer/speaker to establish relationships across sentence or utterance boundaries and which help to link the different parts of the text together. Continuity of meaning is thus achieved.

There are four ways in which cohesion is created. Three of these are grammatical: reference, ellipsis and conjunction; the fourth is lexical.

Common cohesive devices are the use of pronouns (functioning as anaphora), repetition, synonyms and collocation.

To give an example:

(a): Have you seen the books? (b): No, I don't know where they are.

The pronoun 'they' refers back to 'books', thus establishing a cohesive tie between the two sentences.

Specialists in discourse analysis make a distinction between the concepts of cohesion and coherence. Whereas cohesion refers to explicit cohesive devices within a text, coherence relates to background knowledge and context. It includes, for example, all those implicit assumptions or presuppositions without which a text would not make sense.

See also *conjunction, ellipsis, lexical cohesion* and *reference.*

Collective

A collective actant is a collection of individuals endowed with a particular narrative role. In accounts of a strike, the strikers could represent a collective actant. They could be the *subject* of a quest (to change working conditions) which is in conflict with an *anti-subject*, also played by a collective actant, the management whose goal it is to maintain the status quo and ensure that work is continued.

The term collective can also be used to describe a semantic universe based on the opposition nature versus culture. An example would be the semantic universe of a traditional American Western.

See also *individual.*

Collocation

Used in linguistics, the term collocation refers to a grouping of all those items in a text that are semantically related. The following items are examples of lexical collocation because they belong to the scientific field of biology: plants, synthesia, organic, sunlight. We can also say that the above terms make up the lexical field of biology.

The term collocation was coined by M. Halliday and is now extensively used in discourse analysis.

See also *lexical field*.

Communication model

For the linguist Roman Jakobson all communication involves six elements or functions which together make up any speech event (speech act). The following diagram, devised by Jakobson, illustrates these elements and their relations:

	CONTEXT	
ADDRESSER	MESSAGE	ADDRESSEE
(Sender)	CONTACT	(Receiver)
	CODE	

Communication, then, consists of a *message*, initiated by an addresser (sender) whose destination is an addressee (receiver). The message requires a *contact* between addresser and addressee which may be oral, visual, etc. This contact must be formulated in terms of a shared *code* – speech, numbers, writing, etc. – that makes the message intelligible. Lastly, the message must refer to a *context* understood by both addresser and addressee which enables the message to make sense. Any one of these elements may dominate in a particular communicative act.

Jakobson's central point is that the 'message' cannot supply all of the meaning of a transaction. 'Meaning' derives also from the context, the code and the means of contact, in other words, meaning resides in the *total* act of communication.

For more details see under individual headings.

Comparative reference

Comparative reference is a means by which cohesion is strengthened in a text. A relationship of contrast is being set up with one entity being compared to another. It may, for example, be the same or different, equal or unequal, more or less, etc. Any expression such as the same, another, similar, different, as big as, bigger, less big, and related adverbs such as likewise, differently, equally, presumes some point of reference in the preceding text.

Examples: 'John has a beautiful, expensive car. Paul's car is different, less expensive but more practical. Peter has the same car but an older model.'

Comparative reference items can also be used cataphorically (to point forward). In the phrase 'much more beautiful than her picture', for instance, the reference point for 'more beautiful' lies in what follows. The same applies to the sentence 'John has a bigger apple than Lizzy'.

Competence

By competence is meant the possession of those qualities that make it possible to carry out an action. These qualities are known as the modalities. A subject needs first:

> (a) a wanting-to-do (*vouloir faire*) and/or (b) a having-to-do (*devoir faire*).

All action presupposes the desire and/or the necessity to act. The decision to look for buried treasure on a desert island, for example, must be motivated by a particular desire or need: it could be economic deprivation that impels me to embark on the quest – as indeed is the case in many fairy-tales.

A subject in possession only of the desire and/or need to act is known as a *virtual* subject. To become an actualized subject and to become fully competent, the subject must in addition possess the capability to act. It must therefore possess at least one of the following modalities:

> (a) a being-able-to-do (*pouvoir faire*) and/or (b) a knowing-how-to-do (*savoir faire*).

Thus, doing itself presupposes a wanting-to-do (or having-to-do) as well as a being-able-to-do (and/or knowing-how-to-do). In my quest for the buried treasure, for example, I will need to acquire a ship or other means of transport. Maps and tools such as a shovel could also be my helpers providing me with the necessary competence.

The four modalities can be considered as objects with which the subject must be conjoined in order to carry out the performance. Modal objects – which constitute competence – can thus be distinguished from the object of value (which is at stake in the performance). The abstract representation of the competent subject is as follows:

S ⌒ Om

The qualifying test is the series of narrative programmes in which the subject acquires or manifests competence.

See also *modalities* and *qualifying test.*

Complementary

A complementary term is a term that is implied by another within the same semantic category. In the semantic category of 'existence', for example, 'death' and 'non-life' are complementary terms, as are those of 'non-death' and 'life'.

See also *semantic category* and *semiotic square.*

Conative function

When a communication is angled towards the addressee or receiver of the message, drawing him/her into the exchange, then it is the conative function that dominates. This function is indicated by the use of direct questions, warnings or persuasive devices. Questionnaires gathering information about their addressees are an example of texts whose predominant function is conative. The primary function of a party political broadcast may be conative in that it is trying to persuade the listener/viewer to adopt a particular set of opinions and vote for a particular party.

Dominance of the conative function in a text does not preclude the other speech functions being present to varying degrees.

See also *communication model.*

Conceptual

The term conceptual refers to the sphere or inner mental world of abstract ideas. In semiotics the term thematic is frequently employed in the place of conceptual to denote the world of abstract concepts such as those of good and evil, totalitarianism and democracy, freedom and imprisonment, etc.

The conceptual can be contrasted with the figurative, that is, with those elements representing the physical and concrete world that can be apprehended through the five senses.

See also *figurative.*

Concrete

A term is concrete if it possesses a referent in the external physical world, i.e. if it refers to a reality that can be perceived by the five senses. Concrete terms make up what is known as the figurative level of meaning. They are contrasted with abstract, conceptual terms to be found on the deep level.

Concrete terms can have a wealth of meanings depending on the context in which they are used, in other words they have a high semic density. Abstract terms, on the other hand, are much simpler and have low semic density. The term 'car', for instance, in addition to the concrete object may also signify 'speed', 'freedom' or 'prestige', etc., whereas the abstract concepts 'freedom' or 'prestige' are restricted in their meanings.

See also *abstract* and *semic density.*

Configuration

Semiotic theory distinguishes between discursive configurations and lexical configurations. *Discursive* configurations centre on particular expressions or discursive figures revealing underlying immutable structures. The term 'strike', for instance, implies a polemical confrontation staging opposing subjects who are motivated by a sender and an anti-sender. Manipulation, persuasive and interpretative doing are involved, leading to quests failing or being accomplished. Thus the configuration accompanying 'strike' presents itself as a micro-narrative programme (PN *d'usage*) which is to be integrated into larger discursive units within which it acquires functional significance. In this sense, the term configuration in semiotics signifies in a similar way to that of the nineteenth-century concept *motif.*

On a *lexical* level, the term configuration designates the relationships different semantic fields (isotopies) entertain with each other within a particular textual space. For example, a text may be about 'birth' and 'death', about 'work', 'subsistence', 'feelings' and 'time'. All these isotopies would therefore be found independently on the figurative level. In conjunction, however, they can be viewed and evaluated in a configurative perspective.

See also *motif* and *narrative programme.*

Confrontation

The term confrontation describes the polemical structure underpinning narrative programmes in opposition. There are always at least two subjects pursuing quests that are in conflict. The outcome of confrontation, however, varies: either it results in the domination of one or the other of the subjects and their quests, or it leads to an exchange or, more generally, a contract.

To offer a few examples: industrial strikes or wars between nations frequently illustrate confrontation culminating in the domination of one or the other side. Employers achieving a return to work without granting an increase in salary, for instance, is a case in point. On the other hand, negotiations, agreement or a peace treaty, can also be – and sometimes are – the consequence of confrontation in personal quarrels or even between warring nations.

Conjunction

Conjunction is a cohesive device for marking logical relationships in discourse. According to the linguists Michael Halliday and Ruqaiya Hasan (1976) there are four types of logical relationship: additive (designated by conjunctions such as 'and'); adversative (indicated by words such as 'but', 'nevertheless', 'however'); causal (e.g. 'because', 'for'); and temporal (e.g. 'firstly', 'then', 'next', 'while').

Example: 'Very few people are eating beef at present. This is <u>because</u> they are afraid of catching mad-cow disease.' 'Because' here is a causal conjunction.

In discourse analysis, the term conjunction is frequently replaced by the word 'connective' or 'connector'.

See also *cohesion* and *connector.*

Conjunction and disjunction

In semiotic theory, the terms conjunction and disjunction articulate two possible relationships between a subject and an object. In the utterance 'Cinderella is happy', the subject, Cinderella, is in a relationship of conjunction with the object, happiness. In the utterance 'Cinderella is not happy', the relationship between Cinderella and her object, happiness, is one of disjunction.

A narrative programme can be described as the transformation of a syntactical relationship between a subject and an object from one of conjunction to one of disjunction, or vice versa.

See also *narrative programme.*

Connector

A connector is a link word (or a group of words) that binds the parts of a text together thus signalling (i.e. rendering explicit) a logical relationship. It constitutes a key device, therefore, in the creation of textual cohesion.

Connectors may take the form of individual words ('then', 'but'), set phrases and expressions ('as a result', 'the reason is') and conjunctions ('when', 'after'). According to Halliday and Hasan (1976), there are four main groups of connectors (or four types of logical relationship):

1. *Temporal connectors*, e.g. 'first of all', 'then', 'next', 'before', 'after', 'immediately'.

   These express a temporal connection or relationship between parts of the text.

2. *Causal connectors*, e.g. 'because', 'in order to', 'therefore', 'so', 'as a result', 'consequently', 'the reason is'.

   These establish a causal connection, i.e. a relationship of cause and effect between parts of the text.

3. *Adversative connectors*, e.g. 'however', 'but', 'nevertheless', 'in spite of', 'on the other hand', 'yet', 'whereas', 'although'.

   These connectors indicate that what follows is in some sense opposed to, or contrasted with, what has gone before.

4. *Additive connectors,* e.g. 'and', 'also', 'in addition', 'moreover'.

   The connector here expresses a relationship of addition (or variation) between parts of the text.

See also *cohesion* and *conjunction.*

Connotation

Connotation refers to a procedure whereby a term, in addition to meanings allotted to it in a dictionary (denotative meanings), acquires additional significance resulting from the context in which it is applied. In this sense, the signifier 'white', apart from denoting a colour, might connote 'desire', 'absence', 'spirituality', 'death', etc., depending on the conditions of its application. The distinction between connotative and denotative terms is frequently blurred.

The linguist Louis Hjelmslev employs the term connotation in his definition of different types of semiotics, that is, in his terminology, of languages in a broader sense. He calls connotative a semiotic whose expression-plane is a 'language' in its own right. For example, a novel written today but supposed to take place in ancient Greece may evoke ancient connotations by using a way of writing, a vocabulary, syntax and rhythm that copy translations of Homer. Because of its expression-plane and content-plane, Homer's language here connotes the content: ancient reality. Hjelmslev opposes connotative semiotic to denotative semiotic and metasemiotic.

See also *connotator, denotation* and *metasemiotics.*

Connotator

The expression connotator is used by Louis Hjelmslev to describe units of style. These are part of a semiotic system called connotative semiotics. According to Hjelmslev, they include manner of speaking or writing, tone, rhythm, vernacular, medium, etc., and, as stylistic value, they represent the content plane for which the denotative semiotics are the expression. For example, the English language is a denotative form and substance constituting a connotative expression whose content is the connotator 'English'.

See also *denotation.*

Constructivism

Constructivists argue that reality can never be completely independent of the way we perceive the world. Perception itself involves codes and our language and sign systems play a key role in what is termed 'the social construction of the real'. Constructivism is, therefore, an anti-essentialist, anti-realist stance. It does not, however, deny the existence of physical reality.

Through the adoption of a philosophical perspective that highlights the role of human interpretation – especially in the context of media and cultural studies – constructivists give expression to many of the basic principles of semiotics.

Content

According to the Danish linguist Louis Hjelmslev, there are two fundamental planes or levels of language, the plane of content and the plane of expression. These two levels are in a relationship of presupposition. The level of expression relates to the domain of the signifier (sound, image, colour, etc.). The level of content, on the other hand, relates to the concept or idea (the signified) expressed by sound, image or colour, in other words, it concerns their semantic charge.

The expression *content analysis* is normally reserved to the domain of sociology and psychosociology. Content analysis in this case interprets a text (or a group of texts) from an a priori, categorical perspective directed at the mere quantification of data. Present tendencies, in semiotics at least, aim at transforming content analysis into discourse analysis.

See also *discourse* and *expression and content.*

Context

The term context designates any text that precedes or accompanies any specific signifying unit, and on which its meaning depends. Context, in this sense, can be explicit, implied or situational. When making a political speech, for instance, the *explicit* context might be documents on which the speaker bases his arguments; the *implied* context may be events or reasons that give rise to the speech while the *situational* context would refer to the set of circumstances under which it takes place and which also have a bearing on the meaning produced.

Context is one of the six elements or functions that figure in Jakobson's communication model. According to him any message, in order to make sense, must refer to a context understood by both sender (addresser) and receiver (addressee).

We also talk of *contextual* semes (or classemes). These are units of meaning, or bundles of meaning, which occur in both text and context. Thus, in their composition, contextual semes resemble sememes.

See also *classeme, seme* and *sememe.*

Contiguity

This term denotes a relation of touching or adjoining. It refers to things that are directly connected to each other. In semiotics it can describe a relationship of belonging, in particular of part to whole or of part to the same domain. For example, the objects 'sail' and 'ship' are in a position of contiguity. The figure of speech known as metonymy, the substitution of one term for another, is based on a relationship of contiguity. We may use 'pen' to denote 'author', 'No. 10' to denote 'Prime Minister' and 'the crown' to denote the 'monarchy'. Metonymy is contrasted with metaphor, which involves the transposition from one domain to another. An example would be: 'She had mountains of money'. Here money is not connected to, and does not belong to, the natural physical world of mountains.

See also *metonymy.*

Contract

In general terms, a contract could be defined as the establishment of an intersubjective relationship which results in a modification of status (*l'être* and/or *le paraître*) affecting each of the subjects involved. In semiotic metalanguage, a narrative sequence starts with a contract/manipulation between a sender and a subject who undertakes to accomplish an action. The king contracts the knight to slay the dragon and offers him the hand of the princess in return. The knight, on the other hand, is prepared to offer his sword and his services in exchange for the king's promise to give him his daughter in marriage.

Before accepting this contract, however, an agreement of mutual trust must have been established. Otherwise what assurance would the knight have that the king will fulfil his pledge, or, for that matter, what assurance would the king possess that the knight is willing and able to execute his part of the bargain? In other words, without a firm belief in the truthfulness and reliability of the partner, the contract cannot become effective. This *fiduciary agreement*, which takes place on the enunciative level and precedes any actual or projected exchange of objects of value, is termed *contrat de véridiction*.

The fiduciary agreement, moreover, has two parts to it: a conclusion has to be reached as to whether one's partner is telling the truth, hiding something or downright lying, while the true value of the objects to be exchanged must also be ascertained and agreed. The activity involved in reaching consensus in these matters is cognitive: knowledge (*savoir-vrai*) is brought into play, coupled with persuasive doing on the one hand and on the other faith, acceptance (*croire-vrai*) as a result of interpretative doing. Both these manipulate in their own ways, but in the end agreement sanctioning the proceedings must be reached before any actual exchange can be settled.

Since this fiduciary agreement or enunciative contract is a prerequisite for any exchange of objects of value to become effective, it also applies to verbal transactions, that is, written texts or spoken utterances. Examples of this are to be found in normal conversation: the interlocutors' knowledge of each other, the images they project of their own credibility as well as the degree of acquaintance with the subject-matter under discussion affect the successful outcome of any communication.

The *contract/manipulation* refers to the first stage of the canonical narrative schema at which a sender transmits the modalities of desire or obligation to a receiver. Once the proposed modal status has been accepted, the contract is concluded and the receiver becomes a subject pursuing the quest that is to follow.

See also *canonical narrative schema*.

Contradiction

Contradiction is a logical component of the elementary structure of meaning. It is established as the result of the negation of one of the opposing terms, which is thereby rendered absent. The term 'life', for instance, is contradicted or negated by the term 'non-life'. Equally, the contradictory term of 'good' is 'non-good'.

The contradictory term thus produced *implies* the presence of the opposing term necessary to produce meaning. The term 'life' is contradicted by 'non-life', which in turn implies 'death', the latter being the opposing term in the semantic category of 'existence'.

The relationship can be outlined in a semiotic square:

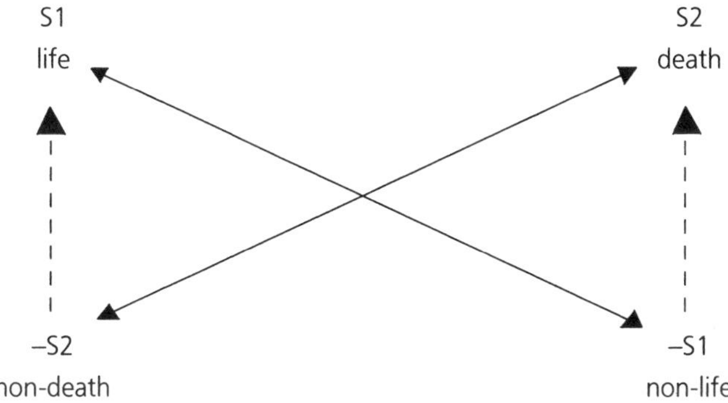

Here the term 'non-life' is in a relationship of contradiction to 'life' and of implication or complementarity to death.

See also *semiotic square.*

Contrary

A term can be described as contrary if its existence presupposes that of its opposite. 'Hot' and 'cold', 'high' and 'low', 'life' and 'death' are contraries, as each term is defined by its opposite which it therefore presumes to exist. In other words, to be contraries, two terms must possess a meaning in common or common denominator. Thus, 'high' and 'low' have the concept of 'verticality' in common, or 'hot' and 'cold' have 'temperature' as their common denominator.

See also *semantic category* and *semiotic square.*

Control-actant

The control-actant relates to the two basic properties belonging to the act of perception: the direction of a perception (source and target) and the control of this direction by an actant, that is, the control-actant. For example, a concert on the radio might be the source of beautiful sound whose target would be the ears of the listener. However, an electricity cut might act as control-actant to prevent the transmission. Or else, the perfume I wear makes me the source of a delicious scent whose strength and impact are controlled by time (the length of time I have been wearing the perfume) and space (how far away the perceiving partner is).

See also *actant, source, target* and *sensory perception.*

Copenhagen School

The Copenhagen School of Linguistics was founded by the Danish linguists Louis Hjelmslev (1899–1965) and Viggo Brondal (1887–1953). The School elaborated a linguistic theory called glossematics which is an attempt to take to its logical conclusion the Saussurean principle that language is form and not substance. Glossematicians argue that linguistic elements are only to be defined by their mutual relations, called their functions. The goal of linguistic analysis is to transform features such as syntactic position or the glottal stop into functions. Glossematics aims therefore at a level of descriptive generality which makes this theory of language applicable to the study of sign systems in general. It is an abstract formalist approach that does not take into account social context.

See also *glossematics.*

Copula

A copula is a grammatical item that is used to link the subject with the complement of the sentence. The most frequently occurring copula in English is the verb 'to be'. The copula can have two functions. First it may serve to express identity such as 'Mary is the tallest girl in her class'. Secondly, it may serve to ascribe some property to its subject: the subject thus becomes a member of a class, for instance 'Anne is a poet', 'The girl is beautiful'. Here

Anne is assigned to the class of poet, and the girl to the class of beautiful people.

Correlation

In semiotic analysis, correlation designates a link being established between different levels of meaning, in particular between the figurative (concrete) level and the thematic (abstract) level. In the works of William Blake, the figurative isotopy of the sea may, for example, be correlated with the abstract themes of freedom, love and unity; the isotopy of the city, on the other hand, may be correlated with themes of imprisonment, hatred or fragmentation.

Cultural assumptions

Cultural assumptions are the cultural presuppositions that underlie a text and that play a key role in the establishment of coherence. Indeed, without the assumption of a shared knowledge of the world, some texts would be totally meaningless. An example would be the newspaper headline: 'Minister condemns spin-doctoring' which, without knowledge of what spin-doctoring connotes, would be meaningless. Cultural assumptions, therefore, relate to the procedure of reference outside the text.

See also *context*.

Cultural relativism

Cultural relativism is the concept that truth is not universal or absolute but differs between cultures. Each culture possesses its own world-view and none of these can be thought more authentic or 'truer' than another. Behind this position lies the semiotic premise that reality is a social construct and that, therefore, no single version of reality can claim a privileged status. This view can be contrasted with the classical essentialist approach.

See also *essentialism* and *postcolonialism*.

Culture

Generally, the term culture designates the sum total of knowledge, attitudes and values which inform a society or characterize an individual. In this sense, culture is the product of human achievements and directly related to the human power of transformation. The arts belong to culture, as do thought products in general or, for that matter, anything produced by human beings.

Semiotic theory contrasts the concept of culture with that of *nature*. Thus when talking about eating habits in the sixteenth century, references to raw meat, fresh blood or killing animals would fall in the category nature, while allusions to cooking, recipes or table manners would be categorized as cultural behaviour.

In accordance with the anthropologist Claude Lévi-Strauss, semiotics posits that the opposing couple 'nature/culture' articulates the semantic category 'social life' whereas the couple 'life/death' characterizes the universe of the individual.

With the growth of zoosemiotics and of biosemiotics in recent years, the sharp distinction between nature and culture has been called into question.

See also *nature*.

Débrayage/disengagement

In semiotic metalanguage *débrayage* refers to the act of projecting an utterance away from its enunciative source. The moment we start speaking we shift as it were into a new set of actorial, spatial and temporal co-ordinates constructed by our discourse. This 'change of gear' or 'disengagement' is called *débrayage*. The sentence 'The government faces an angry electorate' sets up an actor (the government), a space (the whole country, i.e. the seat of the electorate) and a time (the present, as indicated by the tense of the verb) which are separate or different from the actorial, spatial and temporal co-ordinates that apply to the speaker.

Débrayage also applies to the change-over between different discursive units or kinds of discourse as they, too, amount to a change of gear in the narration. If the expression 'Once upon a time ...' marks the initial *débrayage* of a discursive unit named fairy-tale, a dialogue, an interior monologue or a detailed description within the flow of the story would constitute a transformation or new 'shifting out' of the co-ordinates.

See also *embrayage* and *shifter.*

Decisive test

This is the stage of the canonical narrative schema at which the principal performance is enacted. It is the primary event (transformation) towards which the story has been leading. In other words, the decisive test corresponds to the moment where the object of the quest is at stake and the subject acquires (or fails to acquire) the desired goal. In the story of *Bluebeard*, the opening of the forbidden room may be considered the decisive test for the wife. In a general election, the electoral campaign represents the decisive test for the opposing parties, while the casting of votes is the decisive test for the voters.

See also *canonical narrative schema.*

Decoding

In general terms, decoding means identifying the code used to transmit a message and to translate the message concerned into everyday language.

Decoding applies to any kind of code, be it numerical, gestural, linguistic or otherwise. We decode the sign language of the deaf, for example, or the messages sent by the telegraph.

In textual analysis, decoding is often taken to be a synonym for the understanding and interpretation of texts. It also refers to deciphering Jacobson's codes of communication. Semiotics, on the other hand, understands decoding to be either an operation of translation of a fixed code (traffic lights, for instance) or a tool in the construction of the meaning of, for example, a literary text. In that case, the term interpretation is preferable to the term decoding.

See also *code, communication model, encoding* and *interpretation.*

Deconstruction

Deconstruction is a critical reading method associated with the French philosopher Jacques Derrida and with the movement of poststructuralism. The deconstructive method seeks to unmask internal contradictions or inconsistencies in the text (both literary and philosophical), looking for gaps, breaks and discontinuities of all kinds. These breaks can be seen as evidence of the repressed, unconscious within language. In his book *Of Grammatology* Derrida states that a deconstructive reading must always aim at a certain relationship, unperceived by the writer, between what he commands and what he does not command of the patterns of language that he uses; and it should attempt to make the not-seen accessible to sight. A text could be saying something quite different from what it appears to be saying. At the same time, it might possess so many different meanings that it would be impossible to arrive at any final core meaning.

The deconstructive method can be seen as the practical application of Derrida's theory of language. It can be understood within the context of his attack on the 'metaphysics of presence', the belief that the subject can know itself and express itself fully in speech. Derrida contests Saussure's concept of the sign as the self-sufficient and stable union of signifier and signified, introducing instead the notion of *différence/différance*: meaning has no origin or end but is always the product of the difference between signs and is always 'deferred' by a temporal structural process that has no end – words refer to words which in turn refer to other words *ad infinitum*. The application of the deconstructive method has the effect of destabilizing the fixed binary oppositions with which structuralism is associated and which, according to Derrida, are rooted in a belief in a transcendental signified (meaning that transcends language/history). Derrida points out that these oppositions are always hierarchical (i.e. ideological) with one element dominant (male as opposed to female, white as opposed to black). An example of the deconstructive approach is Derrida's own reading of Rousseau's essay on the origin of language in *Of Grammatology*. Rousseau sees music as consisting of two contradictory components, melody and harmony; he regards melody as springing from the passions whereas harmony is the product of articulation and differentiation. Under close scrutiny by Derrida, however, it emerges that in fact Rousseau's definition of melody includes a notion of articulation and differentiation. In other words, through the application of the deconstructive method, logocentric oppositions are questioned and/or neutralized. Derrida's thought has also exerted an important influence on postcolonial theory.

See also *difference*, *différance*, *postcolonialism* and *poststructuralism*.

Deixis

In semiotic analysis the term deixis can have two meanings:

1. Deixis designates one of the fundamental dimensions of the **semiotic square**: through a process of implication it links one of the contrary terms with the contradictory of the other contrary term. There are, therefore, two deixes.

   Let us take the example of the semiotic square of 'existence':

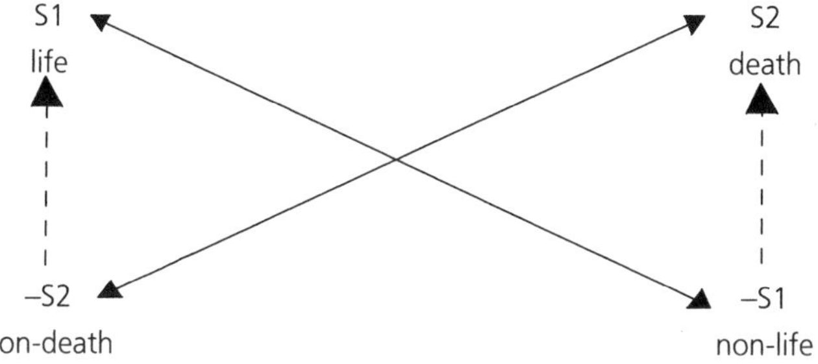

S1 (life) and –S2 (non-death) constitute one deixis. This is termed the *positive deixis.* S2 (death) and –S1 (non-life) constitute the second deixis, termed *negative deixis.* The terms positive and negative in this context are devoid of any axiological investment. This only appears as a result of the projection of the thymic category (euphoria versus dysphoria), that is, the category of feeling, onto the semiotic square.

2. Deixis is also used in a narrative as *deixis of reference.* In this context, temporal positions (now/then) or spatial positions (here/there) can be described as deixes of reference. Thus, for example, what is sometimes described as the 'time of the narrative' appears as a present identifiable with a 'then' deixis in relation to which a past and a future can be installed. In *Treasure Island* the search for the gold could be the deixis of reference in relation to which the preparatory events as well as the later moment of preserving the adventures in writing could be viewed as past and future.

Demonstrative reference

Demonstrative reference is a means by which cohesion is strengthened in a text. It can be expressed by determiners (this, that, these, those) or adverbs (here, then). These are used anaphorically to point backwards to a previously mentioned item or cataphorically to point forwards. The definite article 'the' can be considered as a particular type of demonstrative. Demonstratives can be used on their own or with nouns. Examples:

> 'We must keep him in bed and give him paracetemol three times a day as well as frequent hot drinks. If that fails, we must take him to the doctor.'
>
> 'In my days we took the matter more seriously. We had different ideas then.'
>
> 'This is what he wanted us to do: pick up the money, meet the men at the border, change vehicles and then head for Belfast.'

Denotation

Denotation designates the process of referring to the dictionary meanings of a word. It can be distinguished from connotation which relates to additional meanings resulting from the context in which the word is applied. The word 'rose', for example, denotes a flower or the shrub bearing it. In a particular context, however, the word 'rose' might connote love, or the House of Tudor.

The linguist Louis Hjelmslev employs the term denotation in his definition of different types of semiotics, that is – in his terminology – of languages in a broader sense. He calls a denotative semiotic a language none of whose planes is a semiotic in its own right. In other words, denotation refers to the primary sign of a natural language. Hjelmslev opposes denotative semiotic to connotative semiotic and metasemiotic.

See also *connotation* and *metasemiotics.*

Descriptive

The term descriptive is normally used in connection with **values**. Descriptive values – in opposition to modal values – are attached to objects that can be consumed or hoarded (i.e. *objective* values) or to states of mind or feelings (i.e. *subjective* values). Bananas, for instance, represent descriptive values linked to objects, as do clothes, precious stones or cars. Smoking or listening to music, on the other hand, amount to descriptive values involving subjective feelings or pleasures.

Similarly, statements that deal with descriptive values are referred to as *descriptive statements.* Descriptive statements have to be distinguished from modal utterances that govern them. Thus the sentence 'The monkey wants the banana growing on the tree' contains two statements: a descriptive one ('the banana grows on the tree') and a modal one ('the monkey wants the banana').

See also *modal, modalization* and *object of value.*

Diachrony

The term diachrony designates the arrangement of time in a historical perspective. If we analyse the development of colonialism during the last two or three centuries, for example, our study will be diachronic.

Diachrony is opposed to *synchrony,* which refers to temporal coincidence of events. Thus, if synchrony describes different events all taking place at the same time, diachrony relates to occurrences arranged in sequence or on a vertical/historical axis.

Saussure introduced the dichotomy diachrony/synchrony for the description of language in a historical perspective (dealing with transformations of language over a period of time) and a synchronic perspective (concerning a contemporary language system). When describing abstract systems, however, any notion of time presents problems. Thus present-day linguistics operates within an atemporal or *achronic* framework.

See also *achrony* and *synchrony.*

Dialogism

Dialogism is a term associated with the Russian theorist Mikhail Bakhtin, who argues that all language is inherently dialogic. In other words, language is not the product of an isolated individual but of an interaction with others. It is therefore saturated with the meanings given to it by others. Spoken and written utterances can be likened to multi-layered palimpsests.

Bakhtin draws particular attention to the conflictual nature of dialogue where language is above all a field of ideological contention and the locus of struggle and contradiction. In his first major literary study he argues that the novels of Dostoyevsky are essentially polyphonic, incorporating a range of different voices – by voices is meant the ideas expressed by the different characters or narrators. There is no central voice or privileged point of view. The voices interact and collide in a pattern of continuing dialogue or 'dialogic openness' in which no one has the final say.

Bakhtin's ideas caught the attention of poststructuralist theorists in the 1970s and 1980s and led to the development by Julia Kristeva of the concept of intertextuality. His writings thus contributed to the further undermining of the traditional view of the author as the origin of the text and ultimate authority as to its meaning. The opposite of dialogism is monologism, the denial that there exists another consciousness with the same rights.

See also *intertextuality* and *palimpsest.*

Dialogue

The term dialogue denotes a discursive unit in speech structure. As a verbal exchange, it involves at least two interlocutors or participants who alternately take the parts of sender or receiver of a message. The designation interlocutor here refers to an instance performing a speech act. It has to be distinguished from the terms narrator and narratee, which describe the delegates of an enunciator/enunciatee of an utterance.

To give an example: Little Johnny wants a sweet. Little Johnny: 'I want a sweet.' Mother: 'Why do you want a sweet? You can't have one.' Little Johnny: 'But I want a sweet . . .' In this instance, little Johnny and Mother are participants in an exchange of statements called a dialogue.

Reported dialogue often includes a framework stressing the speech act ('he said', 'she replied'). Additional information relative to the dialogue may also be offered ('nervously', 'with tears in her voice').

See also *communication model, enunciator/enunciatee* and *narrator/narratee.*

Diegesis

Derived from the Greek, the term diegesis relates to 'the narrative aspect of discourse'. For the literary semiotician Gérard Genette, the term designates the narrated events or story, which he also names *histoire* as distinct from the level of narration, i.e. the telling of the story. In other words, the diegetic level of a narrative is that of the main events, whereas the 'higher' level at which they are told is extradiegetic (that is, standing outside the sphere of the main story).

Différance

The expression *différance* was coined by Jacques Derrida to denote the divided nature of the sign. The terms *différence* and *différance* vary only in writing and both derive from the French verb *différer* which signifies to differ (in space) as well as to defer (in time). Deconstructing Saussure's basic principle of difference as the origin of all meaning (*'Il n'y a de sens que dans la différence'*), Derrida proposes that the differences in the meanings of signs are not only the result of static relations with other terms but contends that every semiotic element also contains in itself traces of all other elements or structures. And since every trace exists only by virtue of another trace there cannot be a finite origin of any trace. In other words, signs refer to signs which refer to signs and so on *ad infinitum*. It is to this deferral of meaning that he allots the term *différance*.

See also *deconstruction* and *difference*.

Difference

In his *Course in General Linguistics* (1916), Saussure argues that there can be no meaning without difference. In other words, he sees meaning as residing in relations and their transformation and develops structures as systems of relations. The most elementary relation of difference within a language structure is that of opposition. A. J. Greimas developed differential relationships further by adding contradiction and implication or complementarity. Together they make up the elementary structure of meaning which finds visual representation in the semiotic square.

See also *différance* and *semiotic square*.

Discourse

The term discourse denotes using language or talk generally, treating a subject verbally at length or making a speech.

According to Halliday, the term discourse designates a unit of language larger than a sentence and which is firmly rooted in a specific context. There are many different types of discourse under this heading, such as academic discourse, legal discourse, media discourse, etc. Each discourse type possesses its own characteristic linguistic features. This understanding of the term is generally accepted in discourse analysis.

In strictly semiotic terms, the word refers to the discursive level of meaning as opposed to the narrative level. A discourse is established through the interaction of two dimensions of language:

1) the figurative dimension, relating to the representation of the natural world;

2) the thematic dimension, relating to the abstract values actualized in an utterance.

In this sense, all manifestations of language can be envisaged as a discourse.

Discursive level

The discursive level relates to the process of putting the narrative structures into words, that is, of giving them figurative and linguistic shape. It is on this level that the actants/subjects, for example, are named and become actors, adopting thematic roles such as 'son', 'father' or 'soldier'; transformations enacted are arranged in chronological sequences and placed in a given space; the objects pursued are installed in systems of values which organize the utterance and determine the direction of desires and conflicts.

To analyse the discursive level of an utterance, we have to examine specific words and expressions or grammatical items/structures to discover their semiotic pertinence. Little Red Riding Hood is sent by her mother to take a cake to her grandmother. Thus she is placed in the position of an actant/subject pursuing a quest (narrative level). Her figurative description allots to this actant/subject the thematic role of child with the term 'little' alone establishing her vulnerability (discursive level). The story turns the wolf into an anti-subject (narrative level). The expression 'wolf' – a wild beast – and his figurative portrayal place him in the thematic role of a monster with the wish to harm (discursive level). Child and wolf and their conflicting narrative programmes here illustrate, for example, an underlying value-system which opposes in the shape of 'eating' versus 'being eaten', 'ogre' against 'victim' or 'evil' against 'good'.

There are no abstract formulas for the figurativization of texts or discursive trajectories, since most texts (particularly literary texts) are too complex to be reduced in this manner.

See also *actantial narrative schema.*

Discursive subject

The discursive subject is the subject through whose eyes places and events, etc., are being described. It may be internal (an actor in the story) or external (the position adopted by an imaginary observer). The discursive subject may or may not be identical with the narrative subject, that is, the subject of the main quest in the story. In *Treasure Island*, the discursive subject is Jim Hawkins, who is also a narrative subject in the quest to discover the treasure. In most fairy-tales, the discursive subject is an anonymous narrator who plays no part in the principal quest. In frame narratives, we usually have narrators who, while participating in the narrative they present, do not, or only minimally, function in the main story.

See also *narrative subject.*

Discursive units

In semiotics, the term discursive units covers what was traditionally called 'description', 'dialogue', 'narration', 'interior monologue', 'indirect speech', etc. These units are considered stages in the flow of a text and are analysed in their changing relationship with each other as well as with regard to the enunciative source as point of reference. Operations of ***débrayage/ embrayage*** allow for the stages being shifted from one to the next.

See also *débrayage* and *embrayage.*

Discursivization

This relates to the syntactical organization of discursive elements which are expressed on the textual surface. In this sense, the procedures involved in discursivization are linked to the operations of ***débrayage*** **and** ***embrayage***.

Basically, discursivization can be divided into three sub-components: actorialization, temporalization and spatialization. Together they set up the actorial, temporal and spatial framework in which narrative programmes can function. A narrative quest for love, for example, is put into words or discursivized in the story of Romeo and Juliet by installing actors (Romeo and Juliet), a place (Verona) and a time (long ago) on the textual surface.

See also *actorialization, spatialization* and *temporalization.*

Disjunction and conjunction

In semiotic theory the terms disjunction and conjunction articulate two possible relationships between a subject and an object. In the utterance 'John is poor', John, the subject, is in a relationship of disjunction with the object, wealth. In the utterance 'John has a great deal of money', on the other hand, the relationship between John and his object, wealth, is one of conjunction.

A narrative programme can be described as the transformation of a syntactical relationship between a subject and an object from one of disjunction to one of conjunction, or vice versa.

See also *narrative programme.*

Doing/*faire*

The term doing is synonymous with that of act (or action). The doing of a subject produces a transformation. In the sentence 'John buys a newspaper', the expression 'buys' represents John's doing. It transforms a situation of lack (having no newspaper) into one of reparation of lack (having a newspaper).

The expression **subject of doing** is employed to refer to a subject who in its relationship to an object, brings about a transformation. In the sentence 'John found a coin', John is the subject of doing because he has moved from a position of disjunction to one of conjunction with the object.

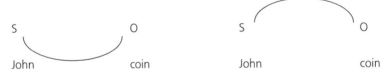

The subject of doing is to be distinguished from the subject of state whose relationship with an object remains unchanged. This kind of relationship is frequently expressed in verbs such as 'to be' or 'to have'. In the sentence 'John is poor', the position of John in relation to the object, poverty, does not vary. John, therefore, is a subject of state.

See also *subject of doing* and *subject of state.*

Donor

The term donor designates one of the seven spheres of action (and hence roles) which, according to Propp, make up the folk-tale. It describes 'the preparation for the transmission of a magical object and the provision of the hero with a magical object'. Other spheres of action include that of the villain, the dispatcher, the auxiliary hero, the false hero, the princess and her father, and finally the hero.

In narrative semiotics, the role of the donor – together with that of the auxiliary – is subsumed in the term 'helper'. The anti-donor, a term used by some semioticians, is related to the role of the opponent.

See also *helper* and *opponent.*

Doxa

The term doxa denotes public opinion, majority prejudice, middle-class consensus. It is linked to the concept of doxology, to everything that is seemingly self-evident in terms of opinion, or conventional practice and habit. In England, for example, talk of the genius of Shakespeare is part of the doxa, as is a meal of fish and chips or a game of cricket.

In his book *Mythologies* (1957), the critic Roland Barthes denounces the French doxa which characterized the 1950s.

Durative

The term durative indicates the continuation of a process. It is frequently expressed in the use of the imperfect tense: 'He was reading a book'; 'We were having a great time'; 'She was a wonderful mother'.

A durative process is usually framed by an inchoative term marking its beginning and by a terminative term marking its end: 'In 1980 I moved to Paris. I lived there until last year.'

See also *inchoative* and *terminative.*

Dysphoria

This is the negative term of the thymic category, that is, the category that relates to the world of feeling and emotions. Dysphoria denotes unpleasant sensations and unhappiness which can be contrasted with their opposite, **euphoria**, the feeling of well-being or joy. In a text, the distinction euphoria versus dysphoria gives rise to an axiological system. An example of dysphoria would be: 'The fall of the democratic government and its replacement by a totalitarian regime was the cause of great misery.'

See also *aphoria, euphoria* and *thymic.*

Ecosemiotics

Ecosemiotics is a branch of the semiotics of nature which emerged in Europe in the 1980s and is currently represented by researchers such as Jean Petitot, François Rastier and Sung-Do Kim. It can be described as the study of the relationship between nature and culture, focusing on questions such as the role of nature for humans, the meaning we give nature and the means whereby we communicate with it.

The notion that nature is made up of sign systems to be interpreted by humans has a long tradition. The most radical manifestation of this is a branch of study known as pansemiotics, the belief that environmental phenomena are semiotic in their essence. This position was adopted by Charles Peirce whose thought undoutedly influenced the growth of ecosemiotics.

Elementary structure of tension

In recent years semiotic theory has developed a model of the elementary structure of tension – or tensive structure – in an attempt to answer questions left open by the classic semiotic models. The semiotic square, for example, provides for an illustration of the apprehension of semantic concepts and the formation of systems of value. However, it represents categories as something fixed, an end-product. It does not account for the actual process whereby meaning emerges from sensations and perceptions as it does, for instance, in the *discours en acte*. In other words, the tensive model is a representation of the manner or process in which *l'intelligible* (meaning) emerges from *le sensible* (the sensible, or sensory perception). In this sense, while being close to the semiotic square, the elementary tensive structure is set up in the perspective of continuing signification.

As explained by Jacques Fontanille, the tensive structure is based on four steps or stages:

1) Before any categorization can take place, awareness of a presence is felt. This presence reveals itself in terms of *intensity* and in terms of *expanse* and *quantity* (*étendue*). Before identifying any kind of object, we will have recognized tactile or visual properties: the hot and the cold, the smooth and the rough, the visible and the invisible, the mobile and the immobile, the solid and the fluid. These qualities can be assessed according to the

degree of their intensity, and to their quantity and position in space. Solidity, for example, is characterized by having the capacity to stay in one position without changing form (expanse) as a result of strong internal cohesion (intensity). Fluidity, on the other hand, shows weak internal cohesion and inconsistency in form, position, space and time. Presence thus makes itself felt and identified in a combination of intensity or force on an internal level and special physical contours externally.

2) If the first stage is one of sensory apprehension, the second stage concerns selecting two dimensions – one on the level of intensity and one on the level of spatial positioning – and bringing them together before even recognizing any figurative shape. In fact it is the *quality of presence* which is here at stake. For example, the element earth could be considered to possess great solidity because of its strong cohesive force as well as weak propensity for dispersal in space or time. Conversely, with regard to the same quality of presence, air has very little strength of cohesion and great expanding capacity in spatio-temporal terms. If we therefore understand the two dimensions of intensity and expanse to be gradual, their correlation can be represented as points in a space controlled by two axes:

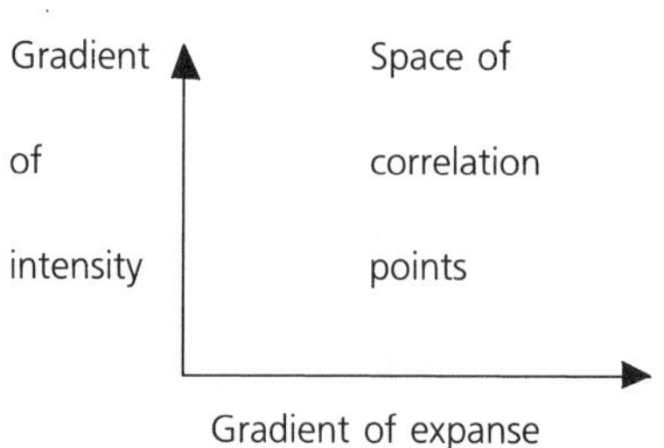

In accordance with the definition of the two levels of language, *intensity* here characterizes the internal, interoceptive domain which will become the level of content while the *spatio-temporal expanse* characterizes the external, exteroceptive domain which will become the level of expression. The correlation of the two is the result of the position taken by a perceiving subject; it is thus proprioceptive.

3) During the third stage, the perceiving, 'feeling' body of the observer not only imposes a division between an internal, intensive domain and an

external, extensive domain, it also imposes a positioning, namely that of awareness or intentionality (*la visée intentionnelle*) coupled with spatial apprehension (*la saisie*). These two operations convert the gradual dimensions of intensity and expanse into axes on a deep level. Thus under the control of intentionality and spatial apprehension the degrees of intensity and expanse turn into degrees of perceptive depth. For example, the sound of the ringing doorbell alerts the perceiving subject (awareness) that there is 'someone' at the door (spatial apprehension).

4) In the final stage the formation of systems of value takes place. The emergence of values, however, relies in the first place on valencies – the preconditions for the apparition of value – and these are to be found in the modes of sensorial perception. Valencies are by nature gradual and exist in two types: the first type is intensive/affective and spans the range from weakest to strongest intensity; the second type is extensive and perceptive and covers expanse and quantity from weakest/smallest to most extensive/concentrated. Correlation between the degrees of each of the two types produces values: each value is defined by one degree of intensity and one degree of spatial expanse or quantity; two values differ because they correspond to both two different degrees of intensity and two different degrees of spatio-temporal expanse. For example, the 'aerial' and diffuse scent of a garden open to the wind contrasts with the concentrated, heady smell in a confined space:

   [weak intensity + large expanse] versus [high intensity + compressed expanse]

   With regard to individual valencies, only degrees differ whereas combinations of valencies equip value systems with a network of discontinuous (or discrete) oppositions. It follows that in the elementary diagram, the two types of valencies are represented as graduated axes in a right-angled relation to each other; values, on the other hand, are the points of intersection of the degrees of projection of the two axes.

See also *presence*, *sensory perception* and *valancy*.

Elementary utterance

The expression elementary utterance refers to the basic unit of meaning, which can be defined as a *relationship* between two actants. This relationship is expressed in a verb. The two actants, subject and object, for example, only exist in relationship to each other.

There are two kinds of elementary utterances:

1) utterances of state, e.g. 'John is poor'; or 'The Queen owns Windsor Castle';
2) utterances of doing, e.g. 'John reads the book', or 'The train arrives in the station'.

See also *actant, function* and *narrative programme.*

Ellipsis

Ellipsis occurs when some essential structural element is omitted from a sentence or clause and can only be recovered by referring to an element in the preceding text. In other words, the sentence can only be understood in conjunction with another utterance that supplies the missing element. For example:

A: I like the blue dress. **B**: I prefer the green.
A: You work too hard. **B**: So do you.

In both cases, the second sentence is incomprehensible without the first one.

Ellipsis is a common cohesive device in texts.

Embedding

The term embedding is sometimes used in semiotics to designate the insertion of a narrative (micro-narrative) into a larger narrative. It is synonymous with the term intercalation.

In Emily Brontë's *Wuthering Heights*, the story of Catherine and Heathcliff as told by the housekeeper is embedded within the story of the tenant Lockwood. Similarly, parables in the Bible story are examples of embedded or intercalated narratives.

Embrayage/engagement

If *débrayage* (disengagement) refers to a shifting away from the enunciative source and into a new set of actorial, spatial and temporal co-ordinates, *embrayage* (engagement) suspends this operation without annulling it, by re-injecting the enunciative presence. The statement, 'Yesterday the forecast said it would be raining in Scotland', for example, marks a *débrayage* by setting up an action, a time and a place different from that of the person who is speaking. The addition 'I went for a walk in the Scottish Hills and got wet', on the other hand, indicates an *embrayage* by making the presence of the actual speaker felt within the newly constructed set-up which it complements rather than cancels.

See also *débrayage* and *shifter.*

Emotion

In semiotic terms, emotion – like passion, which falls under the same heading – is described as a syntagmatic disposition of 'conditions of the soul/mind' (*états d'âme*). Thus we are dealing with states of being (*être*) as opposed to action/doing (*faire*). Cinderella is unhappy. Cinderella cries. There is often a close link between emotional states and preceding or subsequent action.

The connection, however, is even more complex at a stage prior to narrative action. The object of an emotion touches the subject, emotionally. It disturbs the subject, which is moved or disturbed by it. In this sense, an action (*faire*) takes place as a result of which the subject is unbalanced, it is no longer what it was before and even its behaviour may be altered. A gentle, loving husband turns jealous and kills his wife. Joy, happiness give strength to perform deeds one never dreamt of. Emotion is therefore also linked to a micro-transformation, albeit on the level of being (*être*), that precedes the macro-narrative.

See also *semiotics of passion.*

Encoding

In general terms, encoding denotes communicating a message by means of using a code of a linguistic or non-linguistic nature. For encoding to function effectively, both sender (addresser) and receiver (addressee) must be familiar with the code applied, which could be a language, the Morse code, a colour code, or any other conventional practice. In this sense, any written text can be used as an example of encoding since it converts a message into words and relies on agreement between author and reader about the meanings of the words used, and on shared assumptions about their associations and implications. In a more particular sense, encoding within a text refers to the specific use of words emphasizing some meanings while backgrounding others. For example, a passage talking about desert, dust, heat, barren trees, etc., might use these terms to convey loneliness and isolation rather than a picture of the Sahara.

To the linguist Roman Jakobson, the code is one of the six basic functions or elements that make up his model of communication. Encoding here represents making a message intelligible to its receiver.

See also *code*, *communication model* and *decoding.*

Enunciative subject

In semiotic analysis we distinguish between the *enunciator* of an utterance and the *enunciatee* to whom it is addressed. In conversation, two interlocutors take part in an intersubjective exchange, in turn advancing propositions and accepting or rejecting them. On the surface level, therefore, enunciator and enunciatee adopt distinctly different positions: one asking to be believed, the other conferring belief or withholding it. On a deeper level, however, the different participants in the exchange come together in one syncretic figure representing the enunciative performance in its entirety. It is in this context that we talk of the subject of enunciation, or the enunciative subject, which comprises both proposition and acceptance or rejection, like two sides of a whole glued by their fiduciary relation. On the discursive level, this unity is illustrated by, for instance, the syncretism manifest in the expression 'He believed in himself'.

See also *enunciator/enunciatee* and *epistemological subject.*

Enunciator/enunciatee

The term enunciator refers to the instance initiating a speech act. S/he is the author/sender of a message addressed to an enunciatee or receiver.

The enunciator has to be distinguished from the narrator of a written text or verbal communication. The narrator is in fact a construct, an actant to whom the enunciator – by means of the procedure of *débrayage* – has delegated his/her voice. The 'I' in an utterance, therefore, is not identical with the enunciator but a verbal simulacrum of a narrative presence. Correspondingly, the real enunciatee/receiver of the message is represented in a text by an actant/delegate, the narratee. The latter may, or may not, be present on the discursive level with the mention 'you'.

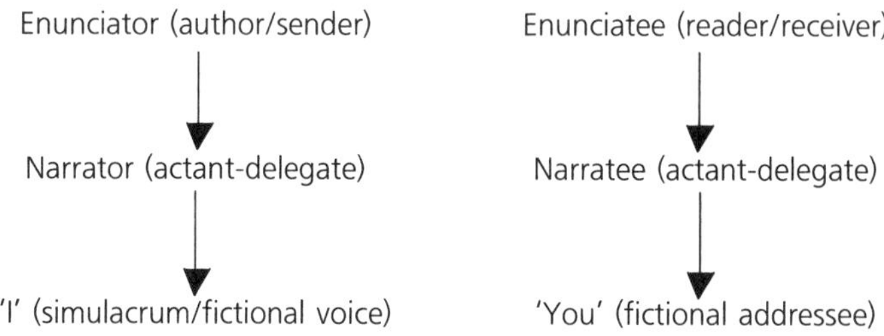

The author Robert Louis Stevenson is the enunciator of the novel *Treasure Island*. Stevenson delegates his voice to a narrating instance, here finding expression in the narrative actant Jim Hawkins. The enunciatee of the novel, on the other hand, the reading public, finds its delegate in the construction of a fictional narratee (model audience) represented in the text by the simulacra of the gentlemen for whom the account is supposedly written.

See also *narrator/narratee*.

Envelope

In semiotic theory the figure of the envelope is used to describe an imaginary surface on which the diverse sensorial contacts are stamped in zones of inscription. This surface, made up of all the sensorial impressions, is both a *memory* and an *envelope* that we all carry with us. A smell or a taste, for example, once experienced, function as traces leading us back to their first encounter. Proust's *A la recherche du temps perdu* is based on this phenomenon.

The sensorial stamp, moreover, also becomes autonomous in the sense that it no longer depends on sensorial types, and has its own form which other contacts, relating to other sensorial types, can reactivate at any moment. For example, touching dark red velvet might evoke the happiness felt at the gift of a bouquet of roses.

In a more general sense, semiotic theory links the envelope and the position of the perceiving body to the semiotic function, that is, the relationship between the two levels of language: the level of expression (or signifier) in this respect is termed exteroceptive, that of content (or signified) interoceptive. The abstract position of the perceiving subject between the two is named proprioceptive because it concerns in fact the position of its imaginary body (*corps propre*). The body, here, represents a sensitive border determining both an interior and an exterior domain. Wherever it finds itself, it determines a distinction between the perception of the external world, the perception of the internal world and the perception of the changes in the border envelope itself. Meaning then results from the act of bringing together the two perceptive domains in the *corps propre* of the perceiving subject. Let us take the novel *L'Etranger* [The Outsider] by Camus as an example: the strength and diversity of sensory experience created by the text might vary; moreover, their correlation, their bringing together with the reader's inner world of notions, emotional responses, impressions and affects will not necessarily be the same in England and France, let alone from one reader to the next.

See also *exteroceptivity, interoceptivity, proprioceptivity* and *semiotic function.*

Environment – Semiotics of the

The semiotics of the environment focuses on uncovering the values that humans attach to the countryside (landscape) and to 'natural space'. For instance, semioticians in this field have examined the myths of 'the noble savage' and the 'return to nature' as well as the ideologies underlying the movement for the protection of the environment.

An important branch of the semiotics of the environment to have emerged in recent years is 'green semiotics'. This is concerned with issues such as the preservation of land and represents a radical critique of the capitalist mode of production and political economy. Green semioticians may thus be said to share many of the political concerns of the ecological and anti-globalization movements.

A further recent area of study focuses on an examination of the individual's perception of the environment throughout the ages. These perceptions can be described as feelings of fear and anxiety in the face of a hostile universe. For example, the Biblical story of the Flood can be seen as an expression of these underlying, often unconscious, fears.

Episteme

The term episteme comes from the Greek and refers to knowledge, a system of understanding. Following Michel Foucault, it has also become accepted as signifying the body of ideas which shape the perception of knowledge at a particular period.

In semiotic theory, episteme has two definitions. Firstly, the term can designate the hierarchical organization of different semiotic systems capable of generating all possible manifestations covered by these systems within a given culture. Greimas, for example, attempted to construct an episteme by hierarchically organizing semiotic systems of sexual, economic and socio-matrimonial relations within the traditional French cultural space.

Secondly, episteme can be defined as a form of cultural meta-semiotics in the sense that it describes the attitude taken by a sociocultural community towards its own signs. Thus in medieval culture, for instance, signs were essentially metonymic, expressing subjacent wholeness. In eighteenth-century French culture, on the other hand, signs were 'natural', simply denoting objects.

Epistemic modalities

The term epistemic relates to knowledge, its theory or scientific study, and the modalities connected involve certainty/uncertainty and probability/improbability.

In semiotic terms, epistemic modalities form part of the competence needed by an enunciatee to evaluate a proposition. In order to establish an enunciative contract (implicit or explicit), an enunciator attempts to persuade (*faire croire*) the enunciatee, who, for her/his part, seals her/his own interpretative doing with an epistemic judgement, that is, with either believing (*croire*) the enunciator or doubting (*ne pas croire*) her/his statements. If I accept the weather forecast and believe that tomorrow the sun will shine, I have judged the prognosis believable.

Epistemic modalities are also part of the necessary competence for a sender-adjudicator to carry out its function in the canonical narrative schema. The epistemic judgement in this instance refers to the assessment of the narrative subject's performance being in accordance with the initial contract. It also relates to cognitive sanction in that it distributes belief or disbelief in statements made within a narrative. The king, for example, who has asked the knight to slay the dragon in return for the hand of his daughter, may not believe (negative epistemic judgement) that the task has been accomplished when the knight returns. On the other hand, he may be persuaded to acknowledge the deed (positive epistemic judgement) when seeing the monster's cut-off heads, or listening to an eyewitness account.

Scientific discourse in particular is characterized by a surfeit of epistemic modalization which appears to take the place of verifying procedures. The same goes for the experimental sciences and all discourse whose hypotheses are difficult to verify.

See also *certainty* and *uncertainty.*

Epistemological subject

The epistemological subject or true subject of enunciation is the underlying voice in a text giving expression to a system of knowlege, ideology, or 'vision of the world'. It is not necessarily the voice of the narrator. The profile of an epistemological subject emerges through an examination of the language and structures of a text, for example, through a study of the spatial element.

Epistemology

In general terms, epistemology denotes the theory or science of the method or grounds of knowledge. In other words, epistemology studies the ways in which a science, for example, erects its axioms and constructs knowledge.

Semiotic theory applies the term epistemology to the analysis of the cognitive dimension not only of scientific discourse but all discourse since all discourse proposes – implicitly or explicitly – an approach to and a theory of knowledge.

See also *cognitive.*

Essentialism

Essentialism is a form of idealism. It upholds the view that concepts such as 'truth', 'freedom' and 'justice' possess an objective existence outside history and outside language. In other words, things are considered to have essential properties independent of our way of looking at them and defining them. For instance, essentialists argue that human nature is unchanging and universal and that sexual identity is fixed rather than a social construct. Semiotics, with its basic tenet that meaning is a human creation, represents a fundamental undermining of this position.

Euphoria

This is the positive term of the thymic category relating to the world of feeling and emotions. Euphoria denotes pleasant sensations and joy and is opposed to the negative term dysphoria which signifies unpleasant feelings and unhappiness. In a text, the distinction euphoria versus dysphoria gives rise to an axiological sytem. An example of euphoria is: 'When Mary passed the examination, she felt happy.' Dysphoria is illustrated by: 'He was horrified by the enormity of the crime.'

See also *aphoria, dysphoria* and *thymic.*

Eurocentrism

Eurocentrism is the view that Europe is the centre of the world and that its culture is the standard with which all other cultures are negatively contrasted. Postcolonial thinkers argue for a decentring of the intellectual sovereignty and dominance of Europe, challenging the assumption that the white male western point of view is the norm and the truth.

See also *postcolonialism.*

Evaluative

Evaluative terms, such as 'good', 'bad', 'beautiful' or 'nice', refer to the instance of enunciation and imply a judgement or particular attitude on the part of the speaker. Their use renders an utterance more subjective.

Evaluative terms frequently take the form of adjectives or adverbs. Examples: I had a nice evening. He has done the work very badly.

The absence of evaluative terms gives an impression of greater objectivity. It is, therefore, a feature of scientific or legal discourse.

Expression and content

According to Hjelmslev, there are two fundamental planes or levels of language, the *plane of expression* and the *plane of content*. These two planes correspond to Saussure's distinction between the signifier (expression) and the signified (content). They are in a relationship of reciprocal presupposition. The level of expression relates to the domain of sound (music, the spoken word), to that of shape or colour or line (graphic icons or images), to that of movement or gestures. The level of content, on the other hand, relates to the concept or idea expressed by these sounds or icons, in other words, it concerns their semantic charge. In our traffic light system, for example, the colours and their spatial layout – green, amber, red – belong to the level of expression. Their significance – green = go, red = stop – belongs to the level of content.

Hjelmslev, however, defines the two planes of language even further:

The level of expression. The level of expression can itself be subdivided into two components, the **substance** of expression and the **form** of expression. Music and the spoken word, for instance, have the same substance of expression: sound. Their form or organization, however, differs: language uses the linguistic system; music employs its own arrangements of opposition and metre. The same applies to the world of colour and shape as a means of expression: the substances – painting, photography, drawing – all take distinctive forms in the way they are organized and applied.

The level of content. This may also be subdivided into the **substance** of content and the **form** of content. The substance of content has been described as an original amorphous continuum of meaning. Hjelmslev gives the example of the general idea of sibling relationship (*fraternité*) considered as a type of nebula. This substance of content takes different forms in different cultures. French (and English), for example, possess the two distinct terms: brother and sister. Hungarian has, in addition, separate terms for younger or older brother or sister, etc. The Mayan language, on the other hand, does not differentiate between brother and sister at all: one term – *sudara* — is used to cover them both.

It must be remembered that the substance of content can only be apprehended through its form: the substance is presupposed but beyond the reach of linguistic investigation. Hjelmslev's concept of language, therefore, supports Saussure's claim that language is a form and not a substance.

See also *signifier and signified.*

Expressive function

If a communication is focusing on the addresser (sender) of the message, calling attention to his/her feelings, beliefs or emotions, then it is the expressive (or emotive) function that dominates. The expressive function is indicated in several ways:

1) Through the use of exclamation marks and interjections.

2) Through the use of modalization, that is, linguistic devices that point to the presence of a narrator, drawing our attention to the subjective source of an utterance. The two principal forms here are:

   - the use of emotive or evaluative terms (expressing judgement) that reveal the presence of a narrator: 'The father had forgotten the poor girl. She was lying awake and unhappy. In the midst of friends . . . she was alone'. (W. M. Thackeray, *Vanity Fair*)

   - the use of terms that nuance or rectify a statement such as 'seem', 'appear', 'perhaps', 'undoubtedly', 'certainly', etc. 'One would certainly suppose her to be further on in life than her seventeenth year – perhaps because of the slow, resigned sadness of the glance . . . perhaps because . . .' (George Eliot, *The Mill on the Floss*)

Dominance of the expressive function in a text does not preclude the other speech functions being present to varying degrees.

See also *communication model.*

Exteroceptivity

The term exteroceptivity describes sensory perception resulting from contact with the outside world. The experience of heat, cold, smell or taste, for example, belongs to the exteroceptive domain.

Exteroceptivity is complemented by interoceptivity which relates to the internal world of impressions, feelings or internal reactions and affects. Both outer and inner world are united by the proprioceptive act, that is, the body of the perceiving subject giving meaning to them by reacting simultaneously to stimuli and to contacts coming from the outside (sensations) as well as from inside (feelings, affects) and taking its position between them. For example, someone puts his hand in the fire which causes a sensation of burning. In the internal world of the affected subject the unpleasant sensation causes feelings or reactions which are recognized as pain, anger or frustration.

See also *interoceptivity*, *proprioceptivity* and *semiotic function*.

Extradiegetic

An extradiegetic narrator is a narrator who is located outside the story, existing on a different narrative level from the level of the events narrated in the story. Examples would be most fairy-tales, or nineteenth-century realist novels such as *Bleak House* by Charles Dickens. The extradiegetic narrator can be contrasted with the intradiegetic narrator who is presented as existing on the same level as the characters in the story which she or he tells.

See *diegesis* and *intradiegetic*.

Fallacy

The term fallacy is derived from the Latin *fallere* [to deceive] and means deceptive appearance, misleading argument, delusion, error. In literary criticism, fallacy occurs in different combinations:

- *Affective fallacy*: encouraging impressionism. The affective fallacy goes back to the nineteenth century when critics were intent on recording their emotional responses to literature, describing the feelings aroused and searching for reasons and explanations for them in the textual language itself. Meaning thus depended on reader interpretation which was considered as some kind of relativism. Today this is not generally regarded as a 'fallacy'.
- *Intentional fallacy*: encouraging biography and relativism. The intentional fallacy holds that the meaning of a text depends solely on the author's intention. This attitude is contested by theorists who doubt whether authors are always aware of their own intentions. Moreover, it dismisses any possible contribution by the reader to the meaning.
- *Pathetic fallacy*: crediting Nature with human emotion. The pathetic fallacy attributes human characteristics to inanimate matter. An example would be to talk of the cruel sea or of the savage storm, the unrelenting winds, etc. It is an attempt to create harmony of Nature with the characters. It is usually considered a device to produce special reading effects.
- *Referential fallacy* or *illusion*: identifying the word/sign with the thing it stands for. The referential fallacy assumes that every sign necessarily has a referent which is self-evidently a wrong judgement since many signifiers have no referent, for example colours, articles or connectives in language, and imaginary terms or signifiers.

Figurative

Figurative elements are those elements in a text that correspond to the physical world and can be apprehended by the five senses (vision, touch, taste, hearing and smell). They are essential ingredients in the construction of a reality effect or illusion of a real world.

Figurative elements operate on the surface level of a text, creating, for example, an impression of time, of place or of character. They should be contrasted with the abstract or conceptual component that belongs to the deep level. In the sentence 'I remember him as if it were yesterday, a tall, strong, heavy nut-brown man', the second part is predominantly figurative while 'remember' and 'yesterday' are abstract notions.

See also *figure.*

Figurativization

Figurativization refers to the process whereby an enunciator invests abstract values in his discourse with figurative shape. When telling the story of a man wishing to be seen to possess power, for example, the enunciator might choose a powerful car as a figurative manifestation of his desire to dominate. Or he might elaborate on how the man acquired the car of his dreams and how he enjoyed his neighbours' or friends' recognition of the power the object 'car' represented.

See also *figurative* and *figure.*

Figure

In semiotic terms, figure refers to the expression of abstract values on the figurative level of discourse. The abstract value 'life', for example, might take shape on the discursive level in the figure of a newly born baby, a growing plant or a flowing river.

See also *figurativization.*

Film – Semiotics of

The semiotics of film emerged in the 1960s in Italy and France and has since become an important branch of film studies. Strongly influenced by structuralism and by the models of Jakobson, Saussure and Hjelmslev, researchers focused initially on films as a signifying whole and on an investigation of the structures of filmic codes. In its acoustic and visual expression-form, a film differs, of course, from books, spoken messages, theatrical presentations or pictures. Combining all these elements, films were seen to create a fixed and repeatable text, in other words, a grammar of filmic language.

During this period research also concentrated on the sign systems of film. Semioticians took the filmic sign to be composed of a Saussurean signifier and a signified. Filmic signifiers, since they are both visual and acoustic, were variously characterized either by heterogeneity (Barthes, 1960) or defined as 'objects, forms, and acts of reality' (Pasolini) or described as simply the image (also called 'imaginary signifier') with its signified as 'what the image represents' (Metz, 1968). The relations between the filmic signifier and its referential reality have occupied a central position in semiotic research.

In a second phase of its development, film semiotics turned to the study of iconicity in the film, of communication and signification in cinema and of the generative process of film production. At the same time, research focused on psychoanalytic interpretations and on topics such as dreams and fantasy as well as the principles of metaphor and metonymy. In recent years attention has been drawn to the relationship between the cinema and the senses. Studies have been made of the films of Jean-Luc Godard (e.g. *Vivre sa vie*) and of those of Krzysztot Kieslowski (e.g. *Three Colours White*), amongst others.

See also *filmic codes, metaphor, metonymy* and *signifier* and *signified.*

Filmic codes

The expression filmic codes usually refers to technological and other devices involved in film production such as camerawork, lighting, colour, sound and graphics, but also genre, manipulation of time and narrative style, etc.

Umberto Eco makes a distinction between cinematographic and filmic codes. According to him technological devices used to reproduce effects of reality are termed cinematographic codes while the filmic code deals with the filmic communication of narrative messages.

See also *code.*

Firstness, secondness and thirdness

The terms firstness, secondness and thirdness were coined by the philosopher C. S. Peirce in an attempt at categorizing signs. Firstness in this context refers to the mode of mere being without reference to anything else. Examples are unreflected feeling, a mere sensation of colour and form, a possibility or quality.

The object or thing that is felt or perceived belongs to the category of secondness involving the relation of a first to a second. It is the category of comparison, factualness, experience of time and space. For example, a vague red patch (firstness) becomes hard, round and bouncing (secondness), although it is not yet identified as something in particular.

Thirdness brings the second category into relation with the first and with a third. It is the category of mediation, memory and habit. Thirdness establishes the red patch that is round and bouncing to be a ball.

Peirce defines the sign in relation to all three categories, placing it in a triadic process called semiosis.

Focalization

The term focalization refers to the angle of vision or position of the observer. It relates to the fundamental question: through whose eyes is the story being told, from whose point of view? There are two principal categories of focalization:

(a) *Internal focalization*, in which events are described as they appear through the eyes of an actor in the story. Examples would be Meursault's account in Albert Camus' novel *L'Etranger*, or the narrator in *A la recherche du temps perdu* by Marcel Proust.

(b) *External focalization*, in which events are described as they appear through the eyes of an external observer/narrator who is not an actor in the story. This is a characteristic of much of nineteenth-century realist or naturalist fiction such as the novels of George Eliot, Honoré de Balzac or Emile Zola.

See also *focalizer*.

Focalizer

The term focalizer refers to the subject through whose eyes events are being described. It is synonymous with the term observer.

See also *focalization*.

Fondement

The term *fondement* was proposed by the semiotician Jacques Fontanille to describe one of the elements of Peirce's definition of the sign. According to Peirce, a sign is something that stands to somebody for something in some respect or capacity. When Peirce described this model of the sign to be triadic (sign/object/interpretant), he omitted to give a name to the last part of his definition 'in some respect or capacity', although he refines this part of his definition further by explaining that it means 'not in all respects, but in reference to a sort of idea'. It is this referential context or placing in perspective of the sign that Fontanille termed *fondement*. To give an example: the sign 'red' means stop in reference to traffic. The context of traffic therefore is the *fondement*. Or, an article about an accident or a particular event signifies differently according to the points of view of the writer, reader, historical circumstances, etc. These points of view – which privilege aspects of the signifying unit – function as *fondement*.

See also *interpretant* and *sign*.

Foregrounding

This term describes the process whereby signifiers draw attention to themselves rather than to the content of a message. Described also as *deautomatization* or *defamiliarization*, it is the act of perceiving differences in comparison with habitual codes and patterns of everyday communication. For the Prague School structuralists, the aesthetic function of language originates in a dialectical process of foregrounding against a background of norms or habitual codes. For Mukarovsky, for example, the function of poetic language consists in the maximum of foregrounding of the utterance and a pushing into the background of communication as the objective of expression. In 'realistic' texts, on the other hand, what is foregrounded is the 'content' rather than the 'form' of expression.

In the linguistics of Halliday, foregrounding refers to the centre of interest or emphasis of an utterance known also as the focus, i.e. the new and thus important information. Focus is opposed to 'theme', normally of a low information value (either because the information has already been given or it is presupposed).

See also *Prague School*.

Form

In semiotic theory, the term form is opposed to that of matter which it 'informs' by 'forming' the recognizable object. Thus the 'form' of any object guarantees its permanence and its identity. An earthenware cup becomes recognizable as a cup only after the clay from which it has been taken assumes the form of a cup. Mountains are not mountains until the original magma shapes itself into a form called 'mountains'.

Saussure defined language as a form composed of two substances. Neither all 'physical', nor totally 'psychological', it is the place where these components converge. As a result, Saussure believed language to be a signifying structure.

The Saussurean affirmation is developed further by Hjelmslev, who postulates the existence of a distinct form for each of the two levels of language: both *content* and *expression* of language are subdivided into their own distinctive substance and form. Accordingly, when investigating language, the form of the expression as well as the form of the content need to be recognized and analysed separately.

See also *expression and content, matter* and *substance.*

Formalism

In general terms, formalism denotes any theory or practice that promotes strict, even excessive, adherence to form, structure or formal rules.

In literary theory, formalism refers to an approach that promotes formal qualities over content. The best known example is an intellectual movement called Russian formalism which originated in the early twentieth century in the Moscow Linguistic Circle and the Petrograd Society for the Study of Poetic Language. The first Formalists believed that the content of written works had no literary value in itself. It was the devices used by the writer that turned them into works of art. According to Shklovsky, for example, artistic devices have the central function of 'making strange', thus causing a renewal of perception. Consequently, new devices needed to be continually introduced into writing to guarantee its *literariness* – a concept developed by Jakobson – and remain a dynamic system. Formalism was thus anti-realist, regarding literature primarily as a special use of language giving an unfamiliar aspect to ordinary experience.

Shklovsky also introduced the distinction between *story*, representing action and events, in other words the writer's raw material, and *plot*, that is their artful arrangement and transformation into a narrative sequence. At the time, the most detailed study of the plot structure was undertaken by Vladimir Propp who, although not officially a Formalist but in line with formalist thinking, examined numerous Russian folk-tales to develop a typology of folk narrative. Altogether a more structuralist approach to formalism emerged with Jakobson and Tynyanov and was continued notably by the Prague Linguistic Circle. Formalism was thus at the root of the development of structural semiotics in Eastern Europe.

See also *literariness*, *Moscow School*, *Moscow-Tartu School* and *structuralism*, and Vladimir Propp in **Key Thinkers in Semiotics**.

Function

In linguistics and in semiotics, the term function has at least three applications: it is used in an instrumental and utilitarian sense; with syntactical meaning; and in a logico-mathematical sense.

1) For the linguist A. Martinet, the predominant function of language is to communicate. Language has a *useful function* as instrument in social interaction.

2) The term function in a *syntactical* context refers firstly to parts played by certain elements in a sentence (subject, object, predicate). The linguist E. Benveniste uses the concept function as a necessary element to define a structure in language (all its constituent parts fulfil a function). Jakobson, for his part, employs the term function to designate the six elements that make up the speech act (expressive, conative, referential, poetic, meta-lingual and phatic). Finally, Propp makes use of the term function to describe syntagmatic units in folk-tales which are common to all stories.

3) Hjelmslev defines the term in a *logico-mathematical* sense, considering function to designate 'the relation between two variables'. Semiotics reserves the term function for the definition of the relationship between

two actants. This relationship is expressed in the verb of the elementary utterance. Any other narrative functions, subject or object for example, are simply named actants.

Semiotic function, according to Hjelmslev, designates the relationship in language between the form of expression and that of content.

See also *actant, communication model, elementary utterance* and *syntax,* and Vladimir Propp in **Key Thinkers in Semiotics.**

Functionalism

Functionalism describes an approach which not only focuses on the structural characteristics of languages but also on the purposes to which language is put. In contrast to Saussure or Hjelmslev, functionalists would analyse semiotic systems in relation to social functions rather than treating them as autonomous forms.

See *Prague School* and *structuralism*, and Roman Jakobson in **Key Thinkers in Semiotics**.

Functive

The expression functive was coined by the linguist Louis Hjelmslev to designate the expression-form and the content-form of the sign function.

See also *expression and content.*

Generative trajectory

The term generative trajectory designates the process whereby meaning is constructed. It is based on the notion of a hierarchy of meaning reflecting the fundamental division between deep and surface structures and between abstract and concrete. According to this model, complex structures derive from simple structures in a process of ever-greater enrichment of meaning.

The starting point (*ab quo*) of the generative trajectory is the deep abstract level associated with Greimas' elementary structure of meaning and the semiotic square. It is from this level that the narrative level is generated which in turn gives rise to the discursive level. We may take the example of the abstract category life versus death situated on the deep level. On the narrative level these values could be articulated in terms of narrative programmes (conjunction and disjunction) and in relationship to an actantial subject. Life, for example, may be the object of a quest. On the discursive level these values are articulated in their most concrete form, and they acquire a figurative shape. Life could be expressed in the figure of light, whereas death could be conveyed in that of darkness.

Each of the three levels of meaning contains two components, a syntactic component and a semantic component. The semantic component relates to the semantic content (signified) of individual words and syntagms which the syntactic component articulates and structures on each of the different levels of signification.

See also *semantics* and *syntax*.

Genre

Referring originally to different styles of literary discourse (sonnets, tragedies, romances, etc.), the term genre has been widened to include all types of oral or written communication such as a casual conversation, a recipe, an advert or a political address. Different genres are characterized by a particular structure, by grammatical forms or special turns of phrases that reflect the communicative purpose of the genre in question. A sermon, for example, has its own distinctive characteristics that would differentiate it from a job interview, a shopping list or a mail-order catalogue. In this sense, the term genre has currently the same meaning as 'discourse type'.

Gift

The term gift describes a discursive figure relating to the communication of objects of value. It refers to a transformation resulting from an attribution (the acquiring of an object) or a renunciation (the deprivation of an object). In other words, as a consequence of a gift, the subject of state (S2) may:

1) Be in possession of an object of value following the act of a subject of doing (S1) other than itself. This is known as *transitive conjunction*. Example: 'Peter gave Paul the ten-pound note he had found.'

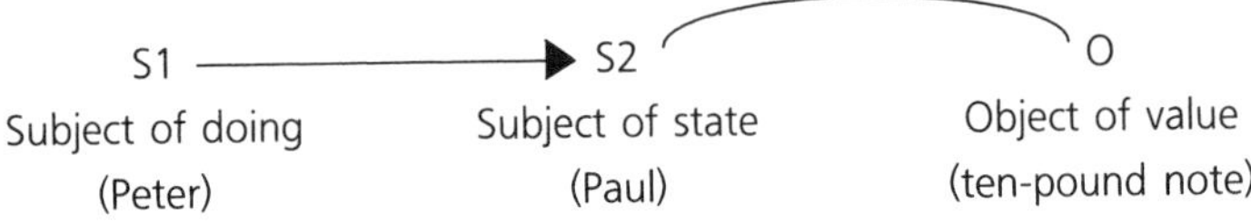

2) Deprive itself of an object of value. This act is known as *reflexive disjunction*. Example: 'Paul gave his life for his country.'

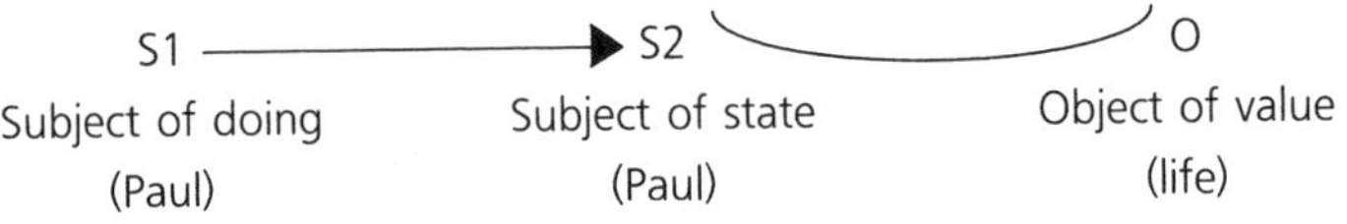

See also *attribution*.

Glorifying test

This is the stage of judgement or sanction in a narrative quest. It corresponds to those episodes where the outcome of an event is revealed. The decisive test has either succeeded or failed, the heroine/hero is acclaimed or punished, the act is deemed good or evil. It is the point at which the performance is interpreted either by the narrator or by an actor in the story. The instance doing the interpreting is known as the sender-adjudicator. S/he judges whether the performance of the subject is in accordance with the original set of values established by the first sender (also known as mandating sender) and whether the contract has been fulfilled or not. In traditional fairy-tales the stage of sanction is frequently enacted in the figure of marriage: the father may reward the hero for his achievements (killing the dragon, for example) by giving him his daughter's hand in marriage.

See also *canonical narrative schema*.

Glossematics

Glossematics is derived from the Greek word *glossa* denoting language. The term is used by the Danish linguist Louis Hjelmslev in order to describe the radically structuralist linguistic theory he elaborated in collaboration with his friend H. J. Uldall. According to Hjelmslev, four particular features characterize the glossematic theory: a) an analytical procedure preceding (and presupposed by) synthesis; b) insistence on form; c) taking account not only of the form of expression but also of the form of content; d) the notion that language is just one semiotic system among many.

Glossematics as a theory of language never became widely accepted. Nonetheless Hjelmslev's theoretical construct could be considered the first coherent and perfected semiotic theory. As such, it became a decisive factor in the development of French semiotics.

See also *Copenhagen School.*

Grammar

The term grammar designates the part of language study that deals with the forms of words, their organization in clauses and sentences, and the rules that govern structures and operations. There are two main components of grammar: morphology (the study of words) and syntax (their arrangement in sentences).

Semiotic theory has adopted the term grammar for the description of semio-narrative structures of signification. Correspondingly, semiotic grammar has two basic components applicable to different levels of signification: (1) *semantics* studying units of meaning and states of being, and (2) *syntax* studying their relationships, organization and transformation.

See also *morphology, semantics* and *syntax.*

Graphocentrism

Graphocentrism denotes an attitude which privileges writing over the spoken word. Text interpretations concentrating excessively on the written form could be considered graphocentric.

See also *logocentrism* and *phonocentrism.*

Having-to-be

See *alethic modalities.*

Having-to-do

This modal structure governs utterances of doing (action). Terms expressing obligation or prescription, prohibition, permission and optionality relate to this category, which can be projected onto the following semiotic square:

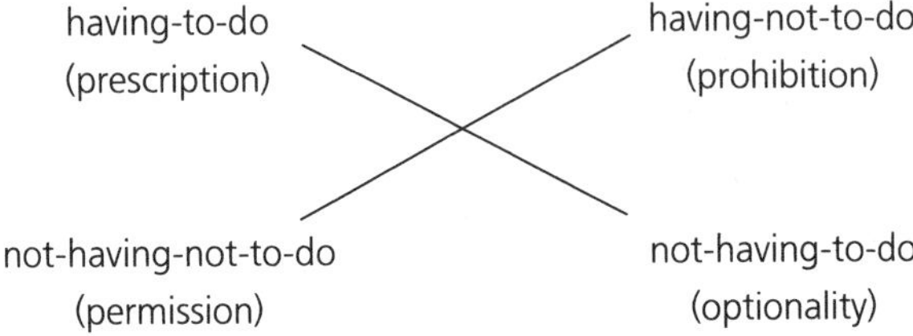

Example: 'Mary felt she had to go (*obligation*) to France the following Wednesday to attend the conference even though it was strictly forbidden (*having-not-to-do*) to take time off for any reason. She did not, therefore, ask permission (*not-having-not-to-do*) to go: it would simply be up to the management (*not-having-to-do*) whether they sacked her or not.'

See also *alethic modalities.*

Helper

Any actant that aids the subject in its quest is known as a helper. In the fairy-tale *Cinderella*, the fairy godmother and the coach function as helpers in Cinderella's quest to go to the ball. During a general strike, pickets or newspaper articles may function as actant/helpers depending on the point of view.

Hermeneutics

The term hermeneutics denotes the interpretation of predominantly religious and philosophical texts. St Augustine's Scriptural exegesis is an example of hermeneutics.

Hermeneutics and semiotics are closely related in so far as they are both concerned with formulating a general theory of signification. In opposition to semiotics, however, which focuses its analysis on the forms that meaning adopts, hermeneutics bases interpretation mainly on the relationship of texts to their referents while paying particular attention to the conditions of textual production and reception and to sociohistorical contexts.

In recent years, the semiotic and hermeneutic methods have found common ground in the thought of the philosopher Paul Ricoeur. For Ricoeur as for Greimas, the structure of narrative is the structure of meaning itself and all human action constitutes a text. Narrative also reflects the lives of subjects who live in time. The aim of hermeneutic philosophy is to reconstruct how a text or narrative arises from the essential unintelligibility of life and of suffering and is transmitted by the writer to readers who change their lives on the basis of what they have learnt about the world and about themselves. The development of a semiotics of passion in France in the 1980s owes much to the stimulus of Ricoeur's thought.

See also *interpretation* and *semiotics*.

Hero

In semiotic theory, the term hero designates the subject actant of a narrative trajectory (or quest) once it has come into possession of a certain competence, that is, of a being-able-to-do and/or knowing-how-to-do. A pilot who sets off to fly around the world in a hot-air balloon must possess the necessary skill and equipment: s/he can then be termed a hero.

An *actualized* hero is a hero who is in possession of this competence but who has not yet passed to the stage of performance. It can be distinguished from the *realized* hero who is in possession of the object of the quest. In our example, the hero is actualized in the act of flying. If the balloon succeeds in going round the world, then the hero can be described as realized.

In a more conventional meaning of a word, especially in oral and classical works, the term hero is endowed with euphoric connotations and is opposed to that of villain (the dysphoric or nasty).

See also *actualization* and *realization*.

Heterotopic space

The term heterotopic space designates those places whose mention in a story precedes or follows the narrative transformation. They are external, therefore, to the events that make up the pivot of the story. In *Treasure Island*, Jim Hawkins' home (from which he sets out and to which he returns after finding the treasure) constitutes a heterotopic space. In *Jack and the Beanstalk*, Jack's home likewise represents a heterotopic space.

See also *topic space* and *utopic space*.

Heuristic

The adjective heuristic means serving to find out, to discover. It is often applied to a method or an argument. For example, a detective applies a heuristic method to find a culprit. In education it describes the method by which pupils are encouraged to find out things for themselves. The semiotic method of exploring the generation of signification is heuristic.

Hierarchy

In semiotic theory, hierarchy appears as the organizing principle of the elementary structure of meaning. The two terms in opposition that are essential for the production of meaning are thus considered hierarchically inferior to their common denominator or the category as a totality. The category 'emotion', for example, may be considered as hierarchically superior to its component parts in a text, say, to the terms of 'love' versus 'hatred'.

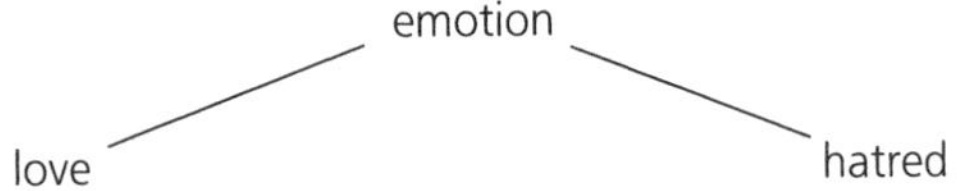

See also *semantic category*.

Homologation

In general terms, homologation designates a process of correlation between different levels of meaning. In a poetic text, the figure of the bird could be homologized with the semes of 'high' and of 'life', for example, whereas the figure of the rat could be homologized with those of 'low' and of 'death'.

See also *correlation*.

Hypertext

The term hypertext was used by Gérard Genette to designate literary texts which allude, derive from or relate to an earlier work or hypotext. For instance, Angela Carter's *The Tiger's Bride* can be considered a hypertext in that it relates to the earlier work, or hypotext, the original fairy-story *Beauty and the Beast*. In the same way Michel Tournier's *Vendredi ou les Limbes du Pacifique* [Friday] is a hypertext, the hypotext being Daniel Defoe's *Robinson Crusoe*.

Hypertexts may take a variety of forms including, for example, imitation, parody, pastiche, transpositions and continuations. A hypertext and its hypotext make up a multilayered palimpsest.

In computing technology the term hypertext refers to a text that links together information from a variety of sources and a variety of media such as sound, graphics, etc. The text thus enables the reader to choose alternatives from a traditional linear reading. In a particular version of a Shakespeare play or a novel of George Eliot, for example, the reader may have access to maps, charts, photographs and pictures of costumes.

See also *hypotext* and *palimpsest*.

Hypotactic

The term hypotactic expresses the relation of a whole to its parts and vice versa. Greimas gives the following example from Maupassant's short story *Two Friends*: 'Paris was blockaded, famished, a death rattle in her throat. The sparrows rarely appeared on the roofs, and even the sewers were being emptied of their regular tenants.' Here the relationship between Paris and her 'roofs' and 'sewers' is hypotactic.

For Hjelmslev the term hypotactic designates the logical relation between a presupposed term and a presupposing term. In the above example, 'roofs' and 'sewers' presuppose Paris.

Hypotext

A hypotext designates a text whose form and/or content inspires – or is reflected in – a later text or hypertext. The medieval exchange of letters between Abélard and Héloïse can be considered the hypotext for Jean-Jacques Rousseau's novel *Julie ou la Nouvelle Héloïse* (1761). The fairy-tale *La Belle et la Bête* is the hypotext on which the film *Beauty and the Beast* is based.

See also *hypertext*.

Icon

In the semiotics of the American philosopher C. S. Peirce, an icon is a sign which resembles the object it signifies. A portrait, for example, is an icon because it resembles the subject represented. A diagram of a house is the icon of a house.

See also *index* and *symbol.*

Iconic

Deriving from icon meaning likeness, image, picture, the term iconic refers to a mode of pictorial representation favouring perception by the senses. Portrait statues of heroes are examples of iconic representation.

In semiotic theory, the term iconic is used in relation to the figurative level of a text. This level corresponds to the physical world and is apprehended through evocation of sensory perception. The expression iconic thus emphasizes an impression of 'reality' and represents a mode of referentiality that seeks in order to involve the reader.

In linguistic terms, iconic establishes a mode in which the signifier imitates or evokes the signified. Examples of this are onomatopoeic words such as 'murmur' or 'babbling brook'. C. S. Peirce refers to iconic representation when categorizing and defining the sign.

See also *figurative* and *icon.*

Iconicity

The term iconicity means resemblance to 'reality', to the natural world outside the text. Its meaning is similar to that of referential impression or illusion. Iconization is the procedure whereby this impression of the referential world is produced and sustained. The evocation of London in Charles Dickens' novels is an example of iconization.

The distanciation (alienation) technique, on the other hand, that characterizes Brecht's theatre is a form of de-iconization.

Identity

The notion of identity is opposed to that of otherness and cannot be defined in any other way. In fact, the terms 'identity' and 'otherness' are interdefinable by relationship of presupposition. For instance, in a biographical novel the reader recognizes the protagonist's identity by setting it off against the 'otherness' of other characters. Moreover, if the story is to make sense, changes provoked by action and plot do not affect the basic identity of actors. Thus identity can also be seen as permanence in opposition to transformation.

Finally, the couple 'identity' and 'otherness' and their relationship form an essential basis for the elementary structure of signification or semiotic square.

See also *semiotic square.*

Ideology

Strictly speaking, the term ideology designates the science of ideas. It is commonly employed, however, to refer to a body of ideas and values characteristic of an individual, a society or a school of thought. We talk of a Marxist ideology or a capitalist ideology, for example, or the ideology of the upper classes.

In semiotic theory, ideology describes the *syntagmatic* arrangement of values, that is, their actualization in a quest. Subjects desire values which become objects of quests. Their selection and setting up as goals define an ideology. Once a quest is realized, we no longer talk of ideology. In other words, the notion of ideology contains a permanent quest as reflected in the actantial structure of its discourse. To offer an example: considering the Christian faith an ideology, we find the Bible stories presenting, again and again, moral values as goals to be achieved.

The notion of ideology in semiotic theory is complemented by, and contrasted with, the term axiology, reserved to describe value systems arranged on a *paradigmatic* axis, that is, signifying either by equivalence or opposition. For example, in such a system 'wealth' signifies in opposition to 'poverty' but on an equivalent level with 'opulence' or 'riches'. Thus the values selected as goals for ideological quests form part of axiological systems.

The Marxist philosopher Louis Althusser defines ideology as a 'representation of the imaginary relationship of individuals to their real condition of existence'. It distorts our view of our 'true conditions of existence', presenting as natural and harmonious what is artificial and contradictory – class differences under capitalism, for instance. Ideology is embodied in all kinds of material practices and works through what Althusser terms the 'ideological State apparatuses', such as the institutions of religion, the law and the political and educational system. Ideology describes then a state of 'false consciousness' and relates to acquired misconceptions about the nature of social reality. It both upholds dominant power groups and is the means through which individuals make sense of the world around them.

See also *axiology*, *essentialsm*, *interpellation*, *realism* and *transparency*.

Idiolect

The term idiolect refers to an individual person's specific use of language or semiotic activity. An idiolect contains individual variations from the norm. Such variations must not be too excessive or else communication will be jeopardized.

See also *sociolect*.

Illocutionary act

According to the speech act theory (J. L. Austin) an illocutionary act is an utterance that involves performing an act. In other words, when I say something, I am not only describing reality, my words are also having a direct effect on this reality. For instance, the speaker performs the act of promising by saying 'I promise'. Illocutionary acts can take the form of threats, warnings, questions, commands or giving advice.

See also *performative* and *perlocutionary act*.

Illusion

On the semiotic square of veridiction, the term illusion subsumes the complementary terms of 'seeming' and 'non-being' which are located on the negative pole or deixis.

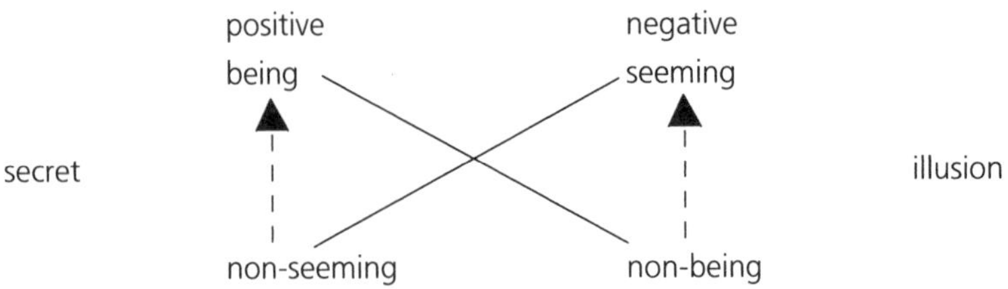

See also *deixis* and *veridiction.*

Imaginary, the

For the psychoanalyst Jacques Lacan, the term '*Imaginary*' describes the initial stage in the constitution of the subject and represents one of the three orders that structure human existence. Between the ages of six and eighteen months, the infant emerges from the realm of the 'Real' where there are no boundaries between self and world to enter the realm of the 'Imaginary' where it begins to acquire a sense of separate identity. The infant looks in the mirror and recognizes its own image. The realization that this image is both itself (its own reflection) and not itself (i.e. only a reflection) means that the infant has become a human subject ready to enter the order of language, or the 'Symbolic'.

See also *semanalysis* and *semiotic/symbolic.*

Immanence and manifestation

Immanent structures are those semantic and logical structures that are situated at the deep level of a text. They can be contrasted with the structures or elements that are manifest on the linguistic surface, that is, with the actual words, pictures or sounds which constitute the text. Immanent structures can be deduced from an examination of elements perceptible on the textual surface.

The relationship between immanence and manifestation is similar to that between content and expression.

See also *expression* and *content.*

Inchoative

An inchoative term is an aspectual term describing the beginning of a process. It indicates that a transformation has taken place and is frequently conveyed through the use of the simple past (the preterite or perfect tense in French), or the narrative present: 'He came into the room'; 'He comes into the room'.

The end of a process, on the other hand, is indicated in the use of a *terminative* term: 'He left the room'.

See also *durative* and *terminative.*

Index

In Peirce's semiotics, an index is a sign that is physically linked to, or affected by, its object. The relationship between sign and object, or signifier and signified, may be causal or sequential. Examples given by Peirce are a weathercock, a barometer and a sundial. A knock at the door indicating that there is someone at the door is another example of a sign seen as an index. Pointing my finger at a dog is the index of a dog. A high temperature may be seen as an index of illness.

See also *icon* and *symbol.*

Individual

An actant is termed individual to mark a contrast with a collective actant defined as a collection of individuals endowed with a narrative role. In Zola's *Germinal*, the miners represent a collective actant whereas Etienne Lantier is an individual actant.

The term individual is also used to describe a semantic universe characterized by the category life/death. The James Bond films would be an example of such a universe.

See also *collective.*

Intensity

The term intensity describes different levels of energy – degrees of heat or light, for example – and relates to the way objects affect us. We first become aware of objects in terms of their intensity and take up a position in relation to them. This primary act of perception is known as intentionality (*la visée intentionnelle*): for instance, headlights may appear to us initially as a blaze of dazzling light.

See also *intentionality, presence* and *spatial apprehension.*

Intentionality

Intentionality or the intentional drive (*la visée intentionnelle*) represents the primary act of perception when the subject becomes aware of the presence of an object in terms of intensity (affect) and takes up a position in relation to it. For instance, a burning sofa may initially present itself to us as intense heat.

See also *intensity* and *presence.*

Interoceptivity

The expression interoceptivity relates to the realm of the internal perception of a perceiving subject. For example, experience of pain, or of fear, joy or anxiety, all form part of our interoceptive world.

The notion of interoceptivity is complemented by that of exteroceptivity, which describes sensory perception resulting from contact with the outer world. The bark of a big dog reaching our ears, for instance, belongs to the exteroceptive domain. The feeling of fear it generates is part of the interoceptive world. Both outer and inner worlds are united in the body of the perceiving subject who reacts simultaneously to stimuli from the outside (sensation) and from the inside (feelings, affects). It is in this act of correlation of external and internal perception (proprioceptive act) that meaning arises. The subject hearing the dog, for example, recognizes his reaction due to the barking and calls it fear.

See also *exteroceptivity, proprioceptivity* and *semiotic function.*

Interpellation

Interpellation is the term coined by the French Marxist philosopher Louis Althusser to describe the process whereby individuals are constructed by pre-given texts or social institutions such as those of the church or the educational system. It is the means by which State power is maintained, without the use of physical violence. A particular commercial or film interpellates/addresses the viewer, positioning her/him (the subject) with regard to their social role and gender. In a liberal capitalist economy, for example, interpellation denotes the way individuals are encouraged to see themselves as entities free and independent of social forces. For instance, the classic realist novel presents its characters as free and autonomous, thereby creating a specific subject position for its readers and giving them the illusion that they, too, are free. The values of the dominant power groups – the status quo – are thus strengthened.

See also *essentialism.*

Interpretant

The term interpretant was coined by the philosopher C. S. Peirce. It refers to one of the three basic elements in his definition of the sign. To Peirce, 'a sign addresses somebody, that is, creates in the mind of that person an equivalent sign, or perhaps a more developed sign. That sign which it creates I call the *interpretant* of the first sign.' The interpretant thus represents the meaning of a sign.

See also *meaning* and *sign.*

Interpretation

Interpretation involves the operations of recognition and identification. 'Re'-cognition or 're'-discovery, in this sense – contrary to acquiring knowledge – is an act of comparing a proposition with what is already known. Recognition as comparison, furthermore, necessarily comprises identifying, in any particular utterance, all or parts of a truth one already possesses. Interpreting any statement means weighing what one already knows to be true against what is being proposed and deciding in the light of this on its meaning and accuracy. For instance, political propaganda anticipates the general public's interpretation being based on comparison of facts personally known to be true (unemployment, rising prices) with those advertised as being correct.

The same applies to the interpretation of literary texts. The story of *Cinderella*, for example, draws on our knowledge of other fairy-tales as well as our familiarity with human behaviour in general, love, jealousy, etc. All this helps to identify essential moments in the story which explain its meaning.

Intertextuality

The notion of intertextuality refers to close relationships of content and/or form between texts. No text stands on its own. It is always linked to other texts. Texts create contexts within which other texts are created and interpreted. Julian Barnes' novel *Flaubert's Parrot* offers an example of intertextuality since its subject and title refer to the literary work of another author. Equally, *Julie ou la Nouvelle Héloïse* by Jean-Jacques Rousseau echoes in both title and form a famous medieval exchange of letters. The practice of epigraphs to introduce texts or textual sections is also evidence of intertextuality.

The idea of intertextuality was originally mooted by Mikhail Bakhtin, who saw textual practice as always involving other texts and described the literary work as a polyphonic multi-layered mosaic of quotations. The concept was established and elaborated in detail by Julia Kristeva, for whom the text is an intersection of texts and codes which cannot be reduced to a simple question of influences.

Intradiegetic

An intradiegetic narrator is a narrator who is presented as existing on the same level of reality as the characters in the story she or he tells. An example would be Meursault in *L'Etranger* [The Outsider] by Albert Camus, or M. S. Fogg in Paul Auster's *Moon Palace*.

See also *diegesis* and *extradiegetic*.

Irony

Irony is a rhetorical device (or trope) whereby language appears to mean the exact opposite of what the speaker intended to say. It is used to convey a message contradicted by the literal meaning of the words that are employed.

For example, on a rainy day the ironic exclamation 'oh what lovely sunshine!' is intended to draw attention to the unpleasantness of the weather.

Irony is also applied in understatements and overstatements to alter the meaning of attributes. To refer to a minute portion of food as a huge meal, for instance, is ironic.

See also *trope*.

Isomorphism

The term isomorphism indicates a correspondence or close similarity in shape or structure between often unrelated elements or compounds. It is frequently applied in chemistry, for example, or in mathematics where it refers to the identity of operations or numerical groups. The term homologation is used by some theorists in place of isomorphism.

In semiotic terms, isomorphism usually relates to formal identity between two or more structures on different semiotic levels. Their isomorphism can be recognized by the homologous nature of the relationships between their constituents. Thus, for example, an isomorphism can be discovered between the level of expression and the level of content within the language system by finding the correspondence of 'phonemes and sememes' or 'a syllable and a semantic utterance'.

See also *homologation*.

Isotopy

The term isotopy refers to recurring semic categories whose presence ensures sustained meaning in the flow of a text. Isotopies thus provide continuity in the deciphering of, for example, a narrative. Their absence, on the other hand, produces an effect of semantic dislocation which may, of course, be what the author intends to achieve. To give an example: frequent reference in a text to times of day, dawn or dusk, to age or eternity coupled with expressions stressing always or never, or detailed dates or pronounced indication of tenses, can be seen as establishing the isotopy of 'time'.

In critical metalanguage, isotopy replaces the traditional terms 'theme' and 'motif'. Isotopies are to be found on the figurative level, allowing for the assembling of semantic fields perceptible on the textual surface; or, by constant repetition of the same lexeme for example, they amount to semantic specification. On the abstract level, isotopies reveal common denominators which structure the deep level of meaning.

Iterative

The term iterative describes a category of narrative frequency where events that have happened many times are recounted once. Traditionally it is used to indicate repeated or habitual actions in an economical fashion; for example, 'Every morning he got up at nine and left the house at ten'.

See also *narrative frequency* and *singulative.*

Jouissance

The French term *jouissance* denotes ecstasy or bliss as well as the more literal orgasm. The term was used by Roland Barthes in his *Le Plaisir du texte*, 1973 [Pleasures of the Text] to distinguish two responses to literature, two different kinds of pleasure. The first he describes as *plaisir* [pleasure]: this is a feeling of comfort and euphoria aroused by having one's basic beliefs and expectations confirmed by the text. The second he terms *jouissance:* this denotes an ecstatic moment, a disruptive violent and orgasmic effect that discomforts the reader and unsettles one's historical and cultural assumptions. It brings the reader into contact with a level corresponding to Julia Kristeva's semiotic (the chora). Generally speaking, *plaisir* is associated with realist writing (the readerly text) and *jouissance* with avant-garde, more experimental writing (the writerly text). However, ecstatic or climactic moments can also be found in the readerly text, when order breaks down and the 'garment gapes'.

See also *readerly and writerly texts.*

Junction

In semiotic theory, the concept of junction regulates the relationship between subjects and objects. Narrative syntax is dominated by two types of relationships: conjunction and disjunction between subjects and objects. In the sentence 'Jack has no money', Jack – the subject – is in a relationship of disjunction from his object, money. On the other hand, the utterance 'Jack is rich' shows Jack to be conjoined to his object of value.

Most narratives start with the subject being in a state of disjunction from the object of value, thus initiating the quest. The narrative programme describes the transformation of this state of privation into a relationship of conjunction with the object, in other words, the completion of the quest.

See also *conjunction and disjunction* and *narrative programme.*

Knowing-how-to-do

The modality of knowing-how-to-do constitutes a key component of narrative competence. In order for the subject to be fully qualified and proceed to the decisive test, it must acquire

(a) the modality of being-able-to-do and/or (b) the modality of knowing-how-to-do.

If the object of a quest is to pass an examination with honours, then the candidate will need to acquire the necessary knowledge and skills (=knowing-how-to-do) to achieve this goal. If the object is winning a shooting competition, there is no point in possessing a gun and presenting oneself at the appointed place and time without knowing-how-to-shoot.

These modalities of knowing-how-to-do and being-able-to-do are known as the actualizing modalities. They can be contrasted on the one hand with the virtualizing modalities (wanting-to-do and/or having-to-do) where the subject is established, and on the other with the realizing modalities ('being' and 'doing') where the subject is realized.

See also *canonical narrative schema* and *modalization.*

Lack

The term lack expresses a state of disjunction between a subject and an object. In abstract terms this is represented thus:

The state of disjunction, the sense of a loss, of something missing is frequently the trigger for the global narrative programme known as the quest. Most stories and indeed human action in general spring from an essential dissatisfaction with the world.

The lack is eliminated by means of a transformation bringing about a conjunction of subject and object. This transformation corresponds to the decisive test or performance.

The term 'lack' was originally coined by Propp, for whom it is closely associated with the 'misdeed' of the villain. It is this misdeed that triggers the quest whose ultimate aim is to remedy a lack and rectify a misdeed.

See also *actantial narrative schema* and *canonical narrative schema.*

Language

The term language designates any signifying whole (system) be it verbal, musical, visual, gestural, etc. We speak of a language of architecture, a language of music or a language of landscape, to mention just a few examples. A language must necessarily bring into play the relationship signifier/signified (Saussure) or (in Hjelmslev's terminology) expression and content. To take the language of traffic lights for instance: the colours green–amber–red in their respective positions and order constitute the signifiers, whereas the signifieds are go–be careful–stop. In other words, a language must always consist of a form and a content, the two facets being deemed inseparable.

Referring to the spoken language (English, French, Italian, etc.), Saussure makes the distinction between *langue* and *parole*. He uses the term *langue* to denote the abstract set of rules and conventions underlying a given language, whereas *parole* designates the concrete manner in which each individual speaker makes use of this system.

See also *expression and content* and *signifier and signified.*

Language act

According to the theories of J. R. Searle all linguistic utterances possess an illocutionary power, that is, they not only communicate a content (ideas, etc.) but also establish a particular relationship – one of intentionality – between enunciator (addresser) and enunciatee (addressee). An utterance, for example, could be an order, a promise, a request, etc., that is, it could be any from a variety of language acts.

Examples: 'It is raining' is an act of affirmation on the part of the enunciator. 'Please do not leave litter on the lawn' – this is a request verging on a command.

See also *illocutionary act* and *perlocutionary act.*

Langue and *parole*

In his theory of language, the linguist Ferdinand de Saussure makes the distinction between *langue* and *parole*. He uses the term *langue* to denote the abstract set of rules and conventions which underlies a given language, while *parole* designates the actual manner in which each individual speaker makes use of this system.

See also *language*.

Law – Semiotics of

The semiotics of law was pioneered in France in the 1970s by the semioticians A. J. Greimas and Eric Landowski. In a seminal chapter of *Sémiotique et sciences sociales* [Semiotics and the Social Sciences], 1976, they explore the commercial laws that govern companies, bringing to the fore the specific properties of legal language, legal grammar and legal production as well as the narrative status of commercial companies. The discipline has been further developed by Landowski and has attained an international status, as evidenced in the publication of the *International Journal for the Semiotics of Law.* A key proponent of Greimassian semiotics in the USA is Bernard Jackson, who in a chapter 'Narrative and Legal Discourse' [*Narrative in Culture*] stresses the importance of narrative structures in persuading a court/jury of the truth of a particular story. His research areas also include the European Convention of Human Rights and a comparative study of Jewish and Islamic law. Recent years have seen a focus on international law and on the construction in law of concepts such as those of 'the people', 'the nation' and 'the international community'.

Lexeme

A lexeme represents the totality of possible or virtual meanings attached to a particular word. Only a select number of these meanings will be actualized in a discourse.

In general usage, the term lexeme has the same meaning as 'word'. 'Apple', for example, is a lexeme/word whose figurative or metaphorical meaning will be actualized in the context of a discursive unit. We call the actualized units of meaning a sememe.

See also *sememe*.

Lexia

For Bernard Pottier the term lexia designates fundamental lexical units (units of meaning). These units can be grouped into three categories:

(a) simple lexias: these are simple lexemes such as 'cat', 'dog', and affixed lexemes such as 'unconstitutional';

(b) compound lexias: these are fixed syntagmes such as 'horse-power', 'shoe-tree', etc.;

(c) complex lexias: these are expressions such as 'to take into account', 'to take care of'.

Lexical cohesion

Lexical cohesion occurs when two (or more) words in a text are semantically related, that is, they are related in terms of their meaning or content. Common devices of lexical cohesion are: pronouns, repetition, collocations and synonyms. An example of repetition would be 'I bought some books because books are my passion'. Collocation, on the other hand, is illustrated by a sentence such as 'His body burnt with the fire of his passion'. The words 'fire' and 'burnt' are both used to express passion.

See also *cohesion* and *collocation.*

Lexical field

A lexical field is formed by grouping together words under one general umbrella term. 'Apple', 'banana', 'strawberry', etc., would all form part of a lexical field headed 'fruit'.

See also *semantic field.*

Lexicology

The term lexicology designates the scientific study of words. Until semantics was recognized as an autonomous branch of science, lexicology was the only area in linguistics to study problems relating to the meaning of words.

See also *lexeme, lexical field* and *semantics.*

Life/death

Life is the positive term of the life/death category whose semantic axis (common denominator of meaning) can be called existence. The category life/death constitutes a thematic elementary structure and can be regarded as universal. It gives rise to the following semiotic square:

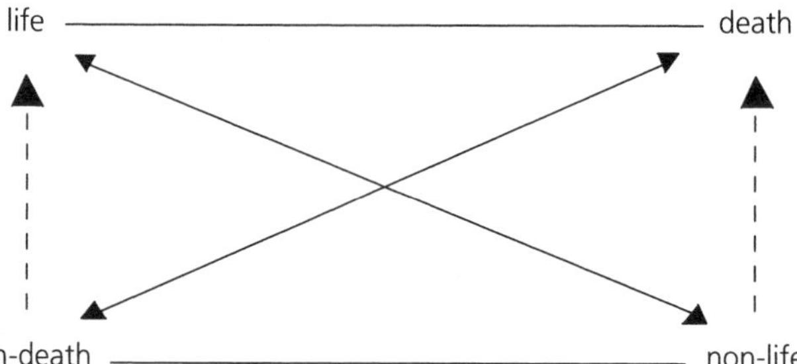

The category life/death can be connoted by the thymic category. Very frequently, the positive and negative terms are coupled, that is, life +

euphoric; death + dysphoric. However, this is not always the case: for someone about to commit suicide, life equals dysphoria.

See also *semiotic square.*

Listener

Like the term reader, the listener designates the receiver of a verbal communication, in this case of an oral nature. In semiotics, the more general term enunciatee is preferred.

See also *enunciator/enunciatee.*

Literariness

The term literariness was introduced by the linguist Roman Jakobson to denote the specificity of literary discourse as opposed to ordinary discourse. According to Jakobson, the object of literary theory should not be literature itself but literariness, in other words, that which allows us to make a distinction between literature and non-literature.

Research, however, has since established that what we call literary form (figures, procedures, discursive or narrative arrangements) may change over time and may also vary according to cultural context. For example, a text considered religious in the Middle Ages is today deemed literature. Thus the concept of literariness belongs to the study of the ethnotheory of genres.

See also *formalism.*

Logocentrism

This term was coined by Jacques Derrida to describe all forms of thought which base themselves on some external point of reference, such as the notion of truth. It implies a challenge to the 'metaphysics of presence', that is, the traditional concept that language is transparent and subservient to some idea, intention or referent that lies outside it. Logocentrism can thus be contrasted with Derrida's concept of language as *différance*, i.e. meaning being a (slippery) play of differences which can never be fully grasped.

Logocentrism, however, can also denote an attitude which values linguistic communication above all other non-verbal forms of expression.

See also *deconstruction*, *graphocentrism*, *phonocentrism* and *transcendental signified.*

Manifestation

See *immanence and manifestation.*

Matter

In semiotic theory, the term matter denotes the formless raw material which allows immanent form to manifest itself. Hjelmslev employs indiscriminately the term matter and the term purport when talking of 'manifestation' of language on both the level of expression and that of content.

See also *form, immanence and manifestation* and *purport.*

Meaning

In general terms, meaning refers to that which is conveyed by a word, a gesture or an operation. It is seen as a synonym of sense, content or referent.

Structuralism sees meaning as residing in the dynamic relations between elements within a structure. The meaning of a text is thus considered to be immanent, that is, to lie within the textual construct, and to be completely independent of the intentions of the author and of historical context or readers' interpretations.

According to semiotic theory, it is not meaning itself that is at stake, but the definition of *meaning effects* and these are 'produced by our senses in contact with meaning'. Importance therefore shifts from meaning to signification, that is, articulated meaning, and it is around this key concept that all semiotic theory is organized.

See also *signification* and *structuralism.*

Medium

The term medium generally denotes a middle position, an intermediate state or a means or instrument. It is widely employed as a noun to indicate a technical means of communication which, while itself being largely transparent, may affect the meaning of the message communicated. For instance, a newspaper article and a radio broadcast could contain the same text but convey somewhat different messages.

Message

In the most general sense, the term message is used to describe any item of cultural information transmitted in any code. In a more restricted sense, a message usually refers to a verbal or written communication by an addresser to an addressee. The linguist Roman Jakobson included 'message' as one of the six functions in his communication model. He also stated that the focus on the message for its own sake represents the poetic function of language and the poetic.

See also *communication model.*

Metalanguage

A metalanguage is a language that is unique to a particular branch of knowledge. It is composed of the specialized concepts or terminology needed to define the discipline. Medicine, for example, has its own metalanguage, as does the science of law, literature, art, etc. Semiotics itself is a metalanguage, in other words, the term refers to the language or concepts that define the manner meaning is produced.

The meanings of terms used in a metalanguage tend to be stable, i.e. independent (as far as possible) of any specific context.

Metalingual function

If a communication is orientated towards the code used – lexical meaning in a verbal text or number symbolism in mathematical discourse, for instance – then it is the metalingual function that dominates. In general, the purpose of the metalingual function is to check that the same code is being used by both parties, that they understand each other. Utterances such as 'in other words', 'do you understand?', 'what I mean to say' are illustrative of this function. Dictionaries are a good example of the metalingual function dominating a text.

Dominance of the metalingual function in a text does not preclude the other speech functions being present to varying degrees.

See also *communication model.*

Metaphor

The term metaphor designates the procedure by which a given sentential unit is substituted for another, thereby transforming its original semantic charge. In other words, a substitute name or descriptive expression is transferred to some object/person to which it is not literally applicable: 'pilgrimage', for instance, is employed instead of 'life', 'burning fire' to express the notion 'love', 'lamb' to describe a child, etc.

See also *metonymy.*

Metasemiotics

The term metasemiotics refers to the theory of meaning produced on a second or higher level of signification. Any utterance which can be semiotically investigated may also cause effects that cannot be explained by analysing linguistic data. For instance: Why do we believe someone's words to be true when they themselves offer no guarantee for such trust? What makes us understand the opening passage of a book as fiction or documentary account, if there is no firm verbal indication as to which way it is to be taken?

According to Hjelmslev, there are two basic types of metasemiotics: a scientific one and a non-scientific one. Non-scientific metasemiotics falls within the domain of philosophy, ontology and even ethics. It concerns, in fact, a fiduciary agreement between an enunciator and an enunciatee which, in everyday life, cannot be analysed in terms of objective science.

Scientific metasemiotics, on the other hand, deals with objects which are themselves already scientific signifying systems, such as mathematics, logic, linguistics. Its main concern, therefore, would seem to be a matter of metalanguage.

See also *contract, metalanguage* and *metaterm.*

Metaterm

Any two terms in opposition that constitute a semantic category will also generate a metaterm. Composed of the oppositional relationship of the two original terms, such metaterms, in turn, find their own opposing terms, thereby creating a new semantic category on a hierarchically higher level. Let us take the term *être*/being opposed by the term *paraître*/seeming to be. Both these terms illustrate different sides of the term *truth*. Truth, on the other hand, has its own opposing term in falsehood. Truth and falsehood thus become metaterms with regard to the original terms of *être* and *paraître*.

See also *veridiction*.

Metonymy

The term metonymy designates the procedure whereby a given sentential unit is substituted for another with which it entertains a necessary relationship of contiguity, i.e. cause for effect, container for contained, part for the whole, etc. We may use 'pen' to denote the notion 'author', 'sail' for 'ship', or refer to 'the crown' to indicate the sovereign, the governing power in a monarchy.

See also *metaphor*.

Mimesis

The term mimesis is used in literary criticism. It relates to a close imitation or simulation of reality in art or literature. The nineteenth-century novel is particularly well known for its attempts at minute observation and meticulous reproduction of bourgeois life in order to create 'realist' pictures. Among famous authors known for their mimetic skill are Flaubert, Zola and George Eliot.

See also *realism*.

Mise-en-abîme

The French expression *mise-en-abîme* describes the procedure whereby a story within a story reflects on the central theme, character or action. For example, we find a *mise-en-abîme* in many comedies where the servants duplicate the love story of their masters.

The *mise-en-abîme* is also frequently used in the French Nouveau Roman as part of the mirroring, multiplying and fragmenting devices meant to draw attention to the narrating process itself.

Mise-en-scène

In the context of film theory, the term *mise-en-scène* refers to the setting or arranging of a scene or to the style of direction of a scene. It thus includes camera position, lighting, costumes, angle of vision, etc. In the Hitchcock film *Rear Window*, the *mise-en-scène* of the opening shot introducing the balcony viewpoint of the backyard determines the direction of the whole film.

The term *mise-en-scène* is often opposed to *montage*.

See also *montage*.

Modal

The term modal is normally used in connection with values or statements. In opposition to descriptive values, modal values are values that contribute to modifying basic statements. Let us take a simple example: 'A monkey sees a banana he wishes to eat. Unfortunately he cannot reach it. So he looks for a stick to help him get the banana within his reach.' In this story the 'stick' which enables the monkey to get the fruit represents a modal value. The banana itself, on the other hand, amounts to a descriptive value.

Similarly, modal statements are used to modify descriptive statements. Thus the sentence 'A monkey wants a banana hanging high in the tree' contains two statements: a descriptive one ('a banana hangs high in the tree') and a modal one ('a monkey wants the banana').

See also *descriptive, modalities, modalization* and *object of value*.

Modalities

The term modalities designates modal expressions such as wanting, having to, ought, may, being able to, knowing how to do. Modalities modify (or overdetermine) basic statements or utterances. These basic statements can be utterances of state or utterances of doing:

(a) utterances of state:
Jack is rich. (basic)
Jack wants to be rich. (modified)

(b) utterances of doing:
Jack killed the dragon. (basic)
Jack had to kill the dragon. (modified)

The modalities can be positive or negative:

Positive: She could swim 50 metres.
Negative: He was unable to do the washing-up.

The basic modalities governing both utterances of state or of doing are:

(a) wanting
(1) utterances of state: wanting-to-be (*vouloir être*) – 'He wanted to be rich.'
(2) utterances of doing: wanting-to-do (*vouloir faire*) – 'They want to find the books.'

(b) having to
(1) utterances of state: having-to-be (*devoir être*) – 'She had to be clever.'
(2) utterances of doing: having-to-do (*devoir faire*) – 'He had to do his homework.'

(c) being able
(1) utterances of state: being-able-to-be (*pouvoir être*) – 'She could not have been there.'
(2) utterances of doing: being-able-to-do (*pouvoir faire*) – 'He was able to swim the Channel.'

(d) knowing
(1) utterances of state: knowing-how-to-be (*savoir être*) – 'He knew how to be evil.'
(2) utterances of doing: knowing-how-to-do (*savoir faire*) – 'She knew how to play the piano.'

In the canonical narrative schema of the quest the modalities of wanting-to-do and/or having-to-do are acquired at the stage of the contract. The subject is described as virtual (the virtual subject) and these modalities become the virtualizing modalities. At the qualifying test or stage of competence, the subject acquires, in addition, the modalities of being-able-to-do and/or knowing-how-to-do. It becomes an actual subject. These modalities therefore are known as the actualizing modalities. The subject is now ready to precede to the next stage, that of the performance.

Further modalities are:

believing: this modal structure governs (or overdetermines) utterances of state – 'She did not believe he would come.'

Mapped out on a semiotic square, the structure of believing would appear as follows:

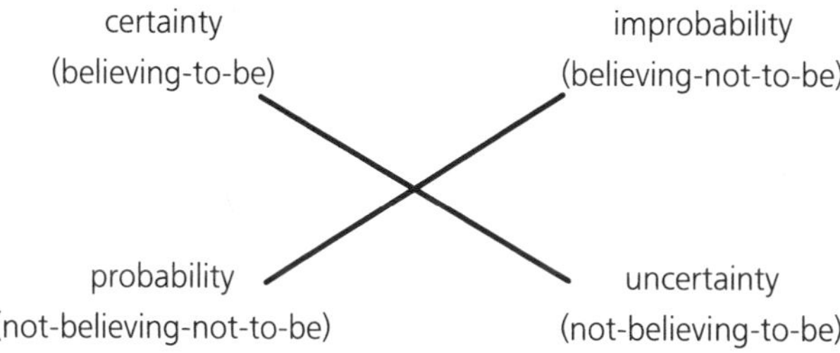

seeming: here one utterance of state modifies another utterance of state – 'He seems to be an honest person.'

Seeming can be described as a veridictory modality, that is, it relates to the process of truth-telling in a story (veridiction).

See also *alethic modalities, epistemic modalities* and *veridiction.*

Modality

Modality is a grammatical category associated with the expression of possibility, certainty, obligation, necessity, etc. It is mainly expressed in the use of modal verbs (to be able, to wish, to have to), adverbs such as 'perhaps' or 'certainly' and verb moods (indicative, subjunctive, imperative, conditional). According to Halliday, sentence types include the following modalities: declarative (for statements), interrogative (for questions), exclamative (for exclamations about one's feelings) and imperative (for commands and requests).

Modalization

The term modalization relates to the procedure whereby a descriptive statement is being modified by means of modal expressions. In the event, phrases articulating a wish, mental or physical capacity, a prescription or a direction (wanting, having to, ought, may, being able to, knowing how to, etc.) adjust and ultimately determine the meaning of utterances describing:

(1) a state of being or a state of affairs

Jack is rich.
Jack wants to be rich.
Jack might be rich.

They are at home.
They have to be at home.
They ought to be at home.

(2) an action

Jack killed the dragon.
Jack should have killed the dragon.
Jack must have killed the dragon.

They build a house.
They are able to build a house.
They intend to build a house.

See also *modalities*.

Mode of existence

The mode of existence defines the various ways and forms in which semiotic objects (actants, modalities, temporality, etc.) manifest their presence in discourse. The Saussurean tradition distinguishes virtual existence (the language system: *langue*) from actual existence (its actualization in speech: *parole*). To these two modes of existence semiotic theory has added a third mode: realization. In the canonical narrative schema, for example, the contract/manipulation grants the subject virtual existence which is actualized during the qualifying test and finally realized in the decisive and glorifying tests; equally, the modalities of believing, having to or wanting install a virtual subject; being able to and knowing actualize the subject which the doing realizes.

In a wider sense, one could say that the modes of existence involve the very formation and adjustment of meaning in speech. In the case of figures of speech such as a metaphor, for example, the tension or competition produced between different levels of meaning is governed by their modes of existence: one might be virtual, another actual, a third potential and a fourth one realizing. Using the expression 'lamb' or 'duckie' as terms of endearment, for instance, actualizes the metaphor.

See also *actualization*, *realization* and *virtualization*.

Modernism

Modernism is the name given to a movement that arose in the West at the end of the nineteenth century and that is associated predominantly with the literature of the early twentieth century and with writers such as James Joyce, Gertrude Stein and Virginia Woolf. Modernist works reject the dominant conventions of the nineteenth century in favour of experimentation or new methods of artistic expression, such as the stream of consciousness and interior monologue in fiction or atonality in music. In many instances, the focus is on the evocation of states of consciousness, on the individual's perception of time and on the role of dream and memory. The modernist text is frequently self-conscious, deliberately reminding the reader or addressee of its status as art. An example here would be Virginia Woolf's *The Waves*.

Montage

The term *montage* is derived from the French *monter* [to assemble]. It is used in film theory to denote the editing of shots to make a film sequence, or the editing of sequences into a whole film.

Early filmologists considered *montage* to be the grammar of a film. They believed filmic images to be homologous with words and their combination comparable to sentences. The theory of *montage* eventually developed into a theory of syntagmatic film analysis which then became the semiotic syntax of film.

See also *semiotics of film* and *mise-en-scène*.

Morpheme

A morpheme is the smallest distinctive unit of grammatical analysis and the smallest unit of meaning. Suffixes and prefixes are morphemes. The word 'misogyny' is composed of two morphemes: 'miso' from the Greek *misein,* which means to hate, and 'gyn' from the Greek *gunē*, which means woman. There are two types of morpheme:

1. Lexical morphemes. All prefixes and some suffixes are lexical morphemes used to build new lexical items, e.g. dry-clean-able; anti-static; pre-shrunk.
2. Grammatical morphemes: -ing, or -ed, e.g. ly-ing; dress-ed; miss-ed.

Morphology

In general, the term morphology designates the study of forms, and in particular, those of words. Morphology is thus one of the two fundamental components of grammar, with syntax representing the other. The description of conjugations, verb tenses, adverbs and adjectives or the declension of nouns forms part of morphology, while syntax is concerned with clauses and sentences.

Semiotic theory, when proposing to apply the concept of syntax to elementary structures of signification, introduced also that of morphology. Morphology here relates to taxonomic (classificatory) terms represented on the semiotic square, and syntax to the operations and dynamics they sanction.

The folklorist Vladimir Propp, author of *Morphology of the Folktale*, applies the term not in a linguistic but in a botanical sense, essentially producing a series of 'dramatis personae'.

See also *grammar, syntax* and Vladimir Propp in **Key Thinkers in Semiotics.**

Moscow School

The Moscow School, or Moscow Linguistic Circle, was founded in 1915 by, among others, the Russian linguist Roman Jakobson and the folklorist Petr Bogatyrev. It is best known for the intellectual movement known as Russian formalism which the Moscow School developed together with OPOJAZ, the Petrograd poetic group whose leading members included Victor Shklovsky, Yuri Tynyanov and Boris Eikenbaum. Initially inspired by the Futurists whose work was directed against decadent bourgeois culture, the Formalists were intent on finding a scientific approach to literature and art. They thus developed a theory of strict adherence to form and structure which they applied to literary writing. Shklovsky expressed this materialistic attitude when he defined literature as 'the sum total of all stylistic devices employed in it'. This early phase of formalism came to an end with Trotsky's criticism of the movement (1924), and official disapproval eventually suppressed the Formalists' work in the 1930s. Jakobson moved to Czechoslovakia where he helped with the foundation of the Prague Linguistic Circle. It was here that the more structuralist side of formalism, initiated by Jakobson and Tynyanov, was continued, and this eventually became highly influential in the development of European semiotics.

See also *formalism*, *Moscow-Tartu School* and *Prague School.*

Moscow-Tartu School

The Moscow-Tartu School of Semiotics, combining the two most important research centres of Soviet semiotics, was founded in the 1960s by Yuri Lotman who worked at Tartu University, Estonia. Building on their formalist heritage, researchers at the School participated in the structuralist-semiotic movement which was developing in Europe and America. Their work became known as 'Soviet structuralism' which, however, was also semiotic from the outset and extended to include 'cultural semiotics'. Strongly influenced by Saussure, Hjelmslev and Jakobson, Soviet semiotics focused on information, communication and systems theory. The field of analysis was broadened to include, apart from language and literature, non-verbal and visual communication such as myth, folklore and religion. Art and culture generally were considered *secondary modelling systems*; 'secondary' because, according to Lotman, 'like all semiotic systems, [they] are constructed *on the model of language*'.

See also *formalism* and *Moscow School.*

Motif

The term motif denotes a distinctive idea or dominant or recurrent theme, feature or pattern in literature, music or the arts. We talk, for example, of the wedding-motif in love stories, of the motif of rags to riches or of the motif of the whore with the heart of gold.

Folklorists such as S. Thompson employ the term *motif* in opposition to *type* of folk-tale in order to designate the smallest story element likely to recur, in its particular form, in popular tradition. Thompson, in fact, is known for his *Motif Index of Folk-Literature*.

Semiotic theory relates the term motif to the concept of configuration because of its particular syntactical and semantic organization as well as its integration into a larger discursive unit.

See also *configuration.*

Myth

The term myth is defined as a symbolic narrative often involving gods or heroes and offering an explanation of some fact or natural phenomenon. Using a different kind of logic, it represents an attempt to impose a graspable shape on human experience and allow for a satisfactory interpretation of human existence. The tale of *Jason and the Argonauts* is a Greek myth and the biblical book of Genesis can be considered a myth with veiled meaning.

Semiotic theory has been influenced by studies of myths from different cultures carried out by Lévi-Strauss. Searching for a semantic structure or 'language system' that underpins culture, he discovered a number of recurrent elements (named 'mythemes') and functions. These seemed to operate like the components of universal signifying structures. Thus Lévi-Strauss found the Oedipus myth to be organized in units set up, like linguistic units, in binary opposition. According to Lévi-Strauss, therefore, it is not the narrative sequence but the structural pattern that gives a myth its meaning.

In today's culture, the term myth has adopted a wider significance. We talk of bourgeois myths generated by the mass media. In this sense, products or ideas are understood and promoted to confirm and reinforce a particular view of the world and its values. Finally, the term myth is also used simply to indicate a figment of the imagination or a commonly held belief without foundation.

Narration

Narration can be defined as the act or process of telling a story. An alternative term is *narrating*. Narrators vary in the extent to which they also participate in the action which they describe. Written narratives may employ third-person omniscient narration where the narrator appears detached from events, as in Charles Dickens' *Bleak House* or *La Cousine Bette* [Cousin Bette] by Honoré de Balzac. On the other hand, they may employ first-person, more 'subjective' narration where events are evoked from the point of view of a particular character or witness in a story. In academic and professional discourse, third-person narration, conventionally viewed as more objective than first-person narration, can become a device for obscuring the subjective source, thereby enhancing the 'truth effect'.

See also *extradiegetic* and *intradiegetic.*

Narrative frequency

Coined by the narratologist Gérard Genette, the term narrative frequency describes the relationship between the number of times an event takes place in a story and the number of times it is actually narrated. He divides the types of narrative frequency into three broad categories: singulative frequency (*le récit singulatif*), repeated frequency (*le récit répétitif*) and iterative frequency (*le récit itératif*).

See also *iterative* and *singulative.*

Narrative pivot point

Within the framework of the three tests (qualifying, decisive and glorifying) the narrative pivot point can be considered as the moment of confrontation between a subject and an anti-subject. This confrontation will lead to the domination or victory of one of the protagonists which in turn will determine who possesses the object of value. The narrative pivot point in *Treasure Island* is the battle between Long John Silver and his treacherous crew, who are rivals of the hero in the search for the gold.

The narrative pivot point can only be determined by reading backwards following a line of presupposition. A hierarchy of narrative programmes is thus established.

Narrative programme

The term narrative programme (*programme narratif*, PN) refers to the abstract representation of syntactical relationships and their transformation on the surface level of the utterance.

There are two basic forms of narrative utterances. The first one expresses a *state* of being/possessing: Jack is rich; John has money. This is an *énoncé narratif d'état*. The second type of utterance relates to a doing/*action*: John works hard; Jack gives money to John. This is an *énoncé narratif de faire*. A narrative programme consists in one utterance relating to action (*énoncé de faire*) affecting two utterances of state (*énoncés d'état*) as a result of transforming a state of being/possessing:

John is poor. Jack gives John money. Now John is rich.

In abstract terms, this is represented in the following way:

$$PN = F\,[S2 \rightarrow (S1 \cap Ov)]$$

F	=	function
S1	=	John (subject of state)
S2	=	Jack (subject of doing)
Ov	=	money (object of value)
$\cap$	=	conjunction with object of value.

In textual analysis, the application of the model of narrative programmes is useful when concentrating on particular aspects of a story. Thus in *Cinderella*, we can analyse the fairy godmother's gifts to the heroine in these terms: the fairy godmother (subject of doing) causes poor Cinderella (subject of state) to be conjoined with an object of value (coach, clothes) which unlike her sisters she does not possess. This narrative sub-programme (PN *d'usage*) can be linked to the basic or macro narrative programme (PN *de base*) of the entire fairy-tale because the fairy godmother's gifts are necessary so that Cinderella (subject of lack) may be conjoined with the objects of wealth, love and happiness at the end of the story.

See also *canonical narrative schema* and *narrative utterance*.

Narrative subject

The term narrative subject designates a particular position in the actantial schema. Other actantial positions are those of object, helper, opponent, sender and receiver.

The narrative subject can be contrasted with the discursive subject and with the epistemological subject or true subject of enunciation.

See also *actantial narrative schema.*

Narrative trajectory

The expression narrative trajectory (or narrative path) describes a movement from one point in a story (quest) to another by way of intermediary stages. In other words, the narrative trajectory of an actant unfolds according to the logical pattern outlined in Greimas' canonical narrative schema. For instance, the stage of competence must always precede that of performance. In Paul Auster's *Moon Palace*, we speak of the narrative trajectory of the actant/subject Marco Fogg which terminates in the finding of his true identity. Before he arrives at his goal, however, he must undergo certain experiences – that of homelessness, for example – which provide him with the necessary competence to achieve his aim successfully.

See also *actant* and *canonical narrative schema.*

Narrative utterance

The term narrative utterance (*énoncé narratif*, EN) is coined to show in abstract terms the relationship/function that exists between two narrative actants: a subject and an object. There are two basic types of narrative utterance: a statement relating to a state of being/possessing and one referring to action.

1. The first one, a narrative utterance of state (*énoncé narratif d'état*) indicates a relationship in existence between a subject and an object, which at any given moment in the course of a narrative can be perceived in terms of being/not being or possessing/not possessing. If the relationship is positive, we speak of the subject being conjoined with

the object. (At the ball Cinderella is conjoined with her object/prince.) If, on the other hand, it is negative, the subject is disjoined from the object. (Cinderella's absence after the ball represents a disjunction.) The abstract representation of a narrative utterance of state is as follows:

EN1 $= S \cap O$ (subject conjoined with object)
EN2 $= S \cup O$ (subject disjoined from object)

All narratives are composed of successive transformations of states of conjunction with objects to those of disjunction and vice versa. These changes are effected and expressed in the second type of basic narrative utterance:

2. A statement of doing/action (*énoncé narratif de faire*): the action/doing which causes the transformation of state of being/possessing does not need to be performed by the subject undergoing the change (Cinderella is conjoined with her object/prince as a result of her fairy godmother's action: she provides the coach). In the abstract formula, therefore, we distinguish S1 (subject of state) from S2 (subject of doing).

$S2 \rightarrow (S1 \cap O)$ or $S2 \rightarrow (S1 \cup O)$

The operation itself, that is, one statement of doing affecting and causing the transformation of two narrative utterances of state, is called a narrative programme (*programme narratif*, PN).

See also *narrative programme.*

Narratology

The term narratology designates a literary science which generalizes the linguistic model and applies it to literary texts. Influenced by structuralism, narratological theory sees the grammatical structure of language reflected in literature: just as we find a sentence composed of a subject and a predicate, so a narrative possesses a syntactical structure recreating this elementary division. The fairy-tale *Cinderella*, for example, is organized, in essence, around a heroine (subject), a doing and a goal (predicate). By pursuing the analogy in greater detail, narratological thought has developed what is now termed a narrative grammar.

The most influential practitioners of narratology have been, apart from Greimas, Tzvetan Todorov, Gérard Genette and Roland Barthes.

See also *structuralism.*

Narrator/narratee

The term narrator denotes an actant in a written text or verbal communication to whom the enunciator – by means of the procedure of *débrayage* – has delegated his/her voice. The 'I' in an utterance, therefore, is not identical with the enunciator but a verbal simulacrum of a narrative presence. Correspondingly, the real enunciatee/receiver of the message is represented in a text by an actant/delegate, the narratee. The latter may, or may not, be present on the discursive level with the mention 'you'.

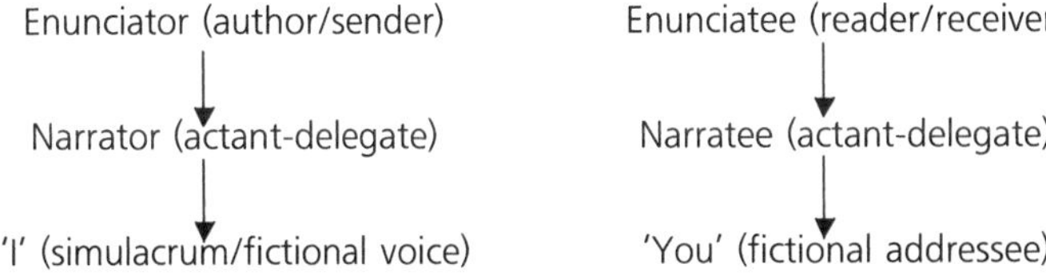

The author Albert Camus is the enunciator of the novel *L'Etranger.* Camus delegates his voice to Meursault, who starts his account with the sentence 'Mother died to-day', and who awaits his execution at the end. Meursault is the narrator, the 'I' in the story, constructed by the enunciator to take his place. The enunciatee of the novel, on the other hand, the reading public, finds its delegate in the construction of a fictional narratee, the implied audience to whom the account is addressed.

See also *enunciator/enunciatee.*

Naturalism

Naturalism is a scientific form of realism that appeared at the end of the nineteenth century. It adopts a documentary, almost photographic, approach to life and stresses how heredity and environment can shape people's lives. In literature, the term naturalistic is used broadly to denote a very detailed illusion of real life. Novels by Zola and Flaubert are examples of naturalistic writing.

Adopting a contemporary perspective, semioticians would challenge the view that a work of art can be 'naturalistic', that is, an innocent neutral reflection of the social, psychological or natural world. Instead, both 'nature' and 'reality' are viewed as cultural constructs or products of language. Far from faithfully reflecting the world, texts draw upon multiple codes from the wider social and cultural context. Photography itself involves the application of conventionalized visual codes.

Literary texts, moreover, are not just the product of other codes: they are themselves signifying systems which structure the larger linguistic system upon which they depend. Movements such as naturalism and realism can be seen as collaborating more closely with contemporary definitions of reality than would, say, the modern or postmodern movements.

See also *essentialism* and *realism.*

Nature

In opposition to anything artificial or man-made, the term nature designates that which is already given or in a state characteristic of being inborn. In that sense, the concept covers all natural phenomena from plants, animals, landscapes, etc., to the inherent and innate characteristics of human beings.

In semiotic theory, the notion of nature is seen as coexisting and contrasting with that of culture. Thus in the description of a seaside town, expressions such as 'coast', 'waves', 'wind' or 'sea' belong to the semantic category *nature* while references to 'houses', 'road', 'cars' and 'boats' relate to that of *culture.* Equally, in a murder story, mention of premeditation and planning the evil deed fall in the category of cultural behaviour while the rendering of the actual killing with its gory details would be classed under violence of natural origin.

Following Lévi-Strauss, semiotics considers the opposing couple nature/culture to articulate the semantic category 'social life' whereas the semantic category 'life/death' characterizes the universe of the individual.

See also *culture.*

Negative

The two terms of the axis of contraries, S1 and S2, are labelled respectively the positive and the negative term. These terms do not imply any thymic connotation (i.e. euphoric or dysphoric). In the category freedom/imprisonment, for instance, freedom is the positive term and imprisonment the negative term:

S1	————————	S2
freedom		imprisonment
positive		negative

However, depending on the context, both terms could have euphoric or dysphoric connotations. The escaped prisoner, for example, feels unhappy about imprisonment (dysphoria) while a starving tramp might be glad to be locked up (euphoria).

See also *positive, semiotic square* and *thymic.*

Nominalization

In Halliday's terminology, nominalization is a structural feature whereby any element or group of elements in a clause is made to function as a nominal group (as a noun). Any nominalization, therefore, constitutes a single element in the message structure: 'What the man did with the violin (= nominal group) was to give it to his friend'; 'The one I like best (= nominal group) is not in the shop'.

Nominalizations are frequently formed from verbs. They express, therefore, a process: 'Stealing from people will not get you anywhere'; 'The building of the department store took six months'; 'The killing took place in the morning'.

Critical linguistics has drawn attention to the ideological weight carried by nominalizations, especially in the field of media discourse. Norman Fairclough, for example, has pointed out that the conversion of verbs to nouns in particular is a means of rendering a discourse more abstract, thereby enhancing its 'truth effect'. The omission of agency also allows one to background (or even ignore) historical detail.

Object of value

The term value has itself several meanings. We differentiate, for example, between value understood through 'valuation', or estimated worth or price, and value understood as 'quality' which makes someone or something worthy of esteem, desirable or important.

Semiotic theory describes value as arising from the relationship between actantial subjects and objects: any subject's need or desire for a particular object makes the latter valuable, turning it into an *objet de valeur* in the process. Moreover, the value it has for the subject comes to be identified with the object. For instance, if someone buys a car, it is probably not so much a question of owning the object/car but rather of acquiring an easy and comfortable means of transport, or a way of enhancing one's social reputation, or enjoying a feeling of power . . . The thing itself, in this case, is merely pretext, a placement for the desired values. Thus, in semiotic analysis, the term object of value has been fashioned to designate objects placed in relation to subjects.

Observer

The term observer refers to the cognitive subject installed in a narrative by the enunciator to receive and transmit information. Its presence in discourse manifests itself in different ways: the observing subject may be implicit and only recognizable by analysis as, for example, the description of an event may imply the point of view of an observer. Accounts of disasters in newspaper reporting often imply an observer who may not even have been there. On the other hand, an observation point may be made obvious in a text by installing a personal reference or voice. In Alain Robbe-Grillet's novel *La Jalousie*, for example, the narrator takes on the position of dispassionate observer while the protagonists A and Franck represent the observed.

The relationship between observer and observed is complex and reversible: a subject that knows it is being observed may well try to manipulate or deceive the observing subject.

See also *enunciator/enunciatee.*

Onomatopoeia

The term onomatopoeia refers to the process whereby a word is formed in imitation of the sound produced by the thing meant. The word 'bang', for instance, sounds like the sudden loud noise to which it is referring. The 's' at the beginning of the words 'snake' or 'serpents' likewise conveys the hissing sound made by these animals. Onomatopoeia is a figure of speech that is often found in poetry, sometimes in prose. 'Myriads of rivulets hurrying thro' the lawn, / The moan of doves in immemorial elms, / And murmuring of innumerable bees' (Tennyson).

Ontology

Ontology is part of metaphysics and relates to the science or study of pure being, of the essence of things. It also refers to philosophical statements about the nature of the things that make up our reality and about their division into separate entities.

Opponent

Any actant who hinders the subject in its quest is known as an opponent. Unlike the anti-subject, the opponent does not have a quest of its own. In an athlete's attempts to acquire a gold medal at the Olympics, for example, physical fatigue and age may act as opponents.

See also *anti-subject*.

Palimpsest

In general terms, palimpsest refers to writing which is superimposed on already existing scripture.

In his later work Gérard Genette uses the term palimpsest to describe a literature made up of hypertexts which derive from, imitate or relate to an earlier work or hypotext. Together a hypertext and its hypotext make up a multi-layered palimpsest. For instance, Joyce's *Ulysses* and Homer's *Odyssey* (the hypotext) together make up a palimpsest. The same goes for Michel Tournier's *Vendredi ou les Limbes du Pacifique* [Friday] and its hypotext *Robinson Crusoe.*

See also *hypertext, hypotext* and *intertextuality.*

Paradigm

The term paradigm refers to a group of sentential units susceptible to occupy the same place, or replace each other, in a syntagmatic chain. In other words, paradigmatic elements exist on the vertical axis of language and could be substituted for one another in the same set. The relationship they entertain is one of equivalence or opposition. Thus 'building', 'house', 'hovel' or 'palace' may be substituted for 'dwelling'; on the other hand, 'out' could be replaced by its opposition 'in' in the sentence 'she stayed in' instead of 'she stayed out'.

See also *syntagm.*

Paradigmatic

Paradigmatic relations are those in which linguistic units are linked by partial resemblances – or oppositions – either in form or in meaning. They can be contrasted with syntagmatic relations in which the units are linked in terms of contiguity or linearity. In its abundant use of repetition and contrast, for example, the French New Novel is exploiting the paradigmatic axis of meaning. This would contrast with the traditional realist novel where more importance would be placed on a linear unfolding of plot.

A paradigmatic analysis of a text would involve the identification of underlying paradigms and of the positive or negative connotations of each linguistic unit. Thematic binary oppositions such as public/private or nature/culture can thus be constructed. The expression isotope in contemporary French semiotics has largely replaced the term paradigm.

See also *isotope* and *paradigm*.

Paraphrase

A paraphrase is a restatement of the text's meaning in different words, i.e. it is a discursive unit that is semantically equivalent to another unit previously produced. Paraphrases are often introduced with 'what I mean to say', 'in other words', 'i.e.', etc.

The operation is one of translation (of meaning) and of expansion.

Paratext

Originally coined by Gérard Genette, the term paratext refers to all those textual elements that surround or frame the text such as titles, subtitles, pseudonyms, forewords, dedications, epigraphs, prefaces, notes, epilogues and afterwords. The paratext can be said to control or influence one's whole reading of a text.

Paratopic space

Paratopic space is the space in which the qualifying test takes place, that is, in which competence is acquired. It is contrasted with utopic space, where the decisive test takes place and the performances are carried out.

In *Treasure Island*, the sea voyage with its encounters with pirates constitutes the paratopic space of the qualifying test. In *Cinderella*, the house where she acquires a new dress, as well as the journey in the coach to the ball, can be considered paratopic spaces.

See also *topic space* and *utopic space*.

Passion – Semiotics of

Semiotics has from the very beginning recognized and incorporated into its theory the contribution made by affective (thymic) states to the production of meaning. Thus it has been accepted that positive or negative assessment of values depends also on a subject's euphoric or dysphoric frame of mind. This is borne out by statements such as 'I know that you are right but I don't believe you'.

When it comes to passion, however, that is, strong feeling or agitation of the mind, semiotic analysis on the narrative and discursive levels of an utterance is more complex. As passion is related to states of mind/conditions of the soul (*états d'âme*) rather than action/doing (*faire*), it does not obey the pattern of the actantial and canonical schemas of the narrative quest. Yet passion does play an important part because it will affect a subject's doing in one of two ways: either impassioned feeling will dominate the action (*dominance pathémique*) or passion will be present yet on the surface be dominated by the cognitive or actional dimensions (*dominance cognitive*) of the narrative. Either way it is analysable on the structural and organizational level of the discourse.

1) Passion dominating action (*faire*) is illustrated by the *crime passionnel*. A discursive utterance governed by passion is marked by:

   - an unstable relationship between the narrative subject and object. Apart from its position of object the latter may also adopt those of sender or manipulator (e.g. 'love' motivates the subject or makes it do something), or even of subject of doing (the object of a passion moves, disturbs, thereby acting on – even transforming – the subject that becomes 'moved'). Thus the subject itself may also take on the function of object (e.g. become a victim of jealousy). Finally, the subject is often affected in its very core by the object of its passion and behaves in an abnormal way (a gentle person having fits of rage or even murdering). Thus we have a subject and an object with altered and changing modal capacities.
   - the importance attached to *absence*: the unstable relationship is accompanied by a proliferation of images focusing on the desired object and dwelling on the absence which it reveals but which also reveals it. 'La sensibilité est une émotion de l'absence' (Bertrand, 1988). 'How like a winter hath my absence been / From thee, the pleasure of the fleeting year! / What freezings have I felt, what dark days seen! / What old December's bareness every where!'

(Shakespeare, Sonnet 97). Most love poetry could serve as an example, as indeed most literature concerned with passion.

- aspectual indications: deep emotion, strong passion are usually characterized by the suddenness of their discovery. One moment the subject does not understand what is happening, the next awareness strikes and all is clear. The very suddenness of the revelation thus becomes a hallmark of the emotion as well as of its strength.

2) Passion dominated by practical or cognitive action is illustrated by subjects giving in to reason/advice in preference to passion. The dutiful daughter complying with her parents' wishes not to marry her unsuitable lover would be a case in point. A discursive utterance in which passion is governed by the cognitive dimension is marked by:

- a stabilization of the object, which becomes, as it were, 'objective'. The object is held at a distance, considered objectively and analysed. Thus after a major accident or a personal tragedy provoking strong emotions, people tend to go over what happened again and again, examining every detail as though the exact restructuring of the event were all-important.
- an epistemic subject concerned with accurate knowledge and the establishment of truth. It is given over totally to a descriptive and analytical competence. In *La Prisonnière*, for instance, Proust's narrator scrutinizes and takes apart one insignificant remark made by the heroine Albertine, endlessly analysing it and hypothesizing about its precise meaning. The underlying motive for this cognitive investigation is, of course, of a passionate nature: jealousy.
- a concern for veridiction. It matters to establish the truth once and for all, thereby trying to dominate emotional uncertainty. It is important to discover a truth that the subject can believe. But this truth, says Stendhal, 'n'est en vérité qu'un soupir' [is actually only a sigh].

It should be noted, however, that passion does not only find expression in verbal discourse. Passion can also be manifest in, for example, spatial, visual or musical utterances.

Finally, in *Sémiotique des passions* (1991), A. J. Greimas and J. Fontanille have developed a canonical schema of passion which – along the lines of the canonical narrative schema – links four sequences of the trajectory of passion.

This schema illustrates a formal coherence which, interlaced with the subject's action (*faire*), throws light on the accompanying states of being (*être*).

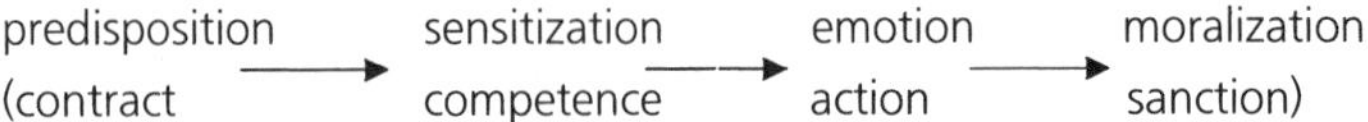

Predisposition: This corresponds to the initial state, that is, the subject's aptitude to accommodate particular passionate effects of meaning. The predisposition of a subject indicates its style of passion, its 'character'. In Flaubert's *Madame Bovary*, for example, the heroine Emma Bovary is from the outset ready to embark on passionate relationships.

Sensitization: This stage corresponds to the 'first impression', the first indication of burgeoning passion. In Emma Bovary's case it relates to her first glimpse of her future lover.

Emotion: This stage prolongs and actualizes the stage of sensitization. Here we have the full-blown emotion as described in Emma's continuing encounters with her lovers.

Moralization: In the final stage, judgement is passed on the emotional crisis: it is either evaluated objectively or subsumed in the passionate feeling which becomes the controlling principle of the narrative. The latter is the case in Prévost's novel *Manon Lescaut*. In *La Princesse de Clèves* by Madame de La Fayette, on the other hand, the moralizing instance remains in control – it is never absorbed by passion itself.

Pathematic role

The term pathematic comes from the Greek and relates to passions or emotions. Thus in contrast to a thematic role which is linked to doing/action (*faire*) a pathematic role relates to a subject's state of being (*être*), namely that characterized by emotion. An actor possessing a pathematic role is often described by reference to a stereotyped passion which renders emotionally geared behaviour predictable. In Dickens' *A Christmas Carol*, for instance, Scrooge has the thematic role of a businessman and the pathematic role of a miser.

In general terms, pathematic roles can be grouped under the overall heading of actors' thematic description on the surface level of an utterance, thereby contributing to actorial individualization. In most instances, socially defined themes or functions outweigh in importance the pathematic input. There are exceptions, however, such as Scrooge, whose stereotyping as a miser overrides his social description.

See also *emotion* and *semiotics of passion.*

Patient

The term patient designates the narrative role of a subject of state, that is of a subject whose relationship with an object remains unchanged. This kind of relationship is frequently expressed in verbs such as 'to be' or 'to have'. In the sentence 'John has blue eyes', 'John' is a subject of state or a 'patient', just as 'Brian' would be in the sentence 'Brian is poor'.

The term patient also designates the narrative role of a subject whose transformation of state in a narrative programme is the result of the action of another subject. In the sentence 'Paul was given a book by his friend', 'Paul' takes the role of a 'patient'.

The term patient contrasts with the term agent, which refers to the narrative role of a subject of doing, that is, of a subject engaged in the carrying out of a particular narrative programme.

See also *agent, subject of doing* and *subject of state.*

Perceptual codes

Perceptual codes are the codes relating to sensory perception by means of which we read or interpret the physical world. They include vision, sound, smell, taste and touch and also telepathy. Perceptual codes may vary between species and also within the same species: therefore they are not universal, but differ according to the sociocultural and environmental context.

Performance

The term performance designates the principal action of the subject, the event to which the story has been leading. It is by carrying out the performance that the subject acquires (or fails to acquire) the object of value. This stage of the canonical narrative schema is also known as the decisive test.

Performance always presupposes competence, doing implies a wanting-to-do as well as an ability-to-do (being able to and/or knowing how to). Sitting an examination (performance) implies the acquisition of a number of skills as well as an initial desire/obligation to succeed (competence).

See also *canonical narrative schema.*

Performative

In Austin's terminology, a performative utterance not only describes the action of the speaker but also performs the same action.

Examples: 'I promise to be there at three o'clock'; 'The chairman declared the meeting open'. In both cases, the utterance embodies the act to which it refers: that of promising or of opening the meeting. Performative utterances, therefore, can be contrasted with those utterances that simply describe an action.

The term performative would seem to be synonymous with illocutionary, a term indicating speech acts that involve commands, questions, warnings, etc.

See also *illocutionary act* and *perlocutionary act.*

Perlocutionary act

The term perlocutionary act is used in the speech act theory (Austin) to describe an utterance that brings about an effect upon the actions, feelings or thoughts of the listener. A political speech, for instance, represents a perlocutionary act in that it produces an effect on its audience that may be one of enthusiasm, conviction or indifference.

A perlocutionary act can be contrasted with an illocutionary act, an utterance that accomplishes something in the act of speaking, such as performing the act of promising by saying 'I promise'. The notion of perlocution belongs partly to cognitive semiotics and partly to the semiotics of emotion.

See also *illocutionary act.*

Personification

Personification refers to a narrative process whereby an object (a thing, abstract or non-human being) is attributed qualities which allow it to be considered as a subject. It is therefore endowed with a narrative programme and capable of performing a doing. To give an example: 'The city opened its mouth and slowly devoured the inhabitants within its entrails.'

Perspective

Unlike the term point of view which implies an observer, the perspective of a text has to do with its composition. It involves the enunciator's choice when selecting the narrative trajectory of a particular actor to the detriment of another actor who is also present in the narrative. In a crime novel, for instance, the choice usually consists in placing the reader in the perspective of the detective, the criminal or the victim.

See also *observer* and *point of view.*

Persuasive doing

Persuasive doing describes the cognitive act whereby an enunciator manipulates an enunciatee, persuading the latter to believe something (*faire croire*) or to act in a certain way (*faire faire*). If someone suggests to me that I might like to enter a fishing contest, that person is exerting a persuasive doing (*faire faire*). If a politician tries to persuade us (*faire croire*) that stringent measures need to be taken to get the economy working, our acceptance of his proposition shows his persuasive doing to have been effective.

Phatic function

If a communication focuses on the contact between addresser (sender) and addressee (receiver), then the phatic function dominates. In general, the phatic function relies on utterances that do not elicit or offer information but simply establish contact (e.g. 'Good morning'), maintain it (e.g. 'How are you?'), or break it (e.g. 'Goodbye'). Most conversation about the weather has this function.

Dominance of the phatic function in a text does not preclude the other speech functions from being present to varying degrees.

See also *communication model.*

Phenomenology

Originating in the work of Husserl, phenomenology can broadly be described as the study of appearances. It is concerned with objects and events as they present themselves to the human consciousness. The focus, therefore, is essentially on concrete reality and on living direct experience rather than on the classical notion of an abstract truth. It calls into question the Cartesian dualism between mind and body, subject and object positing a mutual co-presence and dynamic interaction between the self and the world. For the French phenomenologist Maurice Merleau-Ponty, the subject is above all an embodied consciousness and his thought brings to the fore the central role of the physical body and of the perceptions in our understanding of the world.

The writings of Merleau-Ponty have been extremely influential in the development of semiotics in France. A resurgence of interest in the body led semioticians in the 1980s to move away from narrative towards a concern with figurative elements and with the role of the senses in the emergence of meaning. Recent studies by Jacques Fontanille, Claude Zilberberg and others include an analysis of the role of sight, hearing, touch, taste and smell.

See also Maurice Merleau-Ponty in **Key Thinkers in Semiotics**.

Phoneme

A phoneme is a minimal unit of potentially meaningful sound within a language's system of recognized sound distinctions. It is, for example, the phonemic distinction in English between /l/ and /r/ which enables us to recognize the difference between the words 'level' and 'revel' or 'room' and 'loom'.

For Saussure the linguistic signifier can be described as a collection of sounds or a chain of phonemes, whereas the signified corresponds to the concept or idea conveyed by these sounds.

See also *signifier and signified.*

Phonemics

Phonemics is the branch of linguistics that analyses the sound system of languages.

See also *phonetics.*

Phonetics

Phonetics is the study of the physical sounds of human speech. It includes the production, transmission and perception of sounds. Phonetics can be contrasted with phonology, which is concerned not only with sounds but more importantly with the relationship between sounds and meaning.

Phonocentrism

The term phonocentrism designates a preference for the oral or spoken word over writing. Public speakers may be said to have a bias in favour of phonocentrism.

See also *graphocentrism* and *logocentrism.*

Plane of expression/plane of content

See *expression and content.*

Poetic or aesthetic function

When a communication focuses on its message for its own sake, then the poetic or aesthetic function can be said to be dominant. In other words, the poetic function foregrounds the way a message is expressed rather than concentrating on what is said and the 'reality beyond'. Attention may be drawn, for example, to sound patterns, diction and syntax. In poetry, the poetic function is usually dominant.

Dominance of the poetic function in a communication does not exclude the other speech functions being present to varying degrees.

See also *communication model.*

Point of view

All the procedures which an enunciator employs to select the objects of her/his discourse and to place them in a particular light are termed point of view. In fact the notion, as in ordinary language, covers a wide field and applies to different forms of discourse: narrative, argumentative, descriptive, etc. In each case it involves enunciative positions (*débrayage* and *embrayage*), the relationship installed between the subject (narrator, observer, arguer) and its object as well as structuring strategies which determine textual constraints (what comes first, what comes second, the relationship between the parts and the whole, the passage from the particular to the general or conversely, etc.). The wide area covered by the term point of view is narrowed down with the help of more specific concepts such as focalization, observer and perspective.

See also *focalization, débrayage, embrayage, observer* and *perspective.*

Politics – Semiotics of

The semiotics of politics is a branch of sociosemiotics concerned with the analysis of political discourse, institutions and strategies of persuasion as well as the role of individual actors. It includes the study of political phenomena such as the construction of public opinion and the organization and functioning of election campaigns. Researchers have focused in particular on media representations of power and on the political dimension of institutional discourse. In general terms, the semiotics of politics can be said to concern itself with the signifying practices of dominant power groups in their underlying drive towards social consensus and social cohesion.

Pioneers in this area of study include A. J. Greimas, Eric Landowski and Bernard Alazet, amongst others. The European influence can perhaps be detected in the more recent work of Anglo-Saxon writers such as John Fairclough, manifesting itself in the current preoccupation with the language of politicians and with the phenomenon of spin-doctoring.

Polysemy

The term polysemy designates the presence of more than one sememe (meaning) within a lexeme (word). The word 'head' is polysemic, as it would appear in the dictionary as (a) a part of the body or (b) a leader, as in the expression 'Head of State'.

Polysemic lexemes can be contrasted with monosemic lexemes, which involve only a single sememe. These are characteristic of specialized discourses: the word 'Internet', for example, is monosemic.

Polyvocality

This term refers to the use of multiple narrative voices within a text in order to promote a variety of readings or interpretations. It contrasts with the 'univocal' narrative which offers a single reading of an event. Polyvocality is characteristic of Barbara Kingsolver's *The Poisonwood Bible*, where the reader is presented with five different narrators – all members of the same family – and five different views of Africa. This contrasts with Jane Austin's *Mansfield Park*, where the reader is given one dominant interpretation, that of a third-person omniscient narrator.

The term polyphony is interchangeable with that of polyvocality.

See also *univocality*.

Positive

The two terms of the axis of contraries, S1 and S2, are called respectively positive and negative even though these qualifications do not involve a thymic connotation (euphoric or dysphoric).

In the category life/death, life is the positive term and death the negative:

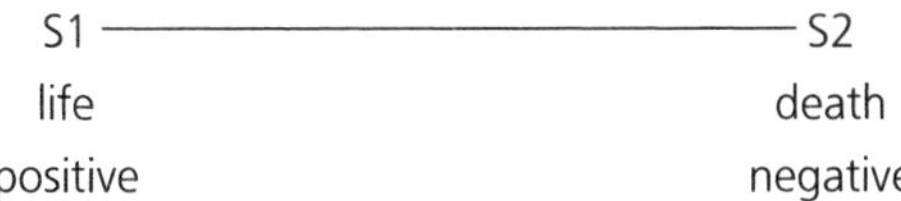

This is equally true of stories where death may be the object of desire (e.g. accounts of martyrdom).

See also *negative, semiotic square* and *thymic*.

Postcolonialism

Postcolonialism is a movement that seeks to explore the effects of European imperialism from the sixteenth century to the present day. Rooted in an attack on Eurocentrism, it challenges colonial representations and ideologies, drawing attention to patterns of cultural and political oppression. An important early influence in the growth of this area of study was the *negritude* movement of the 1940s and 1950s, associated in particular with the writings of Aimé Césaire. A central issue here was the construction of identity. A key role was also played by the works of Frantz Fanon in the 1950s and 1960s (*Black Skin, White Masks,* 1950; *The Wretched of the Earth,* 1961), for whom resistance to colonial power lies in the creation of a national consciousness and in the transformation of traditional culture. He also advocates the adoption of Marxist economic principles.

In 1978 Edward Said published *Orientalism* which, like the writings of Frantz Fanon, was extremely influential in the development of postcolonial theory. Here he shows how the Western creation of the 'myth of the Orient' – exoticism, moral laxity and sexual degeneration – has provided the justification for political imperialism.

It was not, however, until the late 1980s and 1990s that the term postcolonialism was used and that the discipline emerged in its own right. In general, postcolonial theory is heavily influenced not only by Marxism but also by the theoretical discourses of postmodernity such as deconstruction and psychoanalysis as well as by types of discourse analysis derived from Michel Foucault. Other key theorists include Gayatri Spivak who seeks to retrieve the voices of those – especially women – who have been made the subjects of colonial representation, and Homi K. Bhabha who develops, for instance, the concept of hybridity, the notion that the borders between cultures are 'porous' and that we inhabit an 'in-between' space. Recent years have seen the further exploration of the concepts of the transcultural. Peter Hallward, for example, in his *Absolutely Postcolonial*, reassesses in this context the notion of universalism. He shares with Noam Chomsky the view that all languages possess a common core or syntax and his belief that there exists a basic language of feeling (without which intercultural communication would be virtually impossible) recalls recent findings in semiotics.

See also e*urocentrism.*

Postmodernism

Postmodernism describes a trend in art and ideas which challenges and rejects the classic conception of aesthetic beauty based on unity and order. An example of postmodernist architecture is the Pompidou Centre in Paris.

Postmodernism is often dated from Jean-François Lyotard's book *La Condition postmoderne* (1979), which analyses contemporary fragmentation in systems of knowledge. He disputes the notion of the 'grand narrative', the belief that there exists one single true version of events. The trend is neither a firm theory nor a movement but would rather seem to be a general expression for a variety of phenomena in art, architecture, literature and the cinema. These phenomena include textual or visual fragmentation and excessive awareness of production and construction, or playing with types or styles and with texts within texts as well as intertextuality. An example of postmodernist writing is Kate Atkinson's novel *Emotionally Weird* (2000).

Postmodernism is often linked with poststructuralism and deconstruction.

See also *deconstruction* and *poststructuralism*.

Poststructuralism

The expression poststructuralism encompasses developments in literary critical theory from about the late 1960s onwards. The expression is ambiguous in its meaning since it relates to different practices. Thus poststructuralism can be seen simply as succeeding structuralism, as critique of structuralism, as its replacement or as its development. There are three areas of structuralism which poststructuralism challenges in particular: the Saussurean understanding of language as a sign system, the scientific nature of structuralist theory per se, and the idea of the unified subject.

Poststructuralists discover the essentially unstable nature of meaning. They introduce the idea of logocentrism and deferred meaning (Derrida); Barthes proposes 'The death of the author' and hails the plural text. Kristeva and Lacan develop further the notion of the constructed subject. And, with the help of psychoanalysis, they demonstrate how the irrational and the unconscious constantly threaten the unified subject of the ordered text.

Under the influence principally of Derrida, poststructuralism has thus become associated with a critical method known as deconstruction. This approach seeks multiplicities of meaning and includes a 'reading across the grain', an uncovering of the unconscious dimension of internal contradictions or of unsaid implicit ideological assumptions. For instance, in Jane Austin's *Mansfield Park*, the source of wealth behind the property of Mansfield Park itself – its dependence on slavery – is taken for granted by the writer. Poststructuralism is closely linked with postmodernism.

The evolution of poststructuralist semiotics has integrated many of the new findings.

See also *deconstruction*, *postmodernism* and *structuralism*.

Pragmatic

Contrary to the meaning allotted to pragmatic in the English language, semiotic theory uses the term with the meaning given to it in French, that is, as relating to action, to practical doing. Accordingly, the two fundamental dimensions of narrative are termed one pragmatic and the other cognitive. The pragmatic dimension refers to external, physical events such as killing a giant, catching a thief or digging a flower bed. The cognitive dimension, on the other hand, relates to internal mental activities such as knowing, convincing, deceiving, etc. The importance attached to each dimension varies according to the nature of the discourse. In adventure stories, *Treasure Island* for example, it is the pragmatic dimension that dominates, whereas in legal discourse it is the cognitive.

In recent years attention has been focused on a third dimension of narrative known as the thymic dimension. This relates to feelings of euphoria or dysphoria (i.e. pleasant or unpleasant) experienced by the actors. These feelings can be correlated with the stages of a narrative programme. They can, for example, describe a state of disjunction or conjunction with an object of value. In *Romeo and Juliet*, Juliet's disjunction from Romeo, the object of her desire, takes shape in her despair giving rise to her suicide.

See also *cognitive* and *thymic*.

Pragmatics

In the American sense of the word, pragmatics is concerned with the way utterances should be interpreted beyond the meanings of the words used (as defined in a dictionary for instance) and therefore involves looking at the context and particular situation of addresser and addressee. It can thus be loosely defined as the study of language use. Charles Morris divides semiotics into three branches: syntactics, semantics and pragmatics.

Since the 1970s European semiotics has become increasingly concerned with the pragmatic function of a text, with, for instance, enunciative strategies and with the ideological impact of the text on its wider social environment.

See *sociosemiotics*

Prague School

Known originally as The Prague Linguistic Circle, the Prague School was founded in 1926 by V. Mathesius, B. Havranek, J. Mukarovsky, R. Jakobson, N. Trubetzkoy and S. Karcevskij. Other members include the scholars J. Veltrusky and F. Vodicka. Roman Jakobson was vice-president of the Circle until the arrival of the Nazis and his enforced departure in 1939. Influenced by both the Russian Formalists and by Ferdinand de Saussure, the School played a vital role in the development of modern structuralism. Indeed, Jakobson is said to have coined the term 'structuralism' for the group. As well as considering the literary text as a structure generated by dynamic relationships between its component parts, the Prague School adopted a functional approach: language is viewed as a 'system of goal-orientated means of expression' and no linguistic element can be understood without reference to the system to which it belongs. Mukarovsky, for instance, sees art or the artistic system as characterized by its orientation towards the sign rather than towards what it signifies.

Anticipating the work of Greimas and the Paris School, the Prague School also extended the field of analysis to include philosophical texts and non-verbal and visual media of expression. It was concerned with the historical dimension of language and with the functions it serves within the speech community. Some theorists of the pre-Second World War period stressed the importance of social context in the perception of art whilst at the same time maintaining the sharp distinction made by Mukarovsky between poetic language and ordinary language.

The post-war years saw the departure or death of many of the original members of the group and the Circle was disbanded in 1950. However, Mukarovsky and others continued to lecture and undertake research. The 1990s witnessed a revival of the Prague School.

See also *foregrounding.*

Presence

Before identifying an object, we become aware of a presence of physical properties such as hot and cold, smooth or rough, dull or dazzling, mobile or immobile, that affect us with varying degrees of intensity. This presence occupies a space relative to our position and it also possesses spatial limits that confer on it its figurative reality. In other words, objects possess two dimensions, the dimension of intensity (*l'intensité*) and the spatio-temporal dimension (*l'étendue*). The dimension of intensity is an internal one relating to different levels of energy. It is concerned with the way objects affect us. The spatio-temporal dimension, on the other hand, is external and would include questions of number and quantity. Presence involves two fundamental acts of perception, known as intentionality (*la visée intentionnelle*) and spatial apprehension (*la saisie*). For instance, the sun may initially appear to us as a blaze of light – recalling Peirce's notion of firstness – before it takes on the specific figurative contours and we recognize it for what it is.

See also *intensity, intentionality* and *spatial apprehension.*

Process

Along the lines of the Saussurean division of language into *langue* and *parole*, Hjelmslev separates the general practice of giving meaning to objects into a process (*parole*) and a system (*langue*). Process here represents the syntagmatic axis of language and system the paradigmatic axis from which signs are chosen.

In semiotic theory, the term process designates narrative doing which is lexicalized either in the form of a simple verb or enlarged in a sentence, a paragraph or a chapter. 'Running', 'singing' or 'cooking' thus describe a process just as does the full statement 'The cook took flour, eggs, milk and butter and produced a delicious cake.'

A semiotic process always comprises three stages: the inchoative, durative and terminative stages. A strike, for example, analysed as a process has an inchoative stage (tools are put down), a duration (the gates remain closed) and a terminative stage (a solution is found and work restarts).

See also *language* and *system.*

Prolepsis

The term prolepsis designates the narrating or evocation of an event before the time in the story in which it actually takes place. It corresponds to the cinematic notion of a 'flash forward'. In the opening chapter of Arundhati Roy's *The God of Small Things* there is a reference to the incident in which the children will witness the police attacking and killing their closest friend, Velutha:

> They didn't know then, that soon they *would* go in. That they would cross the river and be where they weren't supposed to be, with a man they weren't supposed to love. That they would watch with dinner-plated eyes as history revealed itself to them on the back verandah.

The prolepsis here contributes to the production of suspense and also to the powerful sense of tragedy that permeates the book.

Gérard Genette distinguishes between *internal prolepses* which are cited within the time-span of the story and *external prolepses* which are cited outside of the story's temporal framework.

See also *anachrony* and *analepsis.*

Proprioceptivity

The expression proprioceptivity relates to the imaginary body (*corps propre*) of the perceiving subject and its act of allotting meaning by adopting a position. Linked to the concept of perception, the notion is complemented by those of exteroceptivity – that is, sensory perception of the external world – and interoceptivity, in other words, the internal world of impressions, feelings, emotions. Being part of both outer and inner world, the *corps propre* – the imaginary body – of the perceiving subject is able to take a position between the two and, by uniting them, makes them signify. For example, blinded by lightning and assaulted by heavy rain, you feel terrified, recognize your feeling as fear and seek shelter.

See also *exteroceptivity*, *interoceptivity* and *semiotic function*.

Psychosemiotics

Psychosemiotics is the study of the discourse of pathological human behaviour viewed as discourse. It focuses on the intersubjective relationship between patient and therapist. Although introduced by Greimas in his dictionary as a possible future field of research, psychosemiotics did not emerge as an area of study until the 1980s. Sessions with the patient were to provide the material for an in-depth semiotic analysis. Here the application of the narrative models of Greimas proved of particular significance not only in the understanding but also in the successful treatment of pathological states. For instance, the use of ellipsis by the patient – the inability to give expression to a particular experience or stage of the narrative (such as the sanction) – was especially revealing. Studies were also made of the mechanisms of identification using Greimassian models. Key practitioners in this field include Ivan Darrault-Harris and J.-P. Klein. In recent years research has widened to include the analysis of non-verbal behaviour, such as the examination of the concept of space and of the body in autistic children.

Purport

In general terms, purport designates that which is expressed or conveyed, that is, meaning, substance or gist.

The linguist Louis Hjelmslev makes use of the term purport to indicate a semiotically amorphous matter. This he adds to the division of substance and form. Thus when describing the language sign, he not only refers to the level of expression and the level of content subdividing each one into form and substance, he also attaches a content-purport and an expression-purport to designate the matter from which they are taken. On the level of expression, for example, a word can be divided into form (organized linguistic utterance) and substance (sound). Sound itself, however, is derived from some amorphous sound matter which is here the expression-purport and which Hjelmslev takes to be the phonetic potential of human vocal articulation. Equally, on the level of content, the form of the word 'niece', for instance, is grounded in European culture, its substance is sibling relationships in general, and the content-purport is the 'amorphous thought-mass' from which the English language has taken its ideas.

See also *matter*.

Qualification

Qualification designates the process whereby a subject becomes fully competent, i.e. s/he must be in possession of the modalities of being-able-to-do and/or knowing-how-to-do acquired at the stage of the qualifying test. The process of qualification can be contrasted with those of the establishment of the subject (the contract), the realization of the subject (the decisive test or performance) and the sanction of the subject (the glorifying test).

See also *canonical narrative schema, modalities* and *qualifying test.*

Qualifying test

This is the stage in the canonical narrative schema at which competence is acquired. By competence is meant the qualities that make it possible to carry out an action successfully. These qualities are known as the modalities. They are in the first instance:

(a) a wanting-to-do (*vouloir faire*) and/or (b) a having-to-do (*devoir faire*)

In order to perform an action, the subject must initially desire to act, or feel under an obligation to act. These modalities are usually acquired at the opening stage of the contract/manipulation: they are subsequently manifested (and sometimes challenged) in the qualifying test. James Bond, for example, has been ordered to steal some secret plans (the contract). Embarking on this quest and planning the theft are a manifestation of his desire and represent part of the qualifying test.

The desire or obligation to act, however, is not in itself sufficient. The subject also needs to acquire a further qualification at this stage: it must be in possession of at least one of the following modalities:

(a) a being-able-to-do (*pouvoir faire*): If your object is to break into some premises (decisive test), then you must possess the necessary ability, that is, a key or some other means of entry. This will then become your helper. And/or you must possess:

(b) a knowing-how-to-do (*savoir faire*): Any means of illegal entry is of little value to you if you do not know how to use it. If you are sitting a French examination (decisive test) it is assumed that you have acquired the skills associated with learning French (the qualifying test). If your goal is to find the hidden treasure on a desert island, the qualifying test could take the form of a sea voyage. It could also be represented in episodes where maps of the hidden treasure are acquired. If the subject fails in the qualifying test (e.g. the ship sinks), then the quest is terminated. In *Cinderella*, the fairy godmother functions as helper to provide the young girl with the necessary competence (clothes, coach) enabling her to fulfil her dreams and go to the ball (decisive test).

See also *canonical narrative schema.*

Quest

The quest is a figurative term designating the movement (or displacement) of a subject towards the desired object of value. In general terms, this movement is always from a relationship of disjunction with the object of value towards one of conjunction with it. For instance, Jason's quest for the Golden Fleece begins the moment he leaves home and sets sail for Colchis. It is completed when he is successfully conjoined with his object of value, the Golden Fleece.

For a quest to be successful, a series of logical stages must be completed. These are presented and explained in Greimas' canonical narrative schema.

See also *canonical narrative schema.*

Reader

The term reader describes the receiver of a message or discourse. We speak of a reader of a written text, of sign language or any sign system (colour, dance, music, etc.) that requires decoding to be understood.

In semiotics the term enunciatee is used in preference to reader.

See also *enunciator/enunciatee.*

Readerly and writerly texts

Devised by Roland Barthes, the term readerly (*lisible*) describes literary works such as the classic realist novel which rely upon conventions shared by writer and reader. The text moves inevitably towards an end and to the conclusion of an ordered series of events, where all is revealed. Language seems transparent, acting as a window through which we can see the world. The reader's response, therefore, is more or less passive.

Writerly (*scriptible*) texts, on the other hand, violate the reading conventions, stressing the open-ended, pluralist nature of the text which is irreducible to one final meaning. The text is self-conscious, focusing attention on how it is written and on its status as a work of art. Instead of adopting the role of passive consumer, the reader is compelled to become an active producer of meaning; s/he engages in the process of writing.

The terms 'readerly' and 'writerly' are frequently employed to describe the differences between the classic and the avant-garde, more self-conscious novel, between, for example, Jane Austen's *Persuasion* and James Joyce's *Finnegan's Wake*. However, as Barthes himself shows by choosing to discuss a readerly text – *Sarrasine*, a short story by Balzac – as an example of a writerly one, the distinction between the two concepts is not absolute. The terms may also suggest a reading approach and much of recent nineteenth-century novel criticism has brought to the fore the writerly qualities of the work of George Eliot, for example, or of Henry James.

Realism

In general terms realism refers to a mode of writing that gives the impression of recording an actual way of life or of being a mirror on the world. The text emphasizes the everyday lives of ordinary people within a social context, in contrast, for example, to fantasy, to stories of the supernatural and to myth and science fiction. In historical terms, realism is associated with a trend in the nineteenth-century Western novel in England and Europe. Rooted in Cartesian and essentialist world-views, realist writing claims to be objective and true. The writer is considered the embodiment of a self-determining and knowing self, his/her status that of an individual detached from society and the rest of the world.

Twentieth-century philosophy and critical theory saw a fundamental undermining of the basic premises of realism. Both author and text are viewed as constructs of language, embedded within a wider historical and cultural reality. Texts are thus unable to escape ideology or the literary/cultural conventions within which they operate. The line between fiction and the real can also become blurred. In addition, through advances both in philosophy and science and through the discovery of the unconscious, the classic concept of reason is undermined, the stress now being on the ultimate unknowability of self and world. Language is no longer regarded as static and monosemic but as a dynamic process of production of meaning by the subject in her/his interaction with the environment. Meaning thus becomes polysemic or plural, ambiguous and unstable. This fundamental paradigm shift is reflected to varying degrees in twentieth-century critical theories, from structuralism through to postmodernism and postcolonialism. Semiotics itself is based on the central tenet that meaning is a construct of the observer with its origin in sensory perception and in the feelings.

See also *essentialism.*

Reality

In semiotic theory, the term reality always refers to constructed reality. In everyday life, this relates to the signification with which we invest the world that surrounds us. The *reality effect*, then, corresponds to the relationship between that world and the subject (i.e. us) which is activated by some kind of *embrayage* or engagement, that is, by making our presence felt in the constructed environment.

There are two processes that help setting up reality effects in discourse. The first one is iconization. This relates to the procedure whereby an impression of the referential world outside the text is produced and sustained. The topographical description in Zola's *Germinal*, for instance, creates an illusion of reality.

Figurativization of discourse represents another, though related, way of constructing effects of being real. All elements in a text that refer to the external physical world and can be apprehended by the five senses belong to the figurative level. They are essential ingredients in the creation of an illusion of reality. A journalist seeking to present an event as vividly as possible, for example, might evoke sounds, colours or smells in his description to produce an impression of immediacy and realism.

See also *embrayage, figurativization* and *iconicity.*

Realization

The term realization is used in narrative semiotics when describing modes of junction between a subject and an object. Before any kind of conjunction or disjunction takes place, subjects and objects are placed in a position of virtuality. When they are in a position of disjunction, we talk of actualization. Realization refers to the transformation which reverses an earlier disjunction to bring about a conjunction between a subject and an object. Wishing to possess a car, for instance, and having enough money to purchase the desired object but not having done so yet describes a situation of actualization. However, once the purchase has taken place, the object (car) is conjoined with the desiring subject, reversing the earlier situation of disjunction. This transformation is called a realization.

See also *actualization* and *virtualization.*

Receiver

The receiver represents the actant to whom a desire or obligation is given by a sender. This process or transaction must take place before the receiver can embark on a quest, i.e. before the receiver can assume the function of a subject. In the Falklands War, the soldier/receiver became the subject of a quest only when he had decided to accept his mission or contract to go and fight.

See also *sender.*

Reference

In Halliday's terminology, reference describes the process whereby one element introduced at one place in a text can be taken as a reference point for something that follows. Reference words (or referring expressions) are words which possess only partial meaning: to work out their full significance on any particular occasion we have to refer to something else. Examples of reference words are pronouns and deictics. To give an example: 'I lived in Paris for several years. I was very happy there.' The deictic 'there', in this case, has only limited meaning unless one reads it as referring back to a particular location, i.e. 'Paris'.

See also *cohesion* and *referential cohesion.*

Referent

The referent is the entity to which a word refers or which it stands for in the outside world, or in extra-linguistic reality. The referent can be an object, a quality, actions or real events. The referent of the word 'cow' is the animal, cow.

The referent can also involve the imaginary world, as is the case with the word 'chimera'. Or it can stand for a description, or an idea, expressed in a whole complex of words. The referent of A. J. Ayer's *Language, Truth and Logic* is the philosophical theory of verifiability.

Referential cohesion

In Halliday's theory of discourse, referential cohesion is a type of textual cohesion that is produced by the process of reference. It is characterized by the presence of what is known as reference words (or referring expressions). Reference words are words which do not give their full meaning to the objects of the world (the referent): to work out what they mean on any one particular occasion, we need to refer to something else. There are three categories of reference words:

(a) *personal* reference words or pronouns: 'The girls arrived late at school because they had missed the bus.'

(b) *demonstrative* reference words or demonstratives: 'He bought me the book that I really wanted.'

(c) *comparative* reference words or a reference that is based on contrast: 'I like this dress better than that.'

See also *cohesion.*

Referential function

If a communication is orientated towards the context or world (real or imaginary) outside the text, then it is the referential function that dominates. A good example are texts whose principal aim is to convey information, such as car manuals or recipe books. In literature, it is often when an illusion of the real world is being constructed that the referential function can be said to be dominant. 'The house stood in the best part of town. It had two storeys, five bedrooms and a very big garden that was more like a park' is an example of the referential function dominating.

Dominance of the referential function in a communication does not exclude the other speech functions, which will also be present to varying degrees.

See also *communication model.*

Reiteration

Reiteration designates a form of lexical cohesion in which two cohesive items refer to the same entity or event. Reiterative devices include: repetition, the use of synonyms or near-synonyms, of subordinates and generals.

In the following example, the underlined words refer to the same entity: 'She is having terrible trouble with her car. The thing won't start in the morning.'

See also *cohesion.*

Relativism, epistemological

Epistemological relativism is the view that there exists no fixed or universal truth. Instead there are numerous alternative versions of reality, all of them dependent on context and circumstances. Underlying this stance is the semiotic principle that meaning does not exist per se but is a human construct relative to the subject or observer.

See also *essentialism* and *cultural relativism.*

Relativism, linguistic

Linguistic relativism is the view that each language is a unique system of relations and that phonological, grammatical and semantic distinctions are the expression of differences in world-view. This position is closely associated with epistemological relativism and is the fundamental underlying premise of constructionist theories.

See also *constructivism* and *epistemological relativism.*

Renunciation

The term renunciation characterizes the position of a subject of state when it deprives itself of an object of value. The act is one of reflexive disjunction. For example, 'Mary gives away all her money'. The abstract representation of this relationship is as follows:

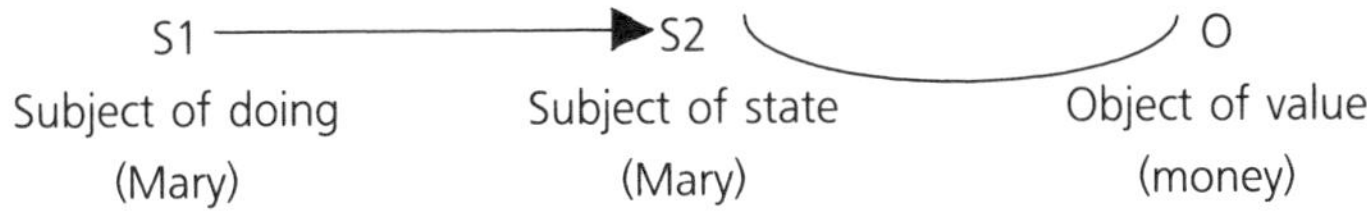

See also *appropriation* and *attribution.*

Representamen

The term representamen was first used by the philosopher C. S. Peirce as the first term in his triadic definition of the sign. Representamen stands for the perceptible object functioning as a sign. Peirce also calls it 'a vehicle conveying into the mind something from without'. A signpost is a representamen, for example, as is a portrait or a written or spoken word.

Other semioticians have likened Peirce's representamen to the signifier (Saussure), to the expression (Hjelmslev) or to the sign vehicle (Morris).

See also *sign.*

Rhetoric

The term rhetoric designates the theory and practice of eloquence, the artful use of language as a means of persuasion. Originally associated with the classics, the art of rhetoric is still alive today. One example is court proceedings, where both prosecution and defence are trying not only with facts but also with words and speeches to convince the jury of the justice of their cause.

In a semiotic perspective, rhetoric is considered a pre-scientific theory of discourse whose organization resembles that of semiotics. Its fundamental three-part structure, however, of *dispositio* (discursive segmentation), *inventio* (discursive themes) and *elocutio* (syntactic and verbal figures and configurations) is applied to persuasive discourse only.

See also *persuasive doing.*

Sanction

The term sanction designates the stage of the quest where the subject's principal action or performance is being evaluated/interpreted by the narrator or an actor in the story. For instance, the performance could be considered a success or a failure, the subject could be rewarded or punished. It is at this stage that the subject undergoes the glorifying test.

See also *canonical narrative schema.*

Secondness

See *firstness, secondness and thirdness.*

Secret

On the semiotic square of veridiction, the term secret subsumes the complementary terms of being and non-seeming which are located on the positive pole or deixis.

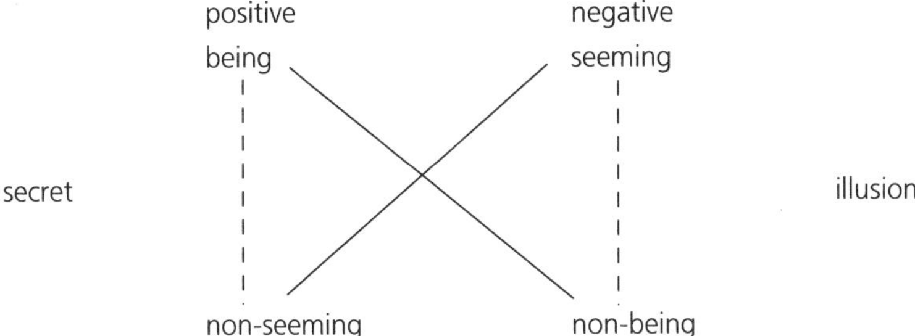

See also *deixis* and *veridiction.*

Seeming

Seeming constitutes one pole of the semantic category 'truth' which combines seeming (*paraître*) and being (*être*). The terms of being and seeming are therefore in a relationship of opposition while also expressing the two faces – or each asserting one aspect – of truth.

See also *veridiction.*

Semanalysis

Derived from the Greek word *sèmeion* meaning 'sign', 'trace' or 'mark', the term semanalysis is the name Julia Kristeva gives to a new critical discourse outlined in her seminal work *La Révolution du langage poétique* [Revolution in Poetic Language], published in 1974. In contrast to Saussure's structural linguistics and to his static formal science of the sign, semanalysis focuses on language as a signifying *process* in which a central role is allotted to the 'speaking historical subject' and the unconscious drives. In other words, Kristeva is not interested in language as a social contract but rather as the expression of affects and feelings such as those of pleasure and desire. Semanalysis is concerned, then, with all those marginal elements that fall outside the signifying norms and that undermine the Symbolic Order, such as 'ellipses, non-recoverable deletions, indefinite embeddings'. In other words, it explores the poetic, subversive dimension of language. The approach focuses above all on the drive-determined primary processes of the unconscious – such as those of displacement and condensation – as they find their way into 'the signifying code and the fragmented body of the speaking subject'. The emphasis is thus on the materiality of language, its sounds, rhythms and graphic disposition rather than on its communicative function.

See also *chora* and *semiotic/symbolic.*

Semantic category

A semantic category is formed by two terms in opposition while possessing at least one common denominator. In other words, they are contraries linked by presupposition in the way that 'in' presupposes 'out' or 'good' presupposes 'evil'. The semantic category itself comprises the two opposing poles in one umbrella term which illustrates their common feature: 'in' and 'out', for example, belong to the semantic category of 'space'; the semantic category of 'temperature' comprises the two poles 'hot' versus 'cold', that of 'verticality' the opposing poles 'up' and 'down'.

Semantic field

A semantic field comprises all the meanings (semes) attached to a particular signifier in the text. The signifier 'fame' may thus include the meanings 'celebrity', 'stardom', 'repute', 'honour', 'glory' or 'eminence', 'illustriousness'; the semantic field of 'joke' might comprise 'witticism' and 'anecdote' or 'prank', 'trick', etc.

The term semantic field is often interchangeable with that of lexical field.

See also *lexical field*.

Semantics

The term semantics designates a branch of linguistics which deals with the meaning given to words or syntagms. In other words, semantics concerns itself with a scientific description of the level of the signified in language rather than the signifier.

In the context of semiotic grammar, semantics represents one of its main components, with syntax making up the other. Semantics, here, relates to the three levels of meaning. Firstly, there is abstract or *conceptual semantics*, which is concerned with meaning at the deep level, the *ab quo* where signification starts. An example are elementary abstract concepts underlying a text such as 'war' and 'peace', or 'virtue' and 'sin', in other words, terms in opposition forming semantic categories. Their organization and dynamics within a text, however, fall under the heading of syntax.

Secondly, there is *narrative semantics*, actualizing values on the story level, selecting them and placing them in conjunction or disjunction with subjects, that is, setting up states of being ready to be transformed. The fairy-tale *Cinderella*, for example, selects happiness and riches as values to aim for, and places these initially in disjunction with the heroine and in conjunction with the nasty sisters. The ensuing narrative programme, on the other hand, the actual process of transformation, in Cinderella's case the achievement of wealth and happiness, is subject to narrative syntax.

Finally, *discursive semantics* puts values into words by giving them figurative and thematic shape. It is here that we encounter reality effects such as references to the senses (vision, touch, etc.) as well as allusion to concrete or abstract worlds. Using *Cinderella* again as an example, we find wealth expressed in lavish clothes and sumptuous balls, and happiness taking the shape of the love of a handsome prince. The syntagmatic organization of these discursive elements belongs to discursive syntax.

See also *grammar* and *syntax*.

Seme

A seme is the smallest common denominator within a unit of meaning. In the sentence 'The summer sun burnt our skin', 'heat' would be the predominant seme; the film title *Trains, Planes and Automobiles* illustrates the seme 'travel'.

See also *lexeme* and *sememe.*

Sememe

A sememe is the totality of semes that are actualized by a term within a given context. In Blake's poetry the following sememe could be attached to the term 'city': industrial, black, crowded, poverty, pain, evil, filth, noise.

See also *lexeme.*

Semic density

The expression semic density relates to the greater or lesser number of semes that enter into the composition of a sememe. The greater the number of semes actualized by a term within a given context, the greater is its semic density. Stanza 2 of Tennyson's 'The Charge of the Light Brigade' offers an example of high semic density: 'Some one had blunder'd: / Their's not to make reply, / Their's not to reason why, / Their's but to do and die.' These four lines evoke the semes of error, unreason, proscription and death in connection with the main seme of obedience.

See also *seme* and *sememe.*

Semiology

In contrast to semiotics, which is concerned with the theory and analysis of the production of meaning, semiology refers to the study of sign systems in operation such as codes, including those of linguistic signs. Explicit meanings resulting from the conjunction of a signifier and a signified are investigated. The traffic code is a case in point: to those familiar with the convention, 'red' means 'stop' and 'green' means 'go'. Nonetheless, there are cases when semiology and semiotics overlap.

The term semiology was coined by Saussure to cover the theory of sign systems, and for a long time was used alongside semiotics with very little difference in meaning. Today the Greimassian School distinguishes clearly between the study of sign *systems* (semiology) and the study of the *process* of the generation of meaning (semiotics).

See also *semiotics.*

Semiotic function/semiosis

The expression semiotic function or semiosis designates the operation whereby a relationship of mutual presupposition between signified and signifier (according to Saussure) or expression and content (in Hjelmslev's terminology) produces intelligible signs: in that sense every language act has a semiotic function.

This definition which is based on logic and fixed meanings has, however, been elaborated and refined by more recent semiotic discoveries, in particular with regard to sensory perception and resulting signifying procedures. It is now understood that semiosis is fundamentally proprioceptive as well as logical, in other words, that the semiotic function rests with the *corps propre* of the perceiving subject, the imaginary body belonging to, and taking a position between, perception of the outer world of sensations and the inner world of feelings and affects. As a result, signification is considered not only stable, conceptual and cognitive but also as a process of an emotional, emotive or passionate nature.

The philosopher Charles Peirce terms semiosis the triadic process by which a sign is defined.

See also *meaning* and *sensory perception.*

Semiotic square

According to Saussure 'il n'y a de sens que dans la différence' and according to Hjelmslev language is fundamentally a system of relationships rather than signs. Thus, in the analysis of meaning, semiotics proceeds from the recognition of differences to the definition of the relationships underpinning them. In the event, the semiotic square is no more than a visual representation of the elementary structure of meaning. It is the logical expression of any semantic category. This elementary structure is defined by three relationships:

1. *Opposition or contrariety.* Meaning is viewed essentially as a product of opposition: there can be no 'up' without 'down', no 'good' without 'evil'. In order to be in opposition or in a relationship of contrariety, two terms (frequently referred to as S1 and S2) must have a feature in common, e.g. 'hot' and 'cold' have the notion of temperature in common: temperature here is known as the complex term. 'High' and 'low' have the notion of verticality in common, their complex term is verticality. S1, therefore, presupposes the existence of S2.

   S1 ———————————— S2

2. *Contradiction.* In order to move from S1 to S2 you must first of all negate S1 (written –S1). If you want to go from 'high' to 'low', for instance, you must move via 'non-high'. 'Non-high' (–S1), then, becomes the contradictory term. If S1 is 'good', then –S1 is 'non-good'. If S2 is 'evil', –S2 is 'non-evil'.

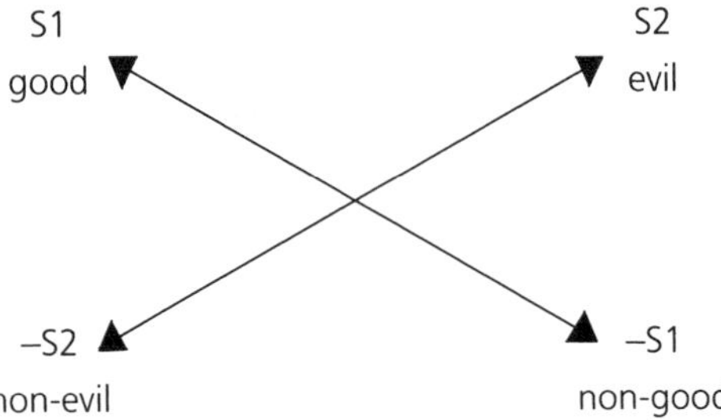

3. The third relationship which seals the square is one of *implication* or *complementarity.* This is built on the connection between a term and the negation of its opposite: 'good' implies 'non-evil', 'high' implies 'non-low'. It is equivalent to the act of assertion, demonstrating the coherence of meaning. For if 'good' does not imply 'non-evil', then our original pair 'good/evil' with their contradictories belong to different semantic categories. S1 and –S2 or S2 and –S1 are therefore defined as complementary terms.

The semiotic square can be used as a tool in the analysis not only of individual semantic concepts but also of longer units of meaning such as paragraphs or whole texts. In this case fundamental semantic oppositions underpinning the unit have to be extracted and placed in the positions of S1 and S2.

Semiotics

Semiotics is the theory of signification, that is, of the generation or production of meaning. In contrast to semiology, which studies sign systems and their organization (e.g. traffic codes, sign language), semiotics concerns itself with *how* meaning is produced. In other words, what interests the semiotician is what makes an utterance meaningful, how it signifies and what precedes it on a deeper level to result in the manifestation of meaning.

Semiotic theory is based on the belief that meaning is not inherent in objects, that they do not signify by themselves, but that meaning is *constructed* by a competent observer – a subject – capable of giving 'form' to objects. To give an example: confronted with an implement from a different culture, say African or Asian, we would probably be incapable of immediately grasping its significance. However, left alone with it, we will give it a meaning that is based on what knowledge we have and what will suit our purposes. The semiotician thus sees the whole of our signifying universe – including statements about it – as the product of a presupposed semiotic competence, the only one able to construct its signification.

The semiotic working method derives from the assumption that the structures underlying – and resulting in – the production of meaning are susceptible to hypothetical representation in the shape of models. The justness of particular models is confirmed or invalidated through testing them against the semiotic object – such as a text – to which they are meant to be applicable. Semiotic analysis by students of literature makes use of such models to decode effects of meaning perceptible on the surface of a text.

See also *semiology*.

Semiotic/symbolic

In *La Révolution du langage poétique* [Revolution in Poetic Language] Julia Kristeva establishes a distinction between the 'symbolic' (*le symbolique*) and the 'semiotic' (*le sémiotique*). The symbolic is the sphere of representation, of images and all forms of articulated language. It is the level of the systematic rules governing denotative language and represents the 'social' domain of signification. The semiotic, on the other hand, designates an archaic layer of meaning that is neither representational nor based on relations between signs. It is associated with the primary processes, with unconscious drives and pulsions and with the workings of the body, with rhythms and sound. Together the symbolic and the semiotic constitute the signifying process. The semiotic plays a subversive role vis-à-vis the symbolic and this subversion is most evident in poetry and in avant-garde literary writing. Here the semiotic may make itself felt in silences and absences, disruptions, syntactical disorder and contradictions.

Kristeva has always made a distinction between her term semiotic (*le sémiotique*) and the conventional use of the term (*la sémiotique*). However, her concern with the emerging subject may suggest a common ground with the thought of the semiotician Jean-Claude Coquet, for example, and recent years have seen the growth of a new area known as psychosemiotics. Moreover, her overall focus on the body and on the signifying process rather than on the sign would suggest affinities with what is known as 'la nouvelle sémiotique' [new semiotics], that is, the theories of the contemporary Paris School that began to emerge in the last decade of the twentieth century.

See also *chora* and *psychosemiotics.*

Semiotic triangle/Peirce's triad

The expression semiotic triangle refers to the triadic model illustrating the definition of the sign. The triangle is based on the notion of mediation: one term is related to another via a third correlate. With regard to the definition of a sign, the correlates or corner points of the triangle are (1) the sign vehicle (Peirce's representamen), (2) the sense (Peirce's interpretant) and (3) the referent (Peirce's object).

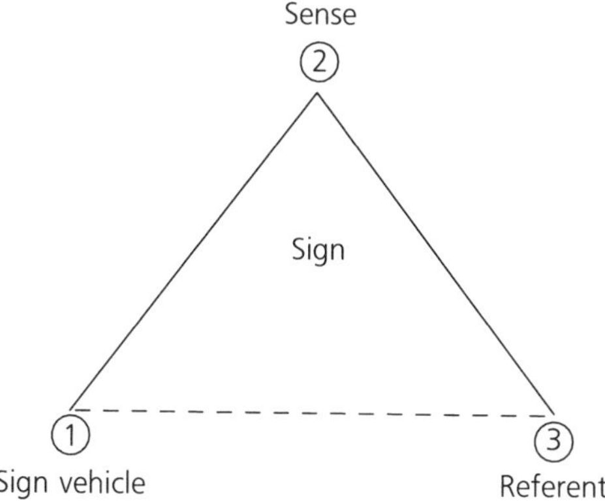

In most sign definitions using the triad model, sense is the mediator of the referent in the standard order of the triad: sign vehicle–sense–referent. Peirce uses his correlates in the same order: representamen–interpretant–object. However in his categorical system, the object relates to secondness and the interpretant to thirdness.

The semiotic triangle was used by many philosophers for the definition of signs, among others by Plato, Aristotle, the Stoics, Bacon, Leibniz, Husserl and Morris.

See also *firstness, secondness and thirdness* and *sign.*

Semi-symbolic

The term semi-symbolic designates a particular relationship between expression and content, or signifier and signified. Nodding one's head to signify 'yes', would be an example, or shaking it to mean 'no'.

The term semi-symbolic is applied in particular to the visual arts, where movement, gesture, colour, etc., acquire specific values. In a particular picture, for instance, light colours and simplicity of outline may be associated with happiness, whereas their opposite – dark colours and blurred lines – may be associated with unhappiness.

The concept semi-symbolic differs from symbolic in that the relationship between signifier and signified relates to categories rather than units. Nodding yes or no, for example, uses the vertical axis to affirm and the horizontal to deny, thus linking the category of spatial axes to that of assertion versus negation. Or a semi-symbolic representation of the category good versus evil may be found in nature where a mountain is associated with God and an abyss with the devil. In the case of a symbol, on the other hand, the relationship between expression and content is one of two individual units: a set of scales symbolizes justice; a rose symbolizes love.

See also *semantic category* and *symbol.*

Sender

The term sender normally belongs to the narrative level of an utterance, where it represents the actantial instance (person or idea) that motivates an action or causes something to happen. The sender not only institutes the values to aim for but also transmits the desire or obligation to pursue them to a subject. Any quest begins with an initial contract between a sender and a receiver/subject accepting the mandate, and ends with a sender's (not necessarily the same as the mandating sender) sanction, that is, an evaluation of the subject's performance.

In their quest to defeat the Argentinians, the soldiers who took part in the Falklands War had two senders: (a) an external sender in the figures of Mrs Thatcher and the rest of the British Government, and (b) an internal sender in the belief in patriotism and in the traditional ideology of warfare.

See also *receiver.*

Sender-adjudicator

The sender normally occupies the positions of mandatory sender and of sender-adjudicator.

At the beginning of a narrative programme, the sender establishes a contract with the future subject and instigates the system of values in accordance with which the subject must act. The sender here is sometimes referred to as the mandatory sender to distinguish it from the later role of sender-adjudicator. The latter is the sender who intervenes at the stage of sanction or the glorifying test. At this point the performance of the subject is being judged with regard to the original mandate. In a fairy-tale, the king (as mandatory sender) asks the knight to slay the dragon. At the end of the story he judges (as sender-adjudicator) the deed to have been accomplished to his satisfaction by giving him his daughter in marriage.

The roles of mandatory sender and of sender-adjudicator, however, are not always held by the same actor. In a military conflict, the defeated army is usually judged not by their mandating government (mandatory sender) but by their victorious enemy (sender-adjudicator). Students in higher education are often awarded degrees not by their teachers (mandatory sender) but by State examiners (sender-adjudicator).

Sensorial modes

According to semiotic theory, the sensorial modes define, by way of a polysensory syntax and the constitution of a semiotic field, a canonical schema of the senses as a logical presentation of sensation. To establish a polysensorial syntax, however, each sense needs to be evaluated separately starting with touch as the fundamental mode of sensory contact.

- **Touch** leads to the elementary distinction between the self (identity) and the other (otherness). There is that which I feel myself and that which is felt to be different. 'I' feel 'you' and between us there is only an envelope, the envelope of 'me-skin' which is affected by the contact. This, then, is the principle of fundamental contact defining a basic transitive field: 'pure presence' and the distinction between what is my own and what is not mine (*propre/non-propre*). This principle, however, does not belong to any sensorial substance in particular.
- **Sensory-motivity** encompasses the internal and external sensations of movement: sensations of walking and jumping, for example, and the innermost sensations of the movement of the flesh, that is, the beating of the heart or taking in breath and expelling it. In the case of the innermost motions, the sensorial centre producing the sensation applies it to itself: the flesh thus syncretizes the actants of source, target and control of sensory perception. The reflexive nature of the sensations, however, introduces a further distinction. By producing an affect on itself, the sensory motory instance splits into an 'ego' (*moi*) and a 'self' (*soi*); it moves itself. Thus sensory-motivity defines a particular semiotic field, a reflexive field, which, as it were, 'invents' the category ego/self

(*moi/soi*) just as the transitive field (the field of touch) 'invented' the category myself/not myself (*propre/non-propre*).

- **Smell** offers a new sensorial property: quantification. If the transitive field required one envelope (the frontier between myself and not-myself), smell multiplies the envelopes: each layer of smell, more or less close or distant, more or less distinct, forms an envelope. In the case of perfume, for example, we have the perfumed body, scented accessories or scented letters. All of them amount to successive olfactory layers; yet all these scents refer back to the source-body. The fact, moreover, that *something smells* and *I myself smell something*, or even that *I smell something that smells*, indicates a reciprocal relation implying an interactive mode between myself and not-myself. The boundaries in the exchange are on the one hand stench, foul smell (the envelope furthest from the body (*corps propre*)), and on the other *penetrating* smell which permeates the envelope of the *corps propre*. Just like fundamental contact, therefore, smell operates by differentiating between myself and not-myself because it distinguishes between the smelling oneself and the smell of the other. In this case, however, the distinction supposes a prior conversion of odours emanating from the other into odours enveloping (or penetrating) the self. Finally, with regard to the constitution of a semiotic field, the plural envelopes of smell occupy an intermediary place between touch and the appearing and disappearing horizons of hearing and sight.

- **Taste** appears first as a mode of contact, a tactile sensation: scalding, stinging, caressing or flowing, hard or soft. This first contact therefore concerns the envelope of the body – even if its location is inside the mouth. Moreover, tasting takes place in stages, that is, it is located in time and space; each stage is distinguished by a predicate such as 'burning' which can be attributed to an identifiable actor (*chilli* burns the palate, for example); careful analysis also recognizes nuances in taste, such as those of different chillis. Tasting thus combines olfactory, tactile and sensory-motory properties.

  On the figurative level, tasting creates an internal theatre where the different parts of the mouth (palate, tip of the tongue, cheeks, throat, etc.), each receiving particular tactile sensations, ensure topological, temporal, actorial and predicative differentiation. The sensorial field of taste, therefore, appears (1) as the interior field of a figurative stage and

(2) as a diagram of correlations between predicates, spaces, moments and actors. It is an *interior* field (because the exploration of the 'not-myself' takes place inside the body); it is *sequentialized* (because after being divided, the target and source parts are put in order); and it is *iconized* (because the exploration consists in distributing predicative stages amid iconic figures such as moments, places and actors). The same kind of semiotic field may be applicable to other interior explorations, such as the inhalation of perfume or to recollection and recall as in Proust's *In Search of Lost Time*.

– **Hearing,** or more precisely the auditory field, is a *sphere*: it generalizes the principle of the exteroceptive envelope but dissociates it from the body (*corps propre*) so that – no longer a corporeal envelope at a variable distance – it becomes an autonomous sphere. However, this sphere retains some of the qualities of the olfactory envelope: it is brought about by another body; it enfolds the body; and, like odour, it also possesses two boundaries – *silence* at the one end, *pain* at the other because sound not only affects the flesh, it may even hurt it. Yet in opposition to sensory-motivity which also moves the flesh, though on its own accord, with hearing the flesh is 'moved' from the outside, a distinction that leads us to oppose *source-flesh* (sensory-motivity) and *target-flesh* (hearing).

At the centre of the auditory sphere, then, is the flesh; the sphere is bordered by appearance and disappearance: here presence (sound), there absence (silence). Moreover, since the horizon has become a boundary, the depth that separates it from the centre can be measured from the centre itself: it becomes a *cognitive* depth in the sense that knowledge of the source and appreciation of the intensity of the sound it emits enable the perceiving subject to evaluate the distance separating it from that source. However, just as with smell, the relationship between the actants is reciprocal: sound has a source, a sound-body, around which a sonorous sphere develops; sound also has a target, the flesh of the perceiving body placed at the centre of the auditory sphere. Yet this perceiving body may become the source of an apprehension whose target is the sound-emitting body: the first evaluates the distance and the position of the second. When hearing a scream, for example, we react by evaluating where it comes from and how close it is. Reciprocity is thus complemented by revertibility and simultaneity of the operations. The auditory sphere thus retains some of the sensorial qualities we already know – totalization and reciprocity – but adds others, revertibility and simultaneity.

– **Sight** functions in accordance with the mode of touch and the tactile envelope (the *haptic* mode), the mode of the olfactory envelope (in the case of visual depth being purely affective and centripetal) or in accordance with the principle of the auditory sphere (when the visual field is bordered solely by a horizon of appearances and disappearances). It functions in a transitive field, a reciprocal or reflexive or internalized field (in the case of the so called 'mental' image), as well as in a squentialized, iconized, reversible and/or simultaneous field. All in all, the fact that for the human race sight has become the dominant sensorial mode is probably due to the way it progressively uses and combines the total of all sensorial properties available. In addition, however, it offers two more qualities which seem to be predominantly part of sight: the *eidetic conversion* and the *actantial conversion of the control-actant*.

When we see *something* or *somebody* it means that we – the perceiving subject – are no longer concerned solely with the envelope of our own body but also with envelopes of other actors (the things, bodies we are perceiving) who take part in the operation of seeing. In other words, the figurative scene is projected away (*débrayage*) from the perceiving source. How we see what we see, moreover, depends on the quality of light by which we see. Light is the actant-source of seeing and in order to identify the form of other bodies, sight appraises the contact zone between the light and the material objects in it – the control-actants of light. That contact zone can also be a zone of conflict: light goes through an object or it does not; it is immediately or totally reflected, or partly and with delay. The different kinds of conflict between the light and the matter we perceive allow us to specify the eidetic (clearly defined, modelled, textured) properties of what we see. The zone of contact therefore becomes a zone of eidetic conversion.

Moreover, the actantial structure of sight appears to be more complex and differentiated than that of the other senses. In fact, the visual field superimposes several kinds of conditions for seeing such as brilliance, glare, moderate lighting, colour and the effects of the eidetic conversion.

> For example, in a dimly lit room we may have difficulty seeing; a flash of lightning, on the other hand, affords only momentary vision; bright sunshine may force us to put on sunglasses to see clearly, etc. To each of these conditions corresponds a particular actantial setup. The diversification and specialization of these actantial structures are based on the principle of the conversion of the control-actant: just as its surface properties can be converted into the form of an envelope (eidetic conversion), so its actantial role can at any moment be replaced by another (actantial conversion). For example, control-actants can become targets (obstacles); obstacles become secondary sources (in the case of a reflecting mirror, for example); light itself becomes a control-actant revealing or dissimulating the structure of objects; targets become control-actants discriminating between colours, etc. Sight still places the body at the centre but mainly because it retains some of the properties of touch, smell, taste or hearing; its distinctive qualities – the eidetic and generalized actantial conversions – work towards the *disengagement* (*débrayage*) of *the figurative dimension*. Although predominantly belonging to sight, these two distinctive qualities are not exclusive to seeing. Sight generalizes the eidetic conversion, yet it only needs a reduction in the intensity of light (at night, for example) for touch to take over; it generalizes the actantial conversion of the control-actant, yet the latter is also liable to change its actantial status in the context of any other actantial regime.

All in all, it seems that none of the properties of the polysensorial semiotic field belong to any sensorial mode in particular. All properties would seem to belong to the senses only tendentiously and by force of use. Also, as a rule the senses are not solicited singly but in concert: seeing, for example, involves hearing; tasting is coupled with smelling. In fact, in our communication with the world, sensorial modes complement or, if need be, replace each other.

See also *débrayage*, *envelope*, *sensory-motivity* and *sensory perception*.

Sensory-motivity

The expression sensory-motivity relates to the sensory-motory sensations, those of flesh in movement (and not of the body itself) which semiotic theory recognizes as one of the sensorial modes. In fact, semiotics holds that the sensory-motory can be divided into external sensations of movement (walking, displacement, moving of the body) and internal sensations of movement (beating of the heart, pulsation, contraction and dilatation). These latter are the innermost motions and it is on their sensation that our perception of being alive is based.

See also *sensorial modes* and *sensory perception*.

Sensory perception

Using the key concepts of the sensible (*le sensible*) and meaning (*l'intelligible*), semiotic theory has developed models to describe the actual process whereby meaning emerges from sensation. Placing the perceiving subject at the centre – the observer reacting to external stimuli – two acts of perception are discovered: there is first of all the intentional drive or intentionality (*la visée intentionnelle*) describing the moment when a subject becomes aware of a presence in terms of intensity. This occurs, for example, when we become aware of a strong smell without knowing what it is. The second act of perception relates to the spatial apprehension (*la saisie*) of the sensation: it describes the moment when the subject becomes aware of spatial-physical contours (*l'étendue*) and the impression acquires figurative shape – a distant repetitive sound, for instance, turns out to be the ringing of a mobile phone.

The fundamental acts of perception, moreover, possess two basic properties allotting actantial positions: a direction (source/target) and a control of this direction. On a narrative level, a bolt of lightning could be the actant-source of light or a clap of thunder the actant-source of sound. At the same time, the eyes or ears of everyone around would be the actant-target of the sound or the light. Equally, the perfume I wear could make me the actant-source of a delicious scent while my surroundings might be the intended actant-target. The direction – source, target – could be controlled by meeting with an obstacle: wearing earplugs (control-actant), for instance, might stop us from hearing the thunder clearly; my perfume might clash with that worn by others (control-actant), or it might have lost its fragrance (time being the control-actant) at the end of a long day.

Finally, meaning (*l'intelligible*) emerging from sensory perception is based on differences. We must therefore be able to perceive variations or differences. On the figurative level this applies to variations in *intensité* (soft light/dazzling light) and/or to *étendue* (near/far). On the axiological level it refers to a correlation of different value systems (light/knowledge).

See also *elementary structure of tension* and *sensorial modes.*

Shifter

Introduced by Jakobson, the term shifter is equivalent in meaning to the semiotic terms engager or disengager. A *disengager* is a word that shifts the discourse away from the point of enunciation by setting up an action, a time and a place different from those of the person who is speaking. For instance, 'at that time' (as opposed to the moment of speaking) 'he' (as opposed to the speaker) 'was living in Paris' (as opposed to the place of enunciation).

An *engager*, on the other hand, is a term that moves the discourse towards the point of enunciation, that is, it sets up an action, a time and a place that coincide with those of the person speaking such as 'I', 'here' and 'now'. For instance, 'I have been living here for three years'.

See also *embrayage* and *débrayage.*

Sign

The term sign is derived from the Greek *sèmeion* denoting a gesture, a signal or something standing deliberately for something else. In the context of semiotics, there are different theories and definitions as to the nature of the sign.

According to the linguist Saussure, a sign – such as a word – is made up of two components: a *signifiant* (signifier) and a *signifié* (signified). The first component, the signifier, the sound and shape of a word, for example, refers principally to the concrete sensorial world. The signified, on the other hand, relates to the idea or concept expressed by the sign. The relationship between the two sides of the sign is one of presupposition; in other words, their indissoluble unity is a precondition for the sign itself. This definition of the sign applies to the linguistic sign but it can be extended to other signs as well. The cross in religious rituals, the crying of a child, or the embrace of a couple are all signs composed of a signifier and a signified.

The Danish linguist Louis Hjelmslev developed an even more complex model of the linguistic sign. He distinguishes between a level of content and a level of expression, the two levels corresponding to Saussure's signifier (expression) and signified (content). Both levels, however, he subdivides further into substance and form. Thus expression has a substance and a form, the substance being colour or shape, for example, while the form may be painting or photography, etc. The same applies to the level of content which also possesses substance (thought input, for example) and a form (a particular idea or concept).

C. S. Peirce, the American philosopher, elaborated yet another definition of the sign. According to him, a sign, or representamen, is something which stands to somebody for something in some respect or capacity. This definition contains three basic elements: 1) the representamen or perceptible object functioning as a sign corresponding to Saussure's signifier; 2) that what it stands for, that is its referent; 3) it addresses somebody, that is, it creates in the mind of somebody an equivalent sign which Peirce calls interpretant. The addition 'in some respect or capacity' – which Peirce understood to mean that the sign stands for an object not in all respects but in reference to some sort of idea – is taken by some semioticians to imply a fourth element. Jacques Fontanille, for example, terms this referential placing the *fondement* of the representamen.

See also *expression and content, fondement, interpretant, representamen, signification* and *signifier and signified.*

Signification

According to Saussure, the term signification denotes the relationship between a signifier and a signified, thus describing the relational aspect of meaning. Peirce also used the term signification to define the meaning of a sign. Charles Morris differentiates between signification and significance as representing two aspects of meaning.

In semiotic theory, signification has both a dynamic and a static aspect. It implies the process of generating meaning as well as the meaning that has been produced. Thus the term applies not only to the signifying process involved in telling a fairy-tale, for example, but also to the signified that is presented by the story.

See also *sign* and *meaning.*

Signifier and signified

According to Saussure, words are not symbols corresponding to referents but signs made up of two components: a mark or signifier and a concept or signified. Things themselves, therefore, play no part in the language system. The significance of words is based solely on a system of relationships.

Signifier and signified represent the two fundamental levels of language. The term signifier refers principally to the concrete world of sound and vision. The term signified, on the other hand, relates to the concept or idea expressed by the sound or icon. The relationship of the signifier to the signified has been described by Saussure as that between the front and back of a piece of paper. In other words, the two levels of language are in a relationship of reciprocal presupposition; form and content cannot be disassociated. The word (linguistic sign) 'tree', to give an example, is made up of a sound or written mark (signifier) and also of the idea or concept of a tree (signified).

See also *expression and content.*

Signifying practices

Signifying practices are systems of meaning (or sign systems), each one of which has its own set of conventions and rules of construction and interpretation. They include the production and reading of texts, as well as cultural activities such as cinema-going, dress, fashion or architecture/design.

See *sociosemiotics* and *semiotics of politics.*

Simulacrum

The term simulacrum designates a semblance, an image of something which it is not. According to semiotic theory, the production of models or simulacra is the means by which we make sense of the world.

Semiotics itself uses the concept simulacrum when analysing reality effects and attempting to visualize, or visually represent, structures of meaning, or systems of interpretation. An example would be the canonical narrative schema describing human interaction.

Singulative

Coined by Gérard Genette, the term singulative (*le récit singulatif*) describes a particular temporal organization of events in a story: what happens *once* is also narrated *once*. It is the most common type of narrative frequency, tending to emphasize narrative progression and the uniqueness of the situation. An example would be 'He came into the room, pulled out his gun and shot the man dead.'

See also *iterative* and *narrative frequency*.

Social determinism

Social determinism is the view that accords central importance to social and political factors in the construction of meaning. It is concerned with issues such as the condition of production, authorial intention and receiver interpretation rather than with the structure of a text. Determinists dispute the position of the New Critics and of the early Barthes, that is, the assumption that a text enjoys complete autonomy occupying a separate domain from the everyday social world.

Contemporary semioticians merge the two positions. Whilst possessing its own internal coherence, the text is also seen to be embedded in a wider sociopolitical discourse. Factors such as the choice of enunciative strategies, pragmatic function and the relationship of the text to dominant ideologies are thus also taken into account.

Sociolect

The term sociolect designates a kind of sub-language that characterizes a particular group or class of society and that contrasts one group with another. Cockney English is a sociolect, as is argot in French.

Sociolect can be compared with the term idiolect. The study of sociolects stems from the discipline of sociosemiotics.

See also *idiolect*.

Sociosemiotics

Sociosemiotics is the study of the different signifying systems within society. A very early example would be Roland Barthes' *Mythologies* (1957) in which he examines the cookery pages of *Elle* magazine, the activity of striptease and electoral photography, among other subjects. The discipline was further developed by the Paris School in the 1970s with seminal studies of law and of political, philosophical and sociological discourse. Pioneers in this area were A. J. Greimas and Eric Landowski. Since then the field has widened to embrace, for instance, the discourse of media and of advertising, the notions of public opinion and of everydayness as well as the conduct of electoral campaigns. Recent research includes an examination of the role of the senses in human interaction. A key concern of sociosemioticians is the relationship of signifying practices to dominant power groups or ideologies.

Somatic doing

Used to describe a figurative actor (character), the term somatic refers to two types of physical activity:

(a) To bodily movements such as running or stealing, accomplished by an actor and directed towards a goal. These movements constitute events in the narrative.

(b) To physical gestures or attitudes or miming, that is, bodily activities that signify in themselves (convey a message), that are communicative. For instance, shaking your head to signify 'no'. A distinction can therefore be made between verbal communication and somatic communication.

Source

The source and the target belong to the basic properties of the activity of perception. On the narrative level, the body could be the source of a smell or a lamp the source of light. The body and the lamp are described as an actant-source. The eyes could be the target of light (the actant-target) emanating from its source, the sun. A smell from a decomposing snake (actant-source) can be so strong that it overpowers everyone in the vicinity (actant-target).

See also *control-actant, sensory perception* and *target.*

Spatial apprehension

Spatial apprehension (*la saisie*) describes the act of perception in which the self becomes aware of an object in terms of physical shape or size. Together with intentionality, it describes the means whereby meaning (*l'intelligible*) emerges from sensory perception (*le sensible*). For instance, we first become aware of a putrid smell (intentionality on the axis of intensity) and then we recognize it as rotting meat (spatial apprehension on the axis of expanse).

See also *intentionality* and *sensory perception.*

Spatial programming

Spatial programming refers to the relationship established in a narrative between particular places and stages in the quest of an actor. For Robinson Crusoe in Daniel Defoe's novel of that title, the decisive test is associated with the island. Parallels may thus be established between places and types of action: Robinson's home may be connected with departure and return, and the island with struggle and confrontation.

See also *canonical narrative schema.*

Spatialization

The term spatialization designates the process whereby places and locations are established in a discourse. Like actorialization and temporalization it is a necessary ingredient for a referential illusion or reality effect to work. In line with the temporal organization of discourse, spatial structuring serves the installation of narrative programmes and their sequence. Stages of Little Red Riding Hood's mission are thus linked to (1) her mother's house; (2) the wood; (3) her grandmother's house.

See also *actorialization* and *temporalization.*

Strategy

The term strategy defines any long-term plan designed to achieve a specific goal. A general follows a strategy when trying to defeat the enemy. The government develops a strategy to cope with economic difficulties.

According to semiotic theory, the notion of strategy presupposes a situation of confrontation. It is thus defined in terms of interaction between adversaries both attempting to manipulate the enemy in order to thwart his/her aims and achieve one's own goal. In this sense, *strategy* is contrasted with *tactics*, which relates to the technique of manoeuvring. To give an example: in a chess game, the act of devising a plan which plays on the opponent's presumed responses amounts to strategy. The actual playing, or moving the pieces and using the rules to one's advantage, involves tactics.

See also *tactics.*

Structuralism (French)

The term structuralism designates a range of research activities inspired by linguists and carried out in France in the 1960s in a variety of branches of knowledge. As an intellectual movement it takes as its premise that the sign is made up of two parts (signified and signifier) and that there can be no meaning without difference (Saussure). In other words, elements do not signify in isolation: they only acquire meaning by virtue of their contrast with other elements within a structure. The structuralist method, therefore, is characterized by a search for immanent (underlying) structures and/or the construction of models. It is from the structuralist method that semiotics has developed.

Because of its initial success, structuralist theory very quickly became a kind of fashionable philosophy. As a result, it has frequently been accused of being totalitarian, static or reductionist. In the late 1960s, a counter-movement originated, poststructuralism, which, based on the discovery of the essentially unstable nature of signification, altered and refined the original theory.

See also *semiotics* and *signifier and signified.*

Structure

The Swiss psychologist Jean Piaget defines structure as an arrangement of entities that embodies the following fundamental ideas: (1) *wholeness*, which means it is internally coherent; (2) *transformation*, which means that it is not a static form but one capable of transformational procedures, or that it is not only structured but also structuring; (3) *self-regulation*, which means that in order to validate its laws, it does not have to appeal beyond itself.

This definition of structure has been used extensively by the structuralist movement.

Subject

In semiotic metalanguage, the subject (without any qualifying adjective) normally denotes a narrative function (actant) in the actantial structure of an utterance. In this context, the subject is defined on the one hand by and opposite the object of value that is being pursued; on the other, it exists in relation to the sender (source of values and mandator of the quest).

In a narrative, the position of an actant/subject may be held by any actor (character) who performs an action. The abbreviation, a capital S, is frequently used to designate this role. In *Robinson Crusoe*, Robinson Crusoe is the principal subject. In an article about the economic situation of the country, the government, pursuing the goal of beating the recession, is the main subject.

The concepts of discursive and epistemological subjects refer to different levels of an utterance: the discursive level and the deep level respectively.

See also *discursive subject, epistemological subject* and *narrative subject.*

Subject of doing

The expression subject of doing designates a subject who, in its relationship with an object, brings about a transformation. In the sentence 'Father bought a new car', 'Father' is the subject of doing because he has transformed his position of being without a new car into one of being in possession of a new car.

The subject of doing is also frequently referred to as 'agent' or 'operating agent'. It contrasts with the 'subject of state' or 'patient'.

See also *agent, patient* and *subject of state.*

Subject of state

The expression subject of state designates a subject whose relationship with an object remains unchanged. This kind of relationship is frequently shown in verbs of being or possessing. In the sentence 'My father owns several properties', 'My father' is the subject of state, illustrated by his possessions. Equally, in the sentence, 'Nordic women are blue-eyed and have blond hair', 'Nordic women' is the subject of state.

The term subject of state is also referred to as 'patient' in a narrative programme. It contrasts with the 'subject of doing' (or operating agent) whose performance causes a transformation of state.

See also *agent, patient* and *subject of doing.*

Substance

In the vocabulary of Hjelmslev, the term substance denotes the semantic charge assumed by a semiotic form in order to produce meaning. Meaning, moreover, signifies only in the joint manifestation of two distinct forms which correspond to the two planes (or levels) of language: the level of content, composed of a *form* and a *substance*, and the level of expression, also made up of a *form* and a *substance.*

In speech, for example, the sound we make represents the substance while the separate words we pronounce are based on the linguistic system giving form to the sound. Together, substance (sound) and form (linguistic system) amount to our speech on the level of its expression. Equally, the content of our speech is composed of general ideas or semantic raw material – its substance – which is organized in accordance with rules of grammar, that is, its form.

See also *form* and *expression and content.*

Syllepsis

The term syllepsis describes a figure of speech whereby the words of a sentence are applied in accordance with their meaning rather than following strict grammatical rules, for example 'The town, and the president, bewails the catastrophe' or 'The horses and riders shied away from the obstacle'.

Symbol

In traditional literary usage, a symbol relates a word or idea to a concrete object, scene or action with which – though essentially different – it entertains some kind of semantic connection. Thus, in a particular culture, a rose may be a symbol of love, a bird of freedom, a forest of madness, or water of life. A symbol, therefore, is based on a relationship between two individual units – one figurative, one thematic – whereas a semi-symbol is the product of the relationship between two categories.

In Peirce's semiotics, the term symbol denotes a sign (signifier) whose relationship to its object (signified) is entirely arbitrary or based on convention. An example would be the word 'car' where there is no causal physical link or resemblance between the sign (the word car) and its object. In his system of classification, Peirce distinguishes signs used as symbols from those used as icons or as indices (index).

See also *icon, index* and *semi-symbolic.*

Synaesthesia

In general terms, synaesthesia denotes a confusion of sensory responses: in a narrow sense it can mean that a sensation is produced by one sense in reply to another sense being stimulated. For example, you see music in colours, or you can taste words. But synaesthesia also refers to supplementary sensory perception, the merging of sensations and their proliferation. Baudelaire's poetry is full of synaesthetic references, for example, when he speaks of 'perfumes, colours and sounds answer[ing] each other' or alludes to 'perfumes fresh like the flesh of children, soft as oboes, green as meadows' . . . etc.

Synchrony

The term synchrony denotes simultaneity of action or events. We talk of synchronous occurrences when events coincide in point of time. For instance, the event of President Kennedy being shot took place at the same time as that of onlookers observing the assassination. The two events therefore occurred in synchrony. Equally, a French film with English subtitles requires synchronization of the two languages in order to be fully understood by a monolingual English audience.

Synchrony is opposed to *diachrony* which refers to events arranged in temporal sequence. Saussure used the couple synchrony/diachrony for the description of language in a contemporary and a historical perspective. In particular, he applied synchrony as a working concept with regard to a coherent language system (*langue*). Since any notion of time, however, presents difficulties when applied to abstract systems, present-day linguistics operates within an atemporal or *achronic* framework.

See also *achrony, diachrony* and *language.*

Synecdoche

A synecdoche is a figure of speech in which a part is substituted for a whole and a genus for a species. The process could also work in reverse: the whole could be substituted for the part, etc. A synecdoche thus possesses many of the functions associated with metonymy. Examples:

- Part for whole
  'She bought six head of cattle.'
- Whole for part
  'She was in trouble with the law.'
- Species for genus (the use of a member of the class for the class)
  'I must buy a new Hoover.'
- Genus for species (the use of class to refer to member of the class)
  'Turn that machine off.' (to refer to the computer or vacuum cleaner, etc.)

Synonym

A synonym is a word that has the same meaning as, or is very close in meaning to, another word. Examples: 'She tried to run up the slope but the incline was very steep'; 'He rushed to the bus stop although there was no need to hurry'. In both sentences the underlined words are synonyms.

Synonyms are frequently used to strengthen lexical cohesion within a text.

See also *antonym, coherence* and *cohesion.*

Syntagm

The term syntagm designates two or more lexical units linked consecutively to produce meaning. The combination of an adjective and a noun – such as 'human life' or 'beautiful day' – offers an example of a syntagm. The same applies to the joining of two nouns – as in 'desert wind' – or the sequence of words forming a whole sentence: 'we shall go out'.

See also *paradigm.*

Syntax

The term syntax designates the grammatical arrangement of words and syntagms in a clause or sentence. Traditionally, the term refers to one of the two constituent parts of grammar, the other being morphology, that is, the study of the forms of words. The description of the relationship between words or groups of words, on the other hand, and the establishment of rules governing their organization in a sentence, belong to syntax. Grammatical concepts like 'subject', 'object', 'predicate' or 'attribute' are thus part of the descriptive vocabulary of syntax, just as is the classification of subordinate clauses.

Semiotic theory has adopted the term syntax to define one of the two main components of semiotic grammar, with semantics forming the other. Syntax, here, is relevant to the three levels of meaning. Firstly, there is *elementary syntax*, which together with abstract or conceptual semantics accounts for the production, functioning and understanding of meaning at its deepest level. Camus' novel *L'Etranger*, for instance, deals on the deep level with the themes of 'life' and 'death'. Their relationship and dynamics within the text, however, are illustrated by deep-level syntax, which can be presented visually on a semiotic square.

Secondly, there is the level of story grammar or surface *narrative syntax*, which, according to semiotic theory, underpins all discourse, be it literary, scientific, sociological, artistic, etc. Semiotics, here, makes use of two fundamental narrative models, the actantial narrative schema and the canonical narrative schema, to describe basic structures articulating the quest. In the fairy-tale *Jack and the Beanstalk*, the narrative syntax exhibits positions and stages of action: the actant/subject (Jack), the actant/object of the quest (money and marriage), the actant/opponent (the mayor), etc., or different stages of the quest, for example, that of competence (getting and sowing the bean), or that of performance (climbing the beanstalk and defeating the giant), etc.

Thirdly, there is *discursive syntax*. Here we are concerned with the syntactical arrangement of discursive elements on the textual surface. Narrative structures are put into words, given figurative and linguistic shape and placed in sequence. The actant/subject of *Jack and the Beanstalk* becomes 'Jack' and adopts the thematic roles of 'son' and 'lover'. His actions are arranged in chronological order and placed in a particular space, for instance, at the bottom of the beanstalk or at its top.

See also *actantial narrative schema, canonical narrative schema, discursivization, semantics* and *semiotic square.*

System

Along the lines of the Saussurean division of language into *langue* and *parole*, Hjelmslev separates the general practice of giving meaning to objects into a system (*langue*) and a process (*parole*). System here represents the paradigmatic axis of language from which signs are chosen, while process refers to the syntagmatic axis combining the language signs into speech.

Generally speaking, the term system denotes a coherent whole of interdependent elements. Saussure refined this definition by discovering that the system in language resides not so much in its elements but in the relationships they entertain with each other. According to him, a paradigm is made up of associative semantic fields which are differentiated by way of opposition to other fields in the same structure. On the other hand, the relationship of similarity between parts of one paradigm also functions to distinguish that particular paradigm from other paradigms, which thus signify by opposition.

See also *language* and *process.*

Tactics

The term tactics designates the science or art of deploying forces or performing manoeuvres in situations of confrontation. Thus a general employs tactics in war; or a person might vote tactically, not to support a party but to prevent the election of another party.

Semiotic theory contrasts the notion of *tactics* with that of *strategy*. While tactics refers to a purposeful procedure or the means to achieve an end, strategy relates to the stage of planning and manipulation. Political strategy, for instance, aims to seduce the electorate with promises. Fixing the date of a general election, on the other hand, is the result of tactical manoeuvring.

See also *strategy.*

Target

Together with the source and the control-actant, the target belongs to the two basic properties of the activity of perception: the direction of a perception (source, target) and the control of this direction. On the narrative level of the text, the eyes could be the target of light (actant-target) emanating from its source, the sun. A smell from a decomposing snake (actant-source) could be so strong that it overpowers everyone in the vicinity (actant-target).

See also *control-actant, sensory perception* and *source.*

Taxonomy

The term taxonomy traditionally means a theory of classification. However, the term also describes the systematic ordering and organizing of given data.

See also *categorization* and *classification.*

Temporalization

The term temporalization denotes the process whereby the temporal dimension is installed in a discourse. Like spatialization and actorialization, it is a necessary ingredient for a referential illusion or reality effect to work.

Moreover, the element of time needs to be present to turn a narrative arrangement into a story. If Cinderella's going to the ball did not *precede* the search for the owner of the lost slipper and if her happiness *after* the prince has found her was not opposed to her *earlier* unhappiness, there would be no meaning to the story and no tale.

See also *actorialization* and *spatialization.*

Terminative

A terminative term is an aspectual term describing the end of a process. It indicates that a transformation is completed and is frequently conveyed through the use of the simple past (the past historic and perfect tense in French), or the narrative present: 'He left the room'; 'He leaves the room'.

The beginning of a process, on the other hand, is indicated by the use of an inchoative term.

See also *durative* and *inchoative.*

Text

The word text is used in linguistics and semiotics to refer to any collection of signs which together form a coherent whole. Texts may be films, speeches, novels, adverts, paintings, opera and so on. In contemporary literary theory the term has been broadened to include all uses of language, e.g. historical events and human relationships. Even the sense of self is 'textualized'. In a famous phrase Jacques Derrida states: 'There is no outside-the-text'.

See also *coherence* and *textualization.*

Textualization

The term textualization can be defined as the arrangement of discursive units in accordance with the linear constraints of verbal reporting. For instance, two actions taking place at the same time cannot be narrated simultaneously: their textualization forces us to place one before the other or to neglect one in order to give prominence to the other. This kind of textual programming gives the enunciator a certain amount of freedom in the organization of the text. The choice of a hero's perspective, for example, or that of the anti-hero, will determine the values that are being selected. It is also possible to take advantage of the elasticity of discourse and play with the possibilities of condensing (by way of text reduction or summarizing) or expanding passages (through amplification or verbal development). Textualization is thus relatively independent from narrative programming.

See also *narrative programme.*

Thematic role

An actor possesses a thematic role if s/he is described in terms of 'themes' such as those of doctor, teacher, carpenter, housewife. These 'themes' are socially defined, stereotyped functions. A character in a story building a house has the thematic role of builder.

The expression thematic role relates to the figurative level of a text and should therefore not be confused with that of actantial role, which is more abstract and relates to the function of a narrative position.

See also *actant* and *actor.*

Thematization

The term thematization refers to the process whereby an enunciator or enunciatee invests figurative discourse with abstract themes. When reading a story mentioning 'clothes', for example, the expression remains ambiguous until it is thematized, in other words, until the enunciator tells us whether to interpret these clothes as a sign of 'wealth' or 'poverty'. A narrative about a poor man getting married and finding employment might be said to establish the themes of success and happiness finding their figurative expression in money earned and a beautiful house.

See also *theme and rheme.*

Theme and rheme

Used widely in discourse analysis, these terms concern the arrangement of information in a sentence or utterance and the importance that the speaker/ writer wishes to accord to a particular item.

Theme is a formal grammatical category which refers to the initial element in a clause serving as the point of departure for the message. It is the element around which the sentence is organized and to which the writer/speaker wishes to give prominence. Everything that follows the theme, i.e. the remainder of the message or part in which the theme is developed, is known as the *rheme*. A message, therefore, consists of a theme combined with a rheme. Compare the following sentences:

> (A) The boys mugged the old woman. (B) The old woman was mugged by the boys.

In the first sentence the theme is 'the boys': it is the boys and what the boys did that is of primary interest. Information about who was mugged is secondary, i.e. the rheme. In the second sentence, on the other hand, it is the fate of the victim, the old woman and what happened to her, that is of primary interest (theme).

In semiotic theory, theme is opposed to figure. In other words, where figurative elements in discourse are essential ingredients in the construction of a reality effect, themes relate to concepts, to the signified that cannot be perceived by the senses. Thus themes such as 'love', 'hate' and 'evil' are not perceptible in themselves, while their expression in gestures of 'love' or 'hate', for instance, is figurativized and perceived by the senses.

See also *thematization.*

Thirdness

See also *firstness, secondness and thirdness.*

Thymic

Situated on the deep level of an utterance, the thymic category relates to the world of feeling and of emotions. It spans the notion made up by the two poles euphoria versus dysphoria and forms the basis of positive/negative evaluation. In other words, it gives rise to an axiological system – a characteristic of all discourse. To give an example: believing a statement to be true involves not only weighing what is being said for its accuracy but also evaluating it positively.

In recent years attention has been focused on the thymic dimension of narrative. This relates to the feelings of euphoria or dysphoria (i.e. pleasant or unpleasant) experienced by the actors. In other words, the thymic dimension, on the narrative level, is concerned with states of mind (*états d'âme*) or feelings rather than with actions (which belong to the pragmatic dimension) or knowledge concerning these actions (which belongs to the cognitive dimension).

When undertaking semiotic analysis, these states of mind or feelings can be correlated with the stages of a narrative programme. They can, for example, describe a state of disjunction or of conjunction with the object of value. In the fairy-tale *Cinderella*, the young girl's lack of means and of family sympathy is expressed in her disjunction from these objects of value as well as in her feeling of unhappiness that accompanies the disjunction. Equally, Cinderella's conjunction with the prince, her love, at the end of the tale also shows the transformation of her unhappiness into joy being accomplished.

See also *cognitive* and *pragmatic.*

Topic space

The term topic space designates the place where the narrative transformation takes place, i.e. where the principal subject undergoes a change of state. In *Treasure Island* the sea voyage and the island can be considered topic spaces.

Topic space itself can be divided into two categories:

(1) *Paratopic space*: this is the space where the qualifying test takes place. The sea journey in *Treasure Island*, or the beanstalk in *Jack and the Beanstalk*, can be considered paratopic spaces.

(2) *Utopic space*: this is the space of the principal action where the object of the quest is at stake. The island represents the utopic space in *Treasure Island*, as does the giant's house in *Jack and the Beanstalk*. In Cinderella's quest to go to the ball, the ballroom constitutes an utopic space.

See also *heterotopic space* and *utopic space.*

Toponym

A toponym is a designation of space by a proper noun. The words 'Paris', 'Jupiter', 'Mount of Olives' or 'the Mediterranean Sea', for example, are toponyms. Together with the names of people and time notations, toponyms contribute to the construction of a referential illusion (illusion of the real). They are associated, therefore, with the figurative level of meaning.

See also *anthroponym* and *chrononym.*

Traitor

The traitor or false hero designates one of Vladimir Propp's seven spheres of action. These were later reduced by Greimas to three pairs of opposed actants (the actantial schema). The semiotic terms 'opponent' and 'anti-subject' subsume the Proppian categories of villain and traitor (false hero).

See also *actantial narrative schema* and *villain.*

Transcendence

Generally speaking, transcendence means being superior, rising above, going beyond the limits, often with respect to human knowledge. For example, we are told that the quality of being transcendent should be applied to God alone.

In semiotic theory, a state of transcendence involves the participation of a receiver in the universe of a sender. In popular tales, for instance, the sender belongs to a transcendental universe (where the transmission of values does not obey normal rules), whereas the receiver-subject is placed in an immanent universe regulated by the normal closed system of value exchange in which the receipt of a gift is at the expense of the giver. When Cinderella meets her fairy godmother she receives her objects of value – a dress, the coach, love – from a transcendental sender in whose universe she participates. She is therefore in a state of transcendence.

See also *immanence and manifestation* and *transparency.*

Transcendental signified

The term denotes the final meaning or ultimate referent towards which all the signifiers in a particular signifying system point. This meaning is portrayed as timeless and stable, relying on the illusion that it transcends, or is independent of, the signifying system in question. For instance, religious people may associate the ultimate signifier with the Word of God or Mohammed – the Bible or the Koran – whereas the non-religious might associate it with science and systems of logic.

This view of language came under attack with the advent of structuralism and was further undermined by the development of semiotics and poststructuralist and postmodernist schools of thought. For Jacques Derrida, for example, there is no ultimate signifier, no closure of meaning. Because meaning is a function of differences, it is always deferred: each word leads on to another word and every signified functions as a signifier in an endless play of signification. Meaning, therefore, depends on absence rather than presence.

See also *deconstruction* and *logocentrism.*

Transformation

A transformation is the passage from one state of affairs (State 1) to another, its opposite (State 2).

State 1 ———————— T ——————▶ State 2

The theft of John's money from his house can be expressed thus:

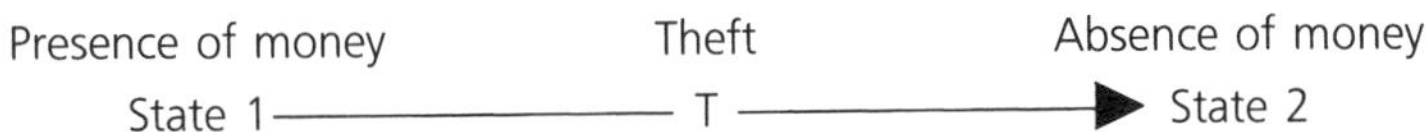

The transformation can correspond to the performance of the subject, who thereby becomes a subject of doing. In order for there to be any story (a narrative) there must be a transformation.

Transparency

The term transparency relates to the belief that texts are a direct expression or reflection of the real world. For semioticians, however, there can be no unmediated experience of the world. Texts are a construct of language and made up of a multiplicity of conventional codes. The classic realist text seeks to hide the presence of these codes whereas a modern or postmodern text may draw attention to its own means of construction and to its status as fiction. An example would be Italo Calvino's *If on a Winter's Night a Traveller*.

See *naturalism* and *realism*.

Trope

A trope is a figure of speech which makes use of a word or phrase in a sense other than its literal meaning. Tropes include metaphors, metonymies, synecdoches and irony. Employing the term 'pilgrimage on earth' to express life's hardship is an example of a trope, in this case, a metaphor.

See also *irony*, *metaphor*, *metonymy* and *synecdoche*.

Truth

In general terms, the word truth designates conformity with fact, agreement with reality. In semiotic theory, the notion of truth is replaced with that of *truth-telling* or veridiction. The process of truth-telling here is connected with the circulation of knowledge and the modes of being (*être*) and seeming (*paraître*). Thus any utterance exhibits signs which allow for it being read as true, false, pretending or a downright lie. Whether or not we believe a political statement to be true, for example, depends on our knowledge of the subject-matter and/or on whether the politician seems truthful to us.

Within the context of truth-telling, the semiotic square of veridiction establishes truth as the metaterm generated by the opposing terms being (*être*) and seeming (*paraître*), both of which illustrate different sides of the concept of truth.

See also *metaterm* and *veridiction*.

Uncertainty

Within the epistemic modal category, uncertainty is the contradictory term for certainty. It designates the modal position 'not-believing-to-be', and can be mapped onto a semiotic square as follows:

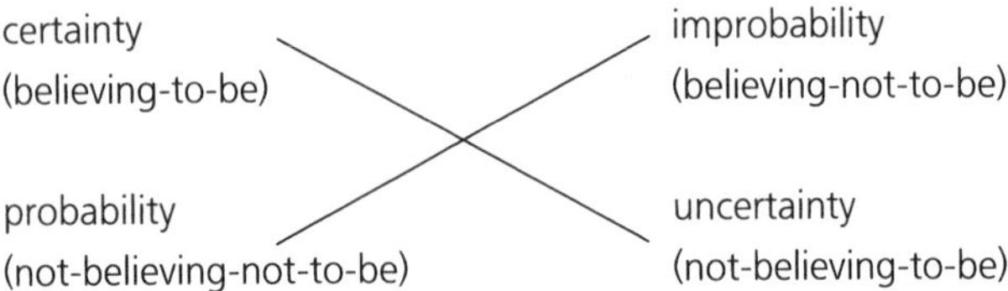

Example: Mother is certain her child is at school = she believes him to be there and does not believe him not to be there. However, the child is not certain his mother is at home = it is probable that she has gone out shopping.

The different (or changing) positions of certainty and uncertainty of the two actors (mother and child) can be plotted on the above square.

See also *epistemic modalities* and *semiotic square.*

Universalism, cognitive

This is the belief that there exists a universal mental structure common to all humankind. The anthropologist Claude Lévi-Strauss argues that this structure is based on binary oppositions transformed in human culture into universal structural patterns and semantic categories such as the oppositions raw/cooked, male/female.

The notion of the existence of universal semantic categories remains a point of contention amongst French semioticians. Some bring to the fore the notion of cultural difference whereas others are more concerned with commonly shared elements. The present focus on the emergence of meaning from sensorial perception would suggest a movement towards the latter position.

Universalism, linguistic

This is the belief that there exists a universal structure underlying all languages. Whatever we say in one language can, therefore, be translated into another. The linguist Noam Chomsky argues that certain basic principles for constructing sentences can be found in all languages and that they are innate or genetically encoded. These principles he terms *universal grammar.*

See *cultural relativism.*

Univocality

This term refers to the use of a single narrative voice within a text. It is a mode of narration that tends to promote a single authoritative reading of a text and that is associated with classic realism. Taken in conjunction with the use of the third person it contributes to the effect of transparency.

See also *polyvocality.*

Utopic space

The term utopic space designates the space in which the decisive test takes place and where performances are realized. Utopic space is contrasted with paratopic space. In Zola's *Germinal*, the mine Le Voreux where the miners fight their principal battle for survival constitutes the utopic space. In *Cinderella*, the ballroom where Cinderella encounters the prince constitutes the utopic space.

See also *topic space.*

Utterance

The term utterance designates any entity that is endowed with meaning. It is usually employed with the broad meaning of statement, both oral and written.

According to semiotic theory, an utterance can be made by any actant able to produce meaning. Thus a spatial utterance would be a statement made about space, objects, their relationship and transformation: e.g. 'The road meanders through the village', or 'The sun burns down from a lead blue sky. The earth is thirsty.' A visual utterance may signify through shape and colours.

Valency

The term valency denotes conditions preliminary to the establishment of values and value systems in discourse. Valencies thus refer to the sensitization of objects and form the basis for the beliefs that are being proposed. Jacques Fontanille has demonstrated, for instance, that valencies in the poetry by Eluard are inchoative. This means that objects are valorized at the moment of their beginning: the birth of a child, the sun rising, the awakening of a lover, etc.

See also *inchoative* and *value*.

Value

See *object of value.*

Veridiction

The term veridiction designates the process of truth-telling in a story. This is connected to the circulation of knowledge, or lack of it, within a text: some actors know more than others about what is happening in the narrative; some are being deceived, others misunderstand, etc. The reader (enunciatee) may also be enlightened or kept in the dark. In Agatha Christie's novels the enunciator witholds vital information from the enunciatee (reader) until the very end. The modal categories of truth, falsehood, of secret and of illusion thus come into play. The following **semiotic square** of veridiction emerges. It is based on the changing modes of being (*être*) and seeming (*paraître*):

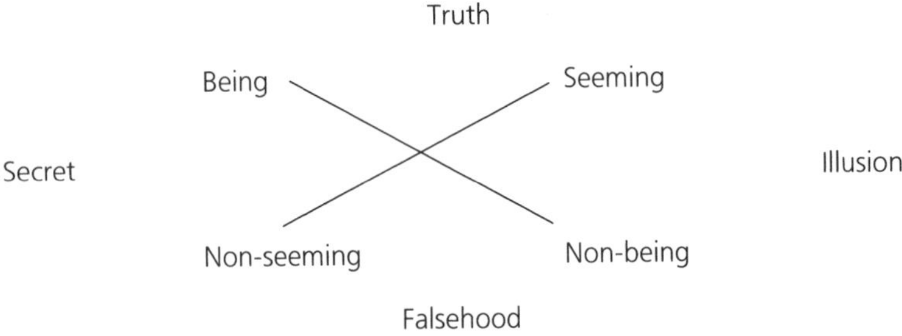

This square allows us to situate modal positions and plot potential trajectories of knowledge. Thus, for example, the detective in a murder story investigates a suspect who seems to have committed the deed but who is not guilty. The true murderer, on the other hand, may at first not seem to be the killer he actually is but is eventually revealed to combine both being and seeming to be a murderer.

See also *modalities* and *semiotic square.*

Villain

In Vladimir Propp's terminology, the villain belongs to one of the seven spheres of action of the folk-tale. Its principal function is the fight or struggle with the hero. In semiotics, the term villain has been replaced with those of opponent and anti-subject. Both opponent and anti-subject are part of the three pairs of opposed actants to which Greimas has reduced and regularized Propp's seven spheres of action of the folk-tale.

Most stories present two narrative trajectories, that of the hero (the subject) and that of the villain (the anti-subject); they are only differentiated by their euphoric or dysphoric moralizing connotation. In the film *Batman*, Batman is the hero and the Joker plays the part of the anti-hero. In *Star Wars*, Luke Skywalker's quest is to save the universe from the Emperor and from Darth Vader whose goal it is to take it over. Subject and anti-subject here have their own narrative programmes. We speak of opponent when a villain's main function is to hinder or obstruct the subject's quest without having a conflicting quest of its own. A locked door is an opponent if you are trying to get out. A storm can be an opponent if you want to reach a port.

See also *actantial narrative schema.*

Virtualization

The term virtualization refers to one of the two basic modes of semiotic existence: virtual or actual. Virtual here denotes that which is in a state of simple possibility, but which in its essence contains the main conditions for its realization, in other words, it means possible/potential. Accordingly, virtualizing modalities are wishing (*vouloir*) and having to do or to be (*devoir*).

Taking language as an example, virtual existence characterizes the paradigmatic axis and actual existence the syntagmatic axis. To put it another way: virtual existence is represented by the language system (*langue*) as opposed to its actualization in the process of speaking (*parole*). The category virtual/actual thus characterizes the relationship between system and process.

With regard to the semiotic model of the narrative, the couple virtualization/actualization has been replaced by the ternary virtualization/actualization/realization in order to describe accurately all possible modes of junction between a subject and an object. Thus before any junction has taken place, subjects and objects are said to occupy *virtual* positions; they are *actualized* when the two actants are disjoined; and they are *realized* once subject and object are conjoined. A person and a car are in virtual positions while the person is only wishing to possess it. We speak of realization once the car has been acquired and of mere actualization if the money has been saved but the car not yet purchased, or if – for non-payment for example – it has been reclaimed by its vendor.

See also *actualization* and *realization.*

Visual semiotics

Visual semiotics comprises the semiotics of architecture or painting, film semiotics, semiotics of the city and aesthetic semiotics generally. It entails the study of the visual components of art and the values attached to them within the context of specific works as well as human cultural behaviour in general. An example would be the semiotic and rhetoric analysis of a work by Rothko which seeks to evaluate the contrasts and oppositions between the colours and shapes in order to make them meaningful to the onlooker ('Approches sémiotiques sur Rothko', *Nouveaux Actes sémiotiques*, 1994). The semiotician Jean-Marie Floch is well known for his extensive studies in the field of visual and plastic semiotics.

Visual semiotics is also relevant to the study of optical and visual communication systems in animals. Many animals have superior eyesight to that of humans and optical signals – such as body shape and colour or movement patterns – form part of intrinsic animal exchanges. The chameleon, for example, communicates through its constant change of colour, while the gestures in the mating dances of birds transmit sexual desire.

See also *advertising – Semiotics of.*

Zoomorphic

The term zoomorphic refers to the attribution of the form or nature of an animal to something, especially a god or superhuman being. In general terms, zoomorphic defines something as having the form of an animal. Characters in fairy-tales taking the form of animals are an example of zoomorphism.

Zoosemiotics

A term coined in 1963 by the semiotician Thomas K. Sebeok, zoosemiotics is the study of messages given off and received by animals. It explores three aspects of language: zoosyntactics (for example the segmentation and classification of bird songs), zoosemantics (the meaning of animal signs) and zoopragmatics (the function of animal signs). Or, to put it another way, research is subdivided into *pure* zoosemiotics or the study of theoretical models of animal signalling, *descriptive* zoosemiotics or the study of animal communication systems, and *applied* zoosemiotics or 'the exploitation of animal communications systems for the benefit of man' (Sebeok, 1972).

According to Sebeok, the entire universe is made up of signs: semiosis is a characteristic feature of all living forms, and an attribute of life itself. Each organism is born and exists within a universe of meaning or semiosphere and must adapt to this semiosphere in order to survive. Zoosemiotics can be seen as a branch of biosemiotics, a discipline that strives to go beyond a purely physical or chemical explanation of the natural world.

Sebeok's thought may be said to possess a strong ethical dimension: the threat now posed to communication between life forms by the economics of capitalist globalization is also for Sebeok a threat to the continuation of life on the earth.

Research in this field has led to a reappraisal of commonly held assumptions, and in particular to a dismantling of the sharp distinction between nature and culture. Animals, for example, like humans, have been found to possess a capacity to lie and deceive.

See also *biosemiotics*.

Key Thinkers in Semiotics

Roland Barthes

1915–1980

Leading French literary theorist, writer and semiotician, Roland Barthes was born in 1915 in Cherbourg, France, to a middle-class Protestant family. His father was killed in action in 1916 and Barthes grew up with his mother and grandparents in Bayonne. At the age of nine he moved to Paris where he completed his baccalauréat in 1934. After the onset of tuberculosis, he spent several years in a sanatorium where he published his first articles on André Gide. After his release in 1945 he taught French in Rumania and in Egypt, where he met A. J. Greimas who introduced him to modern linguistics. Returning to France, he was appointed to a chair of literary semiology at the Collège de France in 1971, a position that he held until his death in 1980. Characterized by a remarkable diversity, Roland Barthes' writings range from studies of semiology or the science of signs, critical literary essays and cultural criticism to more 'personalized' works such as studies on pleasure and reading, on love and on photography.

It was the publication in 1953 of *Le Degré zero de l'écriture* [Writing Degree Zero, 1967] that launched Roland Barthes' career and that established his reputation as a champion of the avant-garde. The book represents a fundamental attack on realism and the notion of *vraisemblance*. Realism like all literary genres is made up of a series of conventions or codes and is held together by the shared knowledge of the reader and the writer. Writing, therefore, can never be innocent: literary traits such as clarity in prose are not absolutes or universals but serve the interests of a rising bourgeoisie anxious to promote its own view of the world as 'natural' or 'normal'.

In his collection of essays, *Mythologies*, published in 1957 [Mythologies, 1967] Barthes applies these ideas to an analysis of everyday media items such as a magazine photograph of an Algerian soldier saluting the French flag. A myth, according to Barthes, operates by confusing nature and history. It thus translates bourgeois norms, which belong to culture, into self-evident laws of nature thereby reinforcing social stereotypes and making them appear inevitable. Through this positioning of items within a wider system of values and beliefs, Barthes' approach represents one of classic structuralism. In *Mythologies* he develops his own semiotic system – or *semiology* – one that is strongly influenced by Hjelmslev's theory of connotation. For Barthes, the primary sign system is one of denotation, the secondary system one of connotation. At the denotative level media texts express primary 'natural meanings'. At the connotative level they conceal secondary, ideological meanings.

Mythologies is followed by the text *Eléments de sémiologie*, 1965 [Elements of Semiology, 1967], a study of non-linguistic semiotic systems, which includes an analysis of cars, architecture, food and clothes. Barthes insists that semiology is part of language and he draws upon the key Saussurean distinction between *langue* or language system and *parole* or speech, the manifestation of that system. In the case of the cultural artefact, for example cooking, the system would include taboos, oppositions (e.g. savoury/sweet) and rules of association at the level of the dish, whereas speech would cover the actual family tradition or national tradition of cookery. This text was followed in 1967 by *Système de la mode* [Fashion System, 1983], a study of fashion in France as presented in two magazines of 1958–1959. Like the writing of books, the wearing of clothes follows a set of conventions: clothes are used to convey messages, to make a statement about oneself and one's preferences.

In the field of literature and literary criticism, Barthes launched a powerful defence of literary structuralism against an attack by the traditionalist Raymond Picard (*Critique et verité*, 1966 [Criticism and Truth, 1987]). Here he stresses the productive nature of language: language is not a means of expression or an instrument for simply conveying messages. Its function is essentially dynamic: it is the means whereby we construct the real – and it is language rather than the individual author that is the source of meaning. At the same time Barthes draws attention to the polysemy or plurality of the literary text, which cannot be reduced to one single meaning. The aim of structuralist criticism then is to reveal the signifying systems at work within a text. These views on literature and interpretation were further developed in

Barthes' collection of essays *Essais critiques*, 1964 [Critical Essays, 1972], and in his 1966 influential essay on the structural analysis of literary narratives, 'Introduction à l'analyse structurale des récits' [Introduction to the structural analysis of narratives, 1979].

In 1970 Barthes published *S/Z*, a detailed line-by-line analysis of *Sarrasine*, a novella by Honoré de Balzac. Here he applies narrative codes derived from the realist text. These are: the hermeneutic code (presentation of an enigma); the semic code (connotative meaning); the symbolic code; the proairetic code (the logic of action), and the cultural code, which evokes a particular body of knowledge. The novella is viewed as an intertextual construct and the product of an interplay of codes rather than simply the expression of a particular individual author. Hence the expression *la mort de l'auteur* [the death of the author]. Barthes also distinguishes between two types of text, the 'readerly' (*lisible*) and the 'writerly' (*scriptible*). The former is predictable, complying with the reader's expectations, whereas the latter is a more unsettling, self-conscious poetic text requiring the reader to become an active participant in the structuring activity: the text becomes an endless play of signifiers where meaning is constantly dispersed. There can, therefore, be no ultimate or 'fixed meaning'. *S/Z* itself played a central role in the emergence of what came to be known as poststructuralism.

In 1973 Barthes published his work *Le Plaisir du texte* [Pleasures of the Text, 1976] in which he outlines a theory of textual pleasure. He makes a distinction between two kinds of pleasure: *plaisir*, which is the comfort or euphoria coming from the readerly text, and *jouissance*, the rapture or ecstasy that proceeds from the more disruptive writerly text. Whilst maintaining this distinction, Barthes frequently suggests that textual pleasure derives from the possibility of finding ecstatic moments in the comfortable texts of pleasure as well as from an attempt to make ecstatic writerly texts sufficiently readable so that their orgasmic effects can be generated: it is not culture or its destruction that is erotic but the gap between them. This concern with meaning and sensory experience was later developed by semioticians in the 1980s and 1990s and continues to occupy a central position in semiotic research.

Barthes' subsequent work includes his semi-fictional 'autobiography' *Roland Barthes par Roland Barthes*, 1975 [Roland Barthes by Roland Barthes, 1977] as well as a meditation on love, *Fragments d'un discours amoureux*, 1977 [A Lover's Discourse: Fragments, 1978]. In 1980 he published a seminal text on photography, *La Chambre claire*: *Note sur la photographie* [Camera Lucida: Reflections on Photography, 1993]. This has been particularly influential in the field of visual analysis. Looking back over his work, Barthes' influence has perhaps been greatest in the field of structural analysis, in particular in the area of cultural and media studies. He brought to the fore the relationship between language and ideology and his deconstruction of myths has become a key weapon in the ongoing struggle against all forms of tyranny. At the same time his own critical theorizing and concern with the way texts construct meaning has deepened our understanding of the avant-garde and postmodern literary text.

Further reading

Culler, Jonathan, *Barthes: A Very Short Introduction* (Oxford: OUP, 2002).

Knight, Diana, *Barthes and Utopia: Space, Travel, Writing* (Oxford: OUP, 1997).

Lavers, Annette, *Roland Barthes: Structuralism and After* (London: Methuen, 1982).

Moriarty, Michael, *Roland Barthes* (Oxford: Polity Press, 1991).

Noam Chomsky

b. 1928–

One of the most influential linguists and philosophers of modern times, Noam Chomsky was born in Philadelphia, USA, in 1928. In 1945 he began studying mathematics, philosophy and linguistics at the University of Pennsylvania where he also came under the influence of the political thought of his professor, Zellig Harris. During this period he became acquainted with the work of Leonard Bloomfield, a leading figure in American structuralism whose behaviourist empiricism dominated American linguistics during the 1930s and 1940s. In 1955 he was awarded a doctorate by the University of Pennsylvania, although most of the research had been completed the previous four years when he was a Junior Fellow at Harvard University. The work on his thesis led to the publication in 1957 of his seminal text *Syntactic Structures*. This brought about a radical shift in thinking about language and established Chomsky's reputation as one of the leading linguists of his age. In 1955 Chomsky began teaching at the Massachusetts Institute of Technology and in 1976 he was appointed Institute Professor of Linguistics, a position that he still holds. Since the 1960s Chomsky has also become more publicly engaged in politics, vigorously opposing the American involvement in Vietnam and more recently the American invasion of Iraq. A left-wing intellectual, he has written over a dozen books dealing with international and domestic political issues as well as continuing to write and teach in the field of linguistics. Indeed, he argues that there is a direct link between his linguistics and politics, contending that language itself is an expression of human creativity and therefore of human freedom.

In his book *Syntactic Structures* (1957) and later in *Aspects of the Theory of Syntax* (1965), Chomsky develops a theory of transformational grammar, which was to revolutionize the scientific study of language. The theory takes utterances (words, phrases, sentences) to correspond to abstract 'surface structures' which in turn correspond to more abstract 'deep structures'. Transformational grammar is a limited set of rules that give rise to sentence transformations and from which it is possible to produce an infinite number of sentences. These rules describe the *competence* of the ideal language-user. The act of production of a finite number of grammatical sentences by an actual language-user Chomsky terms *performance*. In a famous passage written in 1965 (in *Aspects of the Theory of Syntax*) Chomsky describes his position:

> Linguistic theory is concerned primarily with an ideal speaker-listener, in a completely homogeneous speech community, who knows its language perfectly, and is unaffected by such grammatically irrelevant conditions as memory limitations, distractions, shifts of attention and interest and errors (random or characteristic) in applying his knowledge of language in actual performance . . .
>
> We thus make a fundamental distinction between competence (the speaker-hearer's knowledge of his language) and performance (the actual use of language in concrete situations).

Transformational grammar, then, is an attempt to explain how an ideal language user could generate and understand new and unique grammatical sentences without ever having encountered them. It is an attack on behaviourism as propounded by B. F. Skinner, that is, the belief that language is completely learned by cues (stimulus-response theory) and conditioning from the world around the language-user. It is also a reaction to the American structuralist view that language is simply a set of utterances, that is, everything its speakers have said or written. For Chomsky, on the other hand, the set of utterances is potentially infinite and, therefore, does not exist in the real world.

What is more, our knowledge of language is a knowledge that is stored in the brain: Chomsky argues that there are laws or principles governing linguistic competence and that these principles are innate and reflect the structure of the human mind. They constitute what he terms a *universal grammar*.

Chomsky's explanation of the human language faculties was further developed in texts such as as *Reflections on Language* (1975) and *Knowledge of Language* (1986) and subsequently became the model for investigation in several fields of knowledge – in philosophy, cognitive science, computational psychology and computer science, for instance. His theories have exerted an especially strong influence on researchers investigating the acquisition of language in children. Here Universal Grammar presents itself as a system of principles, limiting the range of hypotheses which young people need to try out in the process of learning a language. His theories thus challenge the view that the mind is a 'blank slate' at birth.

Chomsky's thought has always been a source of deep controversy. Some consider his conception of language to be too individualistic or psychological, failing to take into account the social dimension of meaning. Others, Julia Kristeva, for example, argue that his concept of transformational grammar is too static and places too much emphasis on articulated meaning – on performance – and not enough on meaning as a *process*.

In spite of these criticisms, Chomsky's models continue to be widely used. An example would be Niels K. Jerome's Nobel lecture (prize for medicine) in 1983, entitled 'The Generative Grammar of The Immune System'. Over the years Chomsky's thought has considerably evolved and he has been ready to question and reassess his own theories in the light of fresh evidence. He has also been extremely influential in the development of semiotics: his distinction between surface and deep structures is echoed, for example, in Greimas' generative trajectory. From the 1980s onwards, Chomsky's thought has also been instrumental in bringing together semiotics and the natural sciences: it has, for instance, played a key role in the growth of biosemiotics. Central to biosemiotics is the concept that language is not only innate in humans but in all life forms. And as the semiotician Thomas A. Sebeok has pointed out, semiosis is the condition of life itself. Finally, Chomsky's overriding concern with language and the abuse of power lies at the heart of the semiotic enterprise and of its quest to interpret and to reinvent the values by which we live.

Further reading

Alexander, George (ed.), *Reflections on Chomsky* (Oxford: Blackwell, 1990).

Chomsky, Noam, *Language and Mind* (New York: Harcourt Brace Jovanovich, 1968).

Chomsky, Noam, *New Horizons in the Study of Language and Mind* (Cambridge: Cambridge University Press, 2000).

Salkie, Raphael, *The Chomsky Update: Linguistics and Politics* (London: Unwin Hyman, 1990).

Umberto Eco

b. 1932

Italian philosopher and a leading figure in the field of semiotics, Umberto Eco was born in Alessandria, Italy, in 1932. He studied medieval philosophy at the University of Turin and his thesis on the aesthetics of Thomas Aquinas was published in 1956 when he was 24. Three years later he wrote a chapter for a history of aesthetics *Sviluppo dell'estetico medievale,* 1959 [Art and Beauty in the Middle Ages, 1986]. As a medievalist he became interested in the works of James Joyce and in modernity as a cultural and historical phenomenon. In 1959 he published an article *L'opera in movimento e la coscienza dell' epoca* [The Poetics of the Open Work] which later became the first chapter of his book *Opera aperta,* 1962 [The Open Work, 1989]. Here he considers that modern art, under the influence of science, produces 'works in movement' and 'open works'. These are works in which the addressee or reader becomes an active participant in the production of meaning and in which openness itself is brought to the fore. Eco thus came to pioneer a reader-orientated criticism which was further elaborated in his influential *The Role of the Reader: Explorations in the Semiotics of Texts,* published in 1979, and more recently in *The Limits of Interpretation* (1990) and in *Interpretation and Overinterpretation* (1993). In these works, Eco stresses the point that an open text is not one in which the text can mean anything: every literary work proposes a model or ideal reader who represents the range of possible meanings justified in terms of the structure of the text itself.

During the 1960s Eco held faculty appointments at several Italian universities lecturing first in aesthetics, then in architecture, visual communication and semiotics. In 1968 he published a critique of structuralism *La struttura assente* [The Absent Structure], a key influence on the development of semiotics in Italy. Here Eco attacks structuralists such as Lévi-Strauss for ascribing to structures an objective reality: he makes the point that if there were an ultimate structure it could not be defined. Instead, Eco advocates a methodological structuralism, that is, he accepts structures only as operational procedures which can always be replaced by new models should the occasion arise. In 1975 he was appointed to a Chair of Semiotics in the Faculty of Letters and Philosophy at the University of Bologna, a position which he still holds. The publication in English of *A Theory of Semiotics* in 1976, followed later by *Semiotics and the Philosophy of*

Language (1984), established Eco's reputation as one of the leading and most influential semioticians of his age.

In *A Theory of Semiotics* Eco presents a theory of codes and of sign production. His point of departure is Peirce's notion of 'unlimited semiosis', that is, the concept that signs refer *ad infinitum* to other signs. For Eco, however, meanings are not infinite but are established with reference to conditions of possibility. In other words, unlimited semiosis is enacted within the context of the social world of real speech acts and culturally produced and culturally interpreted signs whose meanings are at once fixed, open and arbitrary.

From this position Eco develops the notion of an 's-code'. By s-code is meant the structure of the language, i.e. the code correlates the expression plane with the content plane. To make the s-code more dynamic, Eco introduces a model 'Q' (after Quillian) which accounts for unlimited semiosis within the cultural context. As a result of taking into account the sign's status as a cultural unit, Eco's theory of codes is able to explain how signs can take on a multiplicity of meanings, how meaning is derived from the competence of the user and how, as a result, new meanings can be created. Model Q is, therefore, a model of 'linguistic creativity'.

Eco then goes on to discuss sign production. He focuses again on the tension between elements that can be easily assimilated or foreseen by the code and designated as *ratio facilis* and those that cannot be so easily assimilated, therefore described as *ratio difficilis*. The closer one comes to *ratio difficilis* the more the object is 'motivated' by the nature of the objective situation. However, even the most motivated signs have conventional elements. Eco cites Gombrich's examples of what passed for realism in paintings at various periods in art history. He considers that even a photograph can be seen to possess conventional aspects.

Eco's Model Q and system of sign production brings to the fore, then, the dynamic nature of the sign and the capacity of language for self-renewal and revitalization. He argues that a sign is not only something that stands for something else as in a dictionary. Instead, viewed from the perspective of unlimited semiosis, language can be compared to an encyclopaedia as understood by the eighteenth-century *philosophes*. The encyclopaedia would correspond to a labyrinth from which there is no exit. It is a map-like network of words allowing for the possibility of ever new meanings.

In his more recent work Eco has further developed his notion of interpretation. In the previously mentioned *The Limits of Interpretation* (1990) and in *Interpretation and Overinterpretation* (1992) he attacks deconstruction as a critical reading method. In *Kant and Platypus* (1997) he presents a 'contractarian' form of realism: it is the reader's interpretation – guided by the Peircean concept of objectivity – together with the speaker's undetermined intentions that are needed to fix reference. His current research includes an application of these concepts to the field of translation.

Eco has also established a reputation as a historian and media critic concerned with how modern media and computer technology impact upon literary studies, culture and society. At the same time he is known to a world-wide audience as the author of philosophical novels such as *The Name of the Rose* (1980), *Foucault's Pendulum* (1988) and *The Island of the Day Before* (1994), representing a practical application of his semiotic theories. He has always championed the interdisciplinary approach and has collaborated with the eminent semiotician Thomas S. Sebeok, amongst others.

Further reading

Caesar, Michael, *Umberto Eco: Philosophy, Semiotics and the Work of Fiction* (Malden, MA: Polity Press, 1999).

Capozzi, Rocco (ed.), *Reading Eco: An Anthology* (Bloomington: Indiana University Press, 1997).

Eco, Umberto, *Mouse or Rat: Translation as Negotiation* (London: Weidenfeld & Nicolson, 2003).

Algirdas Julien Greimas

1917–1992

Born in Lithuania in 1917, Algirdas Julien Greimas was the founder of the French branch of semiotics known as the Paris School. After settling permanently in France in 1944, he completed a lexicological study of the vocabulary of dress in 1830 and obtained his State Doctorate in 1948. In 1949 he was appointed lecturer at the University of Alexandria where he was joined a year later by Roland Barthes, with whom he collaborated in research projects. In an article published in 1956 Greimas recognized the importance of Saussure, drawing particular attention to his concept of the sign and to the notion of meaning as difference. Indeed, Saussure's central conviction that meaning does not lie in individual words but in a complex system of relationships or structures will lie at the core of Greimas' semiotic enterprise and of his application of linguistics to texts. In this same article Greimas also advocated the extension of the structuralist method to all branches of social activity, whether it be the visual arts, architecture, politics or music, thus anticipating a future programme for semiotic activity.

From 1962 to 1965 Greimas taught French linguistics at the University of Poitiers, and from 1963 to 1964 he also gave lectures in structural semantics at the Institut Henri-Poincaré in Paris which were later to form the basis of his seminal work *Sémantique structurale* [Structural Semantics, 1976], published in 1966. In this book he proposed a narrative grammar, which was to become one of the basic tools of French semiotic practice. He was elected to the Ecole Pratique des Hautes Etudes in Paris in 1965 where he directed a yearly seminar in semiotics, which subsequently evolved into the Paris School of Semiotics.

During the 1970s Greimas broadened the sphere of his preoccupations to include not only the literary text and myth but also the social sciences, producing, for example, studies of urban space and of legal discourse. In 1979 a first volume of a dictionary of semiotics was produced in collaboration with Joseph Courtés, to be followed in 1986 by a second volume. In the 1980s Greimas developed a semiotics of passion as well as an interest in the concept of the aesthetic. He died in 1992.

Greimas' major contribution to the development of semiotics was the elaboration in *Sémantique structurale* of a set of narrative models that could be applied to all forms of discourse. The first of these models, known as the *actantial narrative schema,* is a reformulation and simplification of Vladimir Propp's 31 functions that were found to be common to all stories. This schema presents six actantial or narrative roles arranged in three sets of binary oppositions: subject/object, sender/receiver, helper/opponent. Together the six actants (narrative roles) and their organization account for all possible relationships within a story and indeed within human action in general. At the same time Greimas introduced a more comprehensive schema outlining the logical stages through which any action or quest must necessarily unfold. This schema, based on Propp's division into narrative sequences, takes the form of three types of event or tests: the qualifying test, the principal test and the glorifying test. These three tests are preceded by the 'contract', the stage at which the subject accepts or embarks on the mission.

In *Sémantique structurale* Greimas also presents a fundamental model known as the *elementary structure of meaning* and situated at the deep level of the text. This model is based on the structure of binary opposition: there can be no 'up' without 'down', no 'good' without 'evil'. In other words, meaning is generated by the oppositions we perceive between two semes (the smallest unit of meaning). Greimas then develops this basic structure to include negating or contradictory terms. In the late 1960s this model was further developed to produce a visual representation known as the *semiotic square.*

The elaboration of the elementary structure of meaning and of the semiotic square led Greimas to formulate what is known as the *generative trajectory*, describing the overall process whereby meaning is produced. The trajectory is based on the notion of a hierarchy of meaning reflecting the fundamental division between deep and surface structures and between concrete and abstract.

In the 1970s Greimas' theories were enriched through the further development of the concept of *modalization* and of the *modalities.* The application of modal theory to the unfolding of narrative sequences (the three tests) led to the production by Greimas of a *canonical narrative schema*, a more comprehensive and more precise description of plot structure. These models were successfully applied by Greimas to an analysis of Guy de Maupassant's short story *Deux amis* [Two Friends] in his book *Maupassant, la sémiotique du texte: exercices pratiques,* 1976 [Maupassant, The Semiotics of Texts, 1988]. Indeed, they have subsequently proved extremely useful in eliciting the core values on which a particular text is based and in the construction of an overall semantic framework.

Greimas, however, was not only concerned with narrativity. In the 1980s his efforts were directed towards the examination of enunciative strategies, with particular emphasis on spatial and temporal organization. Here the concept of aspectualization – the implied presence of the observer in the text – proved to be of particular significance. This focus on aspectualization then led Greimas to undertake a semiotic study of the passions and to the development of the concept of an affective subject. In 1991 Greimas together with his colleague Jacques Fontanille published the book *Sémiotique des passions* [Semiotics of Passions, 1993] which includes studies of jealousy and avarice, presenting in the process general models for the analysis of the passions.

An interest in pre-cognitive states also led Greimas to an exploration of the concept of beauty and of the aesthetic. In his book *De l'imperfection*, 1987 [On Imperfection] he links the experience of beauty with the aspectual moment of the finished or perfect: it is the moment when subject and object fuse in a state of ecstatic indifferentiation. Greimas examines these privileged moments as they appear in passages from, for example, Italo Calvino, presenting a critical method that can be applied to a wide variety of texts.

The impact of Greimas' writings on critical theory has been enormous. His approach is one of scientific rigour, allowing for the uncovering of a multiplicity of fresh layers of meaning in a personal encounter with the text. His work has also opened up avenues for future research. His book *De l'imperfection* has stimulated further examination of the relationship between sensory perception (*le sensible*) and the production of meaning (*l'intelligible*). The recent expansion in the field of sociosemiotics undoubtedly owes much to his legacy.

Further reading

Greimas, Algirdas Julien, *Narrative Semiotics and Cognitive Discourses*, transl. P. Perron and F. Collins (London: Pinter, 1990).

Greimas, Algirdas Julien, *On Meaning: Selected Writings in Semiotic Theory*, transl. and ed. P. Perron and F. Collins (London: Pinter, 1987).

Martin, Bronwen, *Semiotics and Storytelling: An Introduction to Semiotic Analysis* (Dublin: Philomel Productions, 1997).

Perron, P. and Collins, F. (eds) 'Greimassian Semiotics', *New Literary History*, 20.3 (1989) [Special Issue].

Louis Hjelmslev

1899–1965

Born in Copenhagen in 1899, the Danish linguist Louis Hjelmslev spent most of his professional life as Professor of Comparative Philology in Copenhagen (1937–1965). He founded the Linguistic Circle of Copenhagen (1931) and is perhaps best known as the author of glossematics, a theory attempting to radicalize structuralist linguistics, which he elaborated in collaboration with H.-J. Uldall. Glossematics is a formal and abstract theory focusing not only on the spoken language but also, like Saussure's *sémiologie* [semiology], on non-linguistic languages. It is concerned with sign systems and their semiotic significance on a general level. Hjelmslev also developed a glossematic theory of connotation and denotation as it relates to literature and aesthetics. The essentials of his theories are detailed in his most important work *Omkring sprogteoriens grundœggelse*, 1943 [Prolegomena to a Theory of Language, 1953].

Hjelmslev's semiotics and his linguistic approach are grounded in his belief in the importance of formalism and of sign function. His understanding of the sign is a further development of the Saussurean sign model. Without ever having had access to Saussure's detailed notes, Hjelmslev and the Copenhagen Circle would seem to have retraced and developed, on their own, much of Saussure's theoretical discoveries. Saussure's division of the sign into signifier (sound-image) and signified (conceptual image), for example, is replaced by Hjelmslev with two mutually interdependent planes, an expression plane and a content plane. However, in contrast to Saussure's simple distinction, Hjelmslev divides each of these planes further so that we arrive at both an expression-form and an expression-substance as well as a content-form and a content-substance. Each word in a language thus needs a phonetic substance before it adopts a sound form, just as its content requires a content-substance from which the word content-form is derived. But Hjelmslev does not stop there: he discovers beyond what he calls the semiotically formed, structured sign systems a pre-semiotic amorphous world which he names *purport* and which he divides into an amorphous thought mass or continuum (content-purport) and the phonetic potential of human vocal articulation (expression-purport). Altogether then Hjelmslev refines Saussure's theory of the sign by insisting that the two planes of the sign are first of all substances – felt or perceived – which correspond to Saussure's acoustic and conceptual images. The semiotic function of their combined union then converts them into forms: the expression-form and the content-form. In the end, according to Hjelmslev, it is **form**, and not substance, that makes language intelligible.

To Hjelmslev a sign does not stand for something outside the object to which it refers. He thus set about redefining sign function. Holding, like Saussure, that expression and content – the two sides of the sign – make an indissoluble entity, he names the interdependence of expression-form and content-form a relation of solidarity. Moreover, he designates the expression-form and the content-form *functives* of a sign function. In fact, all linguistic elements are determined by their interdependent relations and these are called functions. When it comes to sign systems, Hjelmslev discovers even smaller constituents than the sign on both its planes. These minute semiotic units he calls *figurae*, expression-figurae and content-figurae. Figurae have no content, only their function. He gives the English form *am* as an example. *Am* has two expression-figurae, *a* and *m*; and it has five content-figurae: *be*, *indicative*, *present tense*, *first person* and *singular*. Not all sign systems are languages with interdependent planes. Non-linguistic signs, for instance, cannot be broken down into minimal elements of content and expression. Hjelmslev mentions the example of traffic lights: while 'red' means 'stop', 'green' means 'go' and 'yellow' 'wait', there is no further articulation.

Hjelmslev began his research with developing his theories of the spoken language. Yet his interest soon broadened to incorporate 'language in a far broader way', that is, 'any structure that is analogous to a language and satisfies the given definition'. He used the term semiotic to describe this broader kind of language and defined it thus: 'a semiotic is a hierarchy, any of whose components admits of a further analysis into classes defined by mutual relations'. Among these semiotics, however, a special place is reserved for language because it is a semiotic 'into which all other semiotics may be translated – both all other languages and all other conceivable semiotic structures'.

Within the framework of semiotic relationships, Hjelmslev also developed a theory of connotation and denotation. He distinguished different types of semiotics (that is languages in the broader sense) which he defined thus: a *denotative* semiotic is a semiotic none of whose planes is a semiotic in its own right; a *metasemiotic*, on the other hand, is a semiotic whose plane of content is a semiotic in itself. This applies to all metalanguages concerned with an object language which they aim to describe. Every grammar, for instance, is a metasemiotic. Finally, a *connotative* semiotic is a semiotic whose plane of expression is a whole semiotic. To take the example of a literary text: here style – that is connotators like tone, medium, choice of words, rhythm – is seen to add a semantic charge to the primary semiotic form of expression. Hjelmslev's theory of connotation gave rise to a glossematics of literature based on the assumption that the aesthetic expression plane of a work of art connotes an aesthetic content.

Glossematics and Hjelmslev's linguistic and semiotic theories in general have been of major importance in the evolution of European semiotics. Criticized by many for the abstract formalism and excessive rigour of his approach, Hjelmslev was, on the other hand, applauded for being the originator of a general science of the sign, the *sémiologie* of which Saussure had dreamt. The greatest influence of Hjelmslev's theories is to be found in the work of Algirdas Julien Greimas and the *Ecole de Paris* [Paris School] as well as in the semiotic approach of Umberto Eco. Roland Barthes' *Elements de sémiologie* [Elements of Semiology] is also influenced by Hjelmslev's semiotics, as is Metz's semiotics of film. Eco would seem to be accurate when summing up Hjelmslev's importance to modern semiotics: Hjelmslev, he said, is the only author to have succeeded in proposing a general theoretical framework for a semiotic theory. But, Eco continues, 'his theory was too abstract, his examples concerning other semiotic systems very limited and rather parenthetical, and his glossematic jargon impenetrable'.

Further reading

De Beaugrande, Robert, *Linguistic Theory: The Discourse of Fundamental Works* (London, New York: Longman, 1991).

Hjelmslev, Louis, *Prolegomena to a Theory of Language*, transl. F. J. Whitfield (Madison: University of Wisconsin Press, 1961).

Siertsema, Bettine, *A Study of Glossematics* (The Hague: Martinus Nijhoff, 1955).

Roman Jakobson

1896–1982

Born in Moscow in 1896, the linguist and scientist Roman Osipovich Jakobson was one of the most powerful and most influential minds of the twentieth century. During his long life, Jakobson's work had a major effect on many trends in the evolution of modern literary theory and, in particular, made a significant contribution to the development of structuralism and semiotics. In his early formalist period, he co-founded the Moscow Linguistics Circle (1915) and became a member of the influential OPOJAZ poetic group. In 1920 he moved to Czechoslovakia and helped with the foundation of the Prague Linguistic Circle, renowned for its breakthrough work in structural linguistics and poetics. In the 1940s, his semiotic period, he collaborated with the Copenhagen Linguistic Circle and, having been forced by the Nazis to leave Czechoslovakia, he finally settled in the United States in 1941, where he founded the Linguistic Circle of New York. He spent the last part of his life teaching Slavic languages and literature and general linguistics at Harvard and later held a simultaneous chair at the Massachusetts Institute of Technology, extending his fields of knowledge to include mathematics, neurolinguistics, biology and physics.

The study of language in its relation to poetics was of particular importance in Jakobson's research. He confronted the question: What makes a verbal message a work of art? Poetics deals with verbal structure; hence it may be regarded as an integral part of the science of linguistics. Jakobson set out to define the constitutive factors in any speech event, in any act of verbal communication, replacing the traditional three parts – addresser, message, addressee – with a model comprising six elements:

> The ADDRESSER sends a MESSAGE to the ADDRESSEE. To be operative the message requires a CONTEXT referred to ('Referent' in another, somewhat ambiguous, nomenclature), seizable by the addressee, and either verbal or capable of being verbalized; a CODE fully, or at least partially, common to the addresser and addressee (or in other words, to the encoder and decoder of the message); and, finally, a CONTACT, a physical channel and psychological connection between the addresser and the addressee, enabling both of them to enter and stay in communication. (Paper delivered at conference on 'Style and Language', Indiana University, 1958)

According to Jakobson, each of these factors, which are inalienably involved in verbal communication, determines a different function of language. He names these functions 1) *emotive* relating to the speaker's attitude towards what he is speaking about; 2) *conative* expressing the orientation towards the addressee; 3) *referential* regarding an orientation towards the context; 4) *poetic* focusing on the message itself; 5) *phatic* relating to the establishment of contact; and 6) *metalingual* focusing on the code. While all these functions are present in any speech act, there is usually one (or more) that is predominant on which the structure of a message primarily depends. Thus the referential – cognitive, denotative – is the leading function of many messages, but the other functions also play a role and can be analysed. Equally, in poetry and literature, the poetic function would seem to be dominant and determining. However, one cannot reduce the poetic function to mere poetry. It exists in all other verbal activities, albeit as a subsidiary function.

Jakobson's identification of the rhetorical figures, metaphor and metonymy, as two polar types in the organization of discourse, was another major discovery. He began with the Saussurean basic principle that language involves two operations: selection and combination. In any given sentence, each element is selected from a set of similar elements and can be substituted for another element in the set; the different elements are combined to make the sentence, in other words, they are in a relationship of contiguity. Jakobson found that the vertical (selection) and horizontal (combination) operations of language are illustrated by the figures of metaphor (substitution, similarity) and metonymy (contiguity). Moreover, each person, he held, in manipulating the two kinds of connection, fashions his own style, his verbal predilections and preferences.

His contribution to the evolution of semiotics, however, went beyond linguistic studies. Jakobson's all-pervading interest in communication encompassed other fields of culture and aesthetics. He advanced applied semiotics by writing papers on music, film, theatre, painting and folklore, and participated in the discussion of fundamental semiotic concerns such as the concept of the sign, system and code. He singled out variants of language determining three sign systems connected to language but not an integral part of it: 1) language substitutes such as whistled and drum languages, Morse code; 2) language transforms, for example, formalized scientific languages; and 3) idiomorphic systems including music and gestures which are not directly related to language. For all that, his interest was focused primarily on the study of the larger field of communication within which he saw linguistics and semiotics as having their place.

Jakobson's impact on semiotics was far-reaching in other respects as well. He was the first to draw attention to Peirce's definition of the sign and its importance for linguistics and he re-evaluated Saussure's understanding of language. He also worked closely with the anthropologist Claude Lévi-Strauss and through his influence on him became highly influential in the development of structuralism. An analysis of Baudelaire's poem 'Les chats', on which the two men collaborated, was published in 1962 and became famous as a set piece in structuralist criticism. With Lévi-Strauss, Jakobson also shared ideas on social communication, of which he discovered three levels: exchange of messages, of goods and of women. Finally, Jakobson elaborated many methodological principles in language study that could usefully be applied as guides in other fields of semiotic research.

The many titles Jakobson published during his lifetime bear evidence to his universal genius and the extreme productivity of his intellect. Most of his published work consists of technical articles. Six volumes of his *Selected Works* appeared between 1962 and 1971. Writings of particular semiotic interest include *Main Trends in the Science of Language* (1973), *Six Lectures on Sound and Meaning* (1976) and *Verbal Art, Verbal Sign* (1985).

Further reading

Jakobson, Roman, *Language in Literature*, eds K. Pomorska and S. Rudy (Cambridge, MA: Belknap Press, 1987).

Jakobson, Roman, *On Language*, eds L. R. Waugh and M. Monville-Burston (Cambridge, MA: Harvard University Press, 1995).

Waugh, Linda R., 'Semiotics and Language: the work of Roman Jakobson', in Roberta Kevelson (ed.), *Hi-Fives: A Trip to Semiotics* (New York: Peter Lang, 1998).

Julia Kristeva

b. 1941

Semiotician, psychoanalyst and writer, Julia Kristeva was born in Bulgaria in 1941. After studying at the University of Sofia, she arrived in Paris in 1966 on a doctoral research fellowship. She attended the seminars of Roland Barthes and also became involved with the writers and intellectuals centred around the avant-garde literary journal *Tel Quel*, edited by Philippe Sollers. In the late 1960s she came into prominence as the interpreter of the Russian formalist Mikhail Bakhtin whose central concern was with the dialogic dimension of art. The publication of *Séméiotiké: Recherches pour une sémanalyse*, 1969 [The System and the Speaking Subject, 1973], followed by that of her doctoral thesis *La Révolution du langage poétique*, 1974 [Revolution in Poetic Language, 1984], established Kristeva's reputation as a leading semiotician and poststructuralist thinker. In 1974 she was appointed to a Chair in Linguistics at the University of Paris VII which she still holds. From 1970 to 1983 she served on the editorial board of *Tel Quel* and she also completed professional training in psychoanalysis, opening her own practice in 1979. Eager to make connections between different domains of enquiry, Kristeva has engaged in Freudian and Lacanian psychoanalysis, literary criticism and feminism. Her writing output since the 1980s has been prolific and includes both fiction and non-fiction. She currently (alternate years) lectures at Columbia University whilst retaining her position at the Sorbonne.

In her *Séméiotiké: Recherches pour une sémanalyse,* Kristeva sets out the fundamental principles of her semiotic theory. This theory is a synthesis of elements drawn from psychoanalysis (Freud, Lacan), linguistics (Roman Jakobson, Noam Chomsky) and semiotics (Saussure, Peirce, Hjelmslev). Taking the text as its object of research, semanalysis focuses on the materiality of language – its sounds, rhythms and syntax – rather than simply on its communicative function. The text is envisaged as a generative activity, which Kristeva calls *signifying practice* and *productivity*:

> The text is not the communicative language codified by grammar. It is not satisfied with representing or meaning the real. Wherever it signifies [. . .] it participates in the transformation of reality, capturing it at the moment of its non-closure.

Literary and poetic language is viewed as a prime example of this generative trajectory: Kristeva describes the literary text as *plural,* often polyphonic and as *presenting a potential infinity.* This focus on the polyphonic nature of the text – inspired by the thought of Mikhail Bakhtin – led to the development of the concept of *intertextuality.* For Kristeva, each text exists in relation to others: the text is an intersection of texts and codes, *the absorption and transformation of another text.*

In *Séméiotiké: Recherches pour une sémanalyse* Kristeva also presents what she sees as two fundamental dimensions of meaning in a text: the *phenotext* and the *genotext.* The phenotext is the textual surface structure described by the methods of structural linguistics such as syntax and semantics. The genotext, on the other hand, is the level of the textual deep structure, where the *production of signification* takes place. It is unstructured, exterior to the subject and timeless, containing the possibilities of all languages and all signifying practices.

Kristeva's theory of the semiotic is further developed in her seminal study *La Révolution du langage poétique* in 1974. Here she brings to the fore the psychoanalytic position of semanalysis by introducing a distinction between the *semiotic* and the *symbolic.* The semiotic she relates to Freud's primary pre-Oedipal processes, that is, to the prelinguistic state of instinctual drives. It precedes the symbolic and corresponds to the level of the genotext. The symbolic, on the other hand, relates to language as a rule-governed social system of communication in which signs refer to objects. This would correspond to the phenotext. Genotext and phenotext do not exist in isolation but function together in what Kristeva terms the signifying process.

In contrast to the early structuralist thinkers, then, Kristeva draws attention to the role of the unconscious in the production of meaning. The subject is a *subject in process,* a subject that is not only a subject of consciousness but also a subject in that it is unspeakable, unnameable. To substantiate her position she draws explicitly on Lacanian psychoanalytical theory. She equates the semiotic with the *chora*, a language before language closely related to the mother. The chora exists at the level where the child's basic drives are directed towards the mother. It is a principle of ordering and the home of the signifying drives which serve to structure the semiotic. Although all language is based on the bodily rhythms of the chora, these are more or less repressed when the child enters the symbolic order of representation. The chora can only then be perceived as a pulsional pressure on language when discourse breaks down, emerging, for example, in contradictions, linguistic disruption and silences as well as in the processes of displacement and condensation. In *La Révolution du langage poétique* Kristeva examines how this semiotic basis of language is exploited by nineteenth-century avant-garde writers such as Mallarmé and Lautréamont.

From the 1980s onwards Kristeva has been less concerned with the elaboration of a general theory of language and the subject and more interested in the importance for the individual subject of a successful entry into the symbolic or language. Her subsequent work, therefore, carries forceful implications for ethics and social theory. She has produced studies of the abject, *Pouvoirs de l'horreur. Essai sur l'abjection*, 1980 [Powers of Horror. An Essay on Abjection, 1982], of love, *Histoires d'amour*, 1985 [Tales of Love, 1987], of melancholy and depression, *Soleil Noir. Dépression et mélancholie*, 1987 [Black Sun, 1989], and on the history and experience of being a foreigner, *Etrangers à nous-mêmes*, 1988 [Strangers to Ourselves, 1988]. In *Les Nouvelles Maladies de l'âme*, 1993 [New Maladies of the Soul, 1995] she examines the crisis of moral values in a postmetaphysical age. In 2000 she published *Le Temps sensible*, a magisterial account of Proust's work, and in 2002 an analysis of three major female intellectuals, Hannah Arendt, Melanie Klein and Colette (*Le Génie féminin,* 1999–2002). In all of her work she stresses the importance of art and its role in the formation of subjectivity: the artistic endeavour constitutes the subject as much as the subject constitutes the work of art. A work of art can extend the symbolic and imaginary capacities of the recipient, producing a transformation of identity which is also a becoming 'open to the other'.

Further reading

Becker-Leckrone, Megan, *Julia Kristeva and Literary Theory* (Basingstoke: Palgrave Macmillan, 2005).

Lechte, John and Margoni, Maria, *Julia Kristeva: Live Theory* (London, New York: Continuum, 2004).

Moi, Toril, 'Marginality and Subversion: Julia Kristeva', in *Sexual Textual Politics: Feminist Literary Theory* (London: Routledge, 1988).

Smith, Anne-Marie, *Julia Kristeva: Speaking the Unspeakable* (London: Pluto Press, 1998).

Claude Lévi-Strauss

b. 1908

The French anthropologist Claude Lévi-Strauss was born in Brussels in 1908. Having graduated in law and philosophy, he first lectured at the University of São Paulo, Brazil. It was there that he became interested in social anthropology and undertook several exploratory trips into the Amazon. After a period at the New School for Social Research in New York during the Second World War (where he met Roman Jakobson), he became Director of Studies at the Ecole Pratique des Hautes Etudes in Paris (1950–74) and Professor of Social Anthropology at the Collège de France (1959). He has been associated with the University of Paris for most of his life and is still continuing his research activities in his nineties. Claude Lévi-Strauss is best known for his discoveries in structural anthropology, an innovative approach to the analysis of collective phenomena such as kinship, myth and ritual. His major impact on contemporary thought resides mainly in the application of linguistic principles to non-linguistic material.

Lévi-Strauss' anthropological work is deeply influenced by structural linguistics, in particular by Jakobson's teachings, and by Trubetzkoy's phonology. He believed that all social and cultural phenomena are linked to language and can therefore be analysed in terms of language. As he explains in his autobiographical essay, *Tristes Tropiques,* 1955 [A World on the Wane, 1961]: 'Qui dit homme, dit langage, et qui dit langage dit société' [Being human implies language, and using language implies society]. Inspired by phonology, he thus set out to identify the constituents of cultural behaviour – be they marriage rituals, methods of cooking or political ideologies – considering them, like phonemes, to produce meaning only within a system of opposition and correlation. From the interrelationships of the different systems within a society or societies, he then deduced an overall structure of cultural communication, a total language by which societies express their unconscious attitudes.

In his first work *Les Structures élémentaires de la parenté*, 1949 [Elementary Structures of Kinship, 1969], Lévi-Strauss focuses his linguistic-structuralist approach on the analysis of systems of kinship. He starts with positing that the opposing couple nature/culture articulates the semantic category 'social life'. Following the tradition he defines nature as that which is universal, spontaneous, not dependent on any particular norm whereas culture represents anything that is particular, that regulates society and is capable of varying from one social structure to another. However, he soon discovers something he terms a *scandal*. This scandal is incest prohibition which is both universal, that is, natural and also cultural since it is part of legal systems of prohibitions. From this example he concludes that he has to separate the *truth* of the opposition from the *method* of its application. He thus invents the term *bricolage* [tinkering about, do-it-yourself] to describe the intellectual activity which makes use of materials for their methodological importance without being affected by their ontological non-value. He later further defines *bricolage* as the discourse of this method and, in *La Pensée sauvage*, 1962 [The Savage Mind, 1966], he links it to the primitive mind responding in a non-literate, non-technical way, though not without logic, to the world around it.

In a semiotic context, Lévi-Strauss's most influential work would seem to be his analysis of myths. Searching for their semantic structure, he studied myths intensively and was puzzled by apparent contradictions: on the one hand anything can happen in a myth, there appears to be no logic or continuity; on the other hand, the arbitrariness is belied by the astonishing similarity between myths collected in widely different regions. Also, a myth always refers to events in the past, yet what gives the myth its operational value is that the specific pattern it describes is timeless. In addition, myth is primarily language. And yet it is more than speech – its mythical value is felt even through the worst translations. 'Le mythe est langage; mais un langage qui travaille à un niveau très élevé, et où le sens parvient, si l'on peut dire, à décoller du fondement linguistique . . .' [Myth is language; yet a language which functions at a very high level where meaning, so to speak, succeeds in going beyond its linguistic foundation]. He starts his analysis with establishing constituent units of myth, which he calls mythemes. He finds these mythemes on the sentence level, each one expressing a 'relation' which links a 'function' to a given subject (e.g. Oedipus kills his father). But because of the specific character of mythological time being at once diachronic and synchronic, mythemes do not consist of isolated relations but of bundles of such relations. A 'bundle' can be described as all the versions of a particular 'relation', and it is only as bundles that relations can be put to use and combined so as to produce meaning. By reading them vertically as well as horizontally, Lévi-Strauss finds that they seem to operate like universal signifying structures. He discovers the Oedipus myth organized in units set up, like linguistic units, in binary opposition. According to him, therefore, it is not the narrative sequence but structural pattern that gives a myth its meaning. And because myth always involves the diachronic and synchronic dimensions, Lévi-Strauss compares its working to the interaction between *langue* and *parole*, where the telling of an individual myth represents a particular version (*parole*) of the total of all versions (*langue*). His four volume work *Mythologiques*, 1964–71 [Introduction to a Science of Mythology, 1964–81] represents a study of the practical implications of his theories: he examines individual myths *not* for their intrinsic meaning but for their part in a wider network of myths.

Claude Lévi-Strauss has been called the 'Father of Structuralism' and although this claim is disputable, it is certain that his contribution to the establishment of structuralism in Europe during the 1960s, and to the parallel evolution of semiotics, is of major importance. In particular *L'Anthropologie structurale* (1958) [Structural Anthropology, 1963] and *Le Cru et le cuit* (1964) [The Raw and the Cooked, 1970] were of seminal influence in the development of semiotic theory. A. J. Greimas, for example, elaborated further the concept of universal values underlying all discourse. Within his own fields of anthropology and philosophy, however, Lévi-Strauss' findings were not equally valued. American anthropologists criticized his lack of ethnographic fieldwork and accused him of amateurism. As a philosopher he was not taken seriously, either quarrelling publicly with Sartre, whose *Critique de la raison dialectique* (1960) he contested in *La Pensée sauvage* [The Savage Mind]. The argument between the two was never totally settled. It is certainly true that Lévi-Strauss' philosophico-anthropological formation was unusual. But it is equally undeniable that his abstract findings based on structural-linguistic analysis have contributed significantly to modern thought. Recent years have seen a resurgence of interest in Lévi-Strauss' work. By stressing the complexity of non-Western cultures, his writings serve to challenge the traditional notion of 'the primitive'. At the same time, his belief in universal mythic structures would suggest a common humanity underlying all cultures.

Further reading

Deliège, Robert, *Lévi-Strauss today: an introduction to structural anthropology*, translated from French by Nora Scott (Oxford, UK: Berg, 2004).

Leach, Edmund, *Lévi-Strauss* (Chicago: University of Chicago Press, 1989).

Levi-Strauss, Claude, *Structural Anthropology*, transl. C. Jacobson and G. Grundfest Schoepf (London: Allen Lane, 1968).

Maurice Merleau-Ponty

1908–61

Born in Rochefort-sur-Mer, France, in 1908, Maurice Merleau-Ponty was a leading French philosopher and proponent of existential phenomenology. In 1930 he was awarded the *aggrégation* in philosophy at the Ecole Normale Supérieure, where he returned as a junior lecturer in 1936. During this period he came under the influence of the thought of Husserl as well as that of Hegel and Marx. In 1945 his major work *Phénoménologie de la perception* [Phenomenology of Perception] was published and in 1952 he became the youngest candidate ever to be elected to the Chair of Philosophy at the Collège de France, a position he held until his death in 1961. From 1945 until 1952 he collaborated with his friend Jean-Paul Sartre in the creation of the influential magazine, *Les Temps modernes*, but following a disagreement he resigned from the editorial board in 1952.

In the late 1940s and 1950s Merleau-Ponty came under the influence of Ferdinand de Saussure and was one of the first to bring structuralism and linguistics into a relationship with phenomenology. His concept of human subjectivity as ambiguous marks the beginning of the 'decentring' of the subject in structuralist and poststructuralist thought. His reflections on language and metaphysics were contained in two unfinished texts *Le Visible et l'invisible* [The Visible and the Invisible] and *La Prose du monde* [The Prose of the World] which were published posthumously, in 1964 and 1967 respectively.

In his seminal work *Phénoménologie de la perception*, Merleau-Ponty sets out his interpretation of the phenomenological method. Drawing heavily on the thought of Husserl, he presents phenomenology as a philosophy concerned with 'lived experience', that is, with describing the world as we experience it rather than constructing theories to explain it. By 'lived experience' is meant not the world of the inner self or consciousness but the 'life-world', the pre-scientific and pre-philosophical fully external world in which we act and have our being:

> It [phenomenology] tries to give a direct description of our experience as it is, without taking account of its psychological origin and the causal explanations which the scientist, the historian or the sociologist may be able to provide.

> Truth does not 'inhabit' only 'the inner man', or more accurately, there is no inner man, man is in the world, and only in the world does he know himself.

Merleau-Ponty thus calls into question the fundamental dualism underlying classical philosophy and the idealist concept of language. The stark oppositions body and mind, subject and object, self and world are thereby undermined. For Merleau-Ponty humans are essentially physical beings, 'beings in the world', the self is embodied, a 'body-subject'. All the so-called higher functions of consciousness such as thought or the intellect are anchored in and depend on the subject's pre-reflexive bodily existence, that is, perception. The relationship of the self to the world manifests itself in a dynamic two-way process termed 'aperception'. Through the activity of perception we give meaning to the world and are in turn constructed by it: it is a dynamic intertwining involving proximity and distance, absorption and separation.

The focus on the body and the privileging of perception or sensory experience over rational conceptual thought leads Merleau-Ponty in *Phénoménologie de la perception* to examine the sensory properties of the world, namely colour, taste, sound, odour and touch. He is interested in painting and in the use of colour and writes extensively on Cézanne, whose works epitomize the pre-scientific perception of the natural world. At the same time, colour itself is seen as a prime example of the human subject's 'mingling with the world'. These reflections on painting were further developed in his essay 'Eye and Mind' (1960) and in his book *Le Visible et l'invisible.* They have subsequently made a strong impact on literary studies, where his theories of colour have been applied to the works of contemporary poets such as Yves Bonnefoy and Phillippe Jaccottet.

Merleau-Ponty's thought has played an important role in the emergence of semiotics in France. His rejection of classic idealism and of the separation of body and mind lies at the core of the semiotic enterprise. For Merleau-Ponty, as for the semiotician, meaning is essentially a human construct and relative to the position of the observer. In addition his concept that original differences are perceptual and hence pre-linguistic was to be later developed by the Paris School. Indeed a resurgence of interest in Merleau-Ponty in the 1980s and 1990s contributed to a move away from narrative towards a concentration on the figurative and on the role of the subject and of perception in the construction of meaning. Attention was paid to the position of the observer in the text and a semiotics of the visible was developed. Key contributions were made in this area by Denis Bertrand, Jacques Fontanille and Claude Zilberberg. In a seminal text published in1997, *La Quête du sens* [The Quest for Meaning], the semiotician Jean-Claude Coquet analyses the contribution of Merleau-Ponty to this change in emphasis.

From the late 1980s onwards research has widened to embrace the senses of touch, taste and smell. This interest in pre-cognitive states has also led to an exploration of the concept of beauty and the aesthetic. For instance, Merleau-Ponty's reflections on synaesthesia have been further developed inspiring new readings of Proust. Since the 1980s and 1990s, therefore, semioticians have been less concerned with structure as an end-product or with fixed meaning. The emphasis is now on the *discours en acte* or the process whereby meaning emerges from the senses. In other words, contemporary semiotics draws attention to the interaction between *le sensible* (sensory experience) and *l'intelligible* (meaning). A number of new semiotic concepts have been developed which owe much to the writings of Merleau-Ponty. Foremost amongst these is the notion of *presence*, an examination of physical properties in terms of intensity and spatial volume/shape and time. These concepts have enriched the study of literature – of the texts of Céline and Maupassant, for example – and of the visual arts. The writings of Merleau-Ponty will undoubtedly remain a source of inspiration for semioticians for years to come.

Further reading

Gutting, Gary, *French Philosophy in the Twentieth Century* (Cambridge: Cambridge University Press, 2001).

Langer, Monika M., *Merleau-Ponty's Phenomenology of Perception: A Guide and Commentary* (Basingstoke: Macmillan, 1989).

Matthews, Eric, *The Philosophy of Merleau-Ponty* (Chesham: Acumen, 2002).

Schmidt, James, *Maurice Merleau-Ponty: Between Phenomenology and Structuralism* (Basingstoke: Macmillan, 1985).

Charles Sanders Peirce

1839–1914

Born in 1839 in Cambridge, Massachusetts, Charles Sanders Peirce was an expert in many fields of science and a philosopher of international fame best known for his work on pragmatism (which he later named pragmaticism). For 31 years of his life he worked as a research scientist for the US Coast and Geodetic Survey. Although he lectured in logic and the philosophy of science for brief periods of time, he elaborated his theories in isolation, outside the academic community. Of prime concern to Peirce was the development of universal sign categories, and his production of a theory of signs marked the foundation of an American branch of modern semiotics. His approach, however, differed considerably from that of the European branch of semiotics represented by the *Ecole de Paris* [Paris School], and the linguistic tradition of Saussure and Hjelmslev. In the history of semiotics, Peirce's work has constituted a branch focusing on logic and meaning whereas the Paris School has been concerned with the text and signifying practices in general. In recent years the two positions have merged.

Peirce believed the whole universe to be made up of signs. Even thoughts are signs because they refer to other thoughts and he concluded that 'the fact that every thought is a sign, taken in conjunction with the fact that life is a train of thought, proves that man is a sign'. In this pansemiotic view of the universe, it follows that semiotics, the theory and study of signs, is a universal science comprising all other sciences. Peirce's philosophical approach to semiotics is grounded in a system of three universal categories: *firstness*, that is the mode of being without reference to anything else, such as unreflected feeling, mere potentiality or undifferentiated quality; *secondness* which involves the relation of a first to a second, that is the category of comparison, factualness, action, experience of time and space; and *thirdness* which brings the second category into relation with a third. Thirdness is the category of mediation, memory, habit, continuity, representation and signs. Peirce then defines the sign in relation to all three categories, placing it in a triadic process, called semiosis:

> A sign, or *representamen*, is something which stands to somebody for something in some respect or capacity. It addresses somebody, that is, creates in the mind of that person an equivalent sign, or perhaps a more

> developed sign. That sign which it creates I call the *interpretant* of the first sign. The sign stands for something, its *object*. It stands for that object, not in all repects, but in reference to a sort of idea. (*Collected Papers*, § 2.228, 1931–58)

Representamen in this definition is the perceptible object functioning as a sign and corresponds to Saussure's signifier. Peirce's *object* equals the referent of other models while his *interpretant* denotes the meaning of a sign. Some critics believe that Peirce's definition of the sign contains more than three basic elements. Jacques Fontanille (1998) discovers a fourth element in the final part of the definition: 'not in all respects, but in reference to a sort of idea', which he names *fondement* [foundation]. Umberto Eco brings the number of elements even to six, adding dynamic and immediate object either chosen by the *interpretant* or put in perspective by the *fondement*.

Peirce also developed different ways of classifying signs according to his universal categories. The best known of these is the classification according to the relation between the *representamen* and the object. This led to the division of the sign into icon, index and symbol. In Peirce's understanding, an icon is a sign that resembles the object it signifies, such as a portrait for example. It is a 'qualisign', that is, a quality that is a sign but which cannot actually act as a sign until it is embodied. An icon thus belongs to the category of *firstness*. An index (belonging to the category of *secondness*) is a sign that is physically related to, or affected by, its object. The relationship may be causal or sequential. Peirce gives the examples of a weathercock, a barometer and a sundial. A symbol (*thirdness*), on the other hand, denotes a sign whose relationship to its object is entirely arbitrary or based on convention. An example would be the word 'car', where there is no causal physical link or resemblance between the sign (the word car) and the actual object.

Peirce's interest in the sign focused in particular on a theory of method: how is the sign arranged; how does it function? As far as the application of the Peircean typology of signs to the study of texts is concerned, it has turned out to be rather limiting. Mere classification cannot be exhaustive where, for example, literary texts are concerned. On the other hand, texts themselves are signs classifiable according to their function. Any text is a symbol because it consists of arbitrary signs; it is indexical when its main object is to instruct or to question, or when it creates textual reference to reality as we know it; finally textual iconicity manifests itself in images, diagrams, metaphors, etc.

Peirce died in 1914. He did not publish much during his lifetime. Most of his writings appeared posthumously – an anthology entitled *Chance, Love and Logic*, edited by M. R. Cohen, in 1923, and his collected papers in eight volumes between 1931 and 1958. After his death, his semiotic theories were predominantly pursued in America by, among others, Charles Morris. The European branch of semiotics, on the other hand, heavily influenced by structuralist linguistics and focusing on textual analyses, at first distanced itself from Peirce's philosophical theories, so much so that semioticians in general tended to follow either the European or the Peircean school of thought. Today things have changed. Researchers make use of both the Greimassian and the Peircean theoretical apparatus, not in order to differentiate between the two theories, but with the common aim of exploring the problems of signification. The recently developed elementary tensive model, for example, coincides to a large extent with Peirce's theories.

Further reading

Hoopes, James (ed.), *Peirce on Signs: Writings on Semiotic, by Charles Sanders Peirce* (Chapel Hill: University of North Carolina Press, 1991).

Kevelson, Roberta, *Peirce and the Mark of the Gryphon* (Basingstoke: Macmillan, 1999).

Peirce, C. S., *The Essential Peirce: Selected Philosophical Writings*, vol. 1, eds N. Hauser and C. Kloesel (Bloomington: Indiana University Press, 1992).

Peirce, C. S., *The Essential Peirce: Selected Philosophical Writings*, vol. 2, ed. Peirce Edition Project (Bloomington: Indiana University Press, 1998).

Vladimir Propp

1895–1970

The Russian folklorist and critical theorist Vladimir Propp was born in 1895 in St Petersburg to a family of German descent. After graduating at the University of St Petersburg in 1918, he started teaching Russian and German at secondary school. In 1932 he was called to Leningrad University where he worked until his death. There is early evidence of Propp's interest in folklore. He began researching the 'wondertale' as a genre in the 1920s and in 1928 published his first book, *Morphology of the Folktale*, the work that would eventually make him famous. All his subsequent writings testify to his continued preoccupation with the formation, structure and historical typology of folk narrative. There is no doubt that Propp's work was a theoretical breakthrough and that it exerted a strong influence on structuralism and semiotics.

When Propp set out to write his morphology, he did not see his method of analysis as an end in itself. His overall intention was to compose a work about the history and genesis of Russian folklore. To undertake a diachronic study, however, he believed he needed first to examine the narrative invariants or constant elements synchronically in order to determine the specificity of the genre. Historical research would then provide an explanation for its uniform character. One hundred Russian fairy-tales or 'wondertales' taken from the Afanas'ev collection served as the corpus for analysis. He rejected the 'motif' as the basis for classification, considering it too restrictive a narrative unit. Instead he divided the text into segments according to the most important actions that make up the story. Each segment was condensed into a short sentence, such as 'An interdiction is addressed to the hero', 'The interdiction is violated' or 'The villain is punished'. These narrative units, or types of actions, Propp called *functions* to denote their significance for the progress of the narrative. He discovered 31 such functions which together describe the structure of the Russian wondertale. No tale included all of them but those he found would always follow one another syntagmatically in strict logical order. Propp also found that the functions were distributed among a fixed set of seven character roles, those of villain, donor (provider), helper, princess (sought after person) and her father, dispatcher, hero (seeker or victim), and false hero. These he named spheres of action. By establishing in this way an abstract predicate/

action and subject structure to the folk-tale, Propp had set up what he called the grammar of the folk-tale, albeit relevant only to the subgenre he had analysed.

There were two ways in which the influence of Propp's morphological study manifested itself: as a stimulating example for practical application and as a stimulus to critical discussion of its epistemological foundations. One of the first to realize the significance of Propp's work and apply its principles to other texts was Alan Dundes, who made Propp famous in the United States. In France, on the other hand, the recent development of structural linguistics and semiotics made Propp's scientific discoveries highly attractive to structuralist thinkers and semioticians. By reworking them, criticizing, and adapting them to their particular aims, however, they also tended to modify and reduce their original importance. Claude Lévi-Strauss in his review (1960) reproached Propp with having analysed only the form of the tale and not what he called its 'raw content'. Having in his own study defined myth in bundles of relationships, he found fault with the exclusively linear arrangement of Propp's narrative functions and tried to translate the compositional invariants of the folk-tale into achronic signifying elements. Basically, Lévi-Strauss was looking for universally applicable paradigmatic models while Propp had been concerned with the syntagmatic pattern of a particular genre.

The semiotician A. J. Greimas also attempted to extract universally valid models by streamlining Propp's theory. In his book *Sémantique structurale* [Structural Semantics] he presents a general narrative grammar largely elaborated from Propp's theoretical principles. He simplified the seven spheres of action to produce his own actantial narrative schema based on three sets of binary oppositions: subject/object, sender/receiver, helper/opponent. These six key narrative functions (actantial roles) together account for all possible relationships within a story. His canonical narrative schema, based on Propp's 31 functions, complements this actantial model by describing the logical stages of action in narrative. This schema comprises three tests (acquiring competence, the decisive contest and the final stage of reward or punishment) preceded by a contract. Other eminent French structuralists (Roland Barthes, Claude Bremond, Tzvetan Todorov) followed his example. Looking for universal structures, they adapted Propp's findings and incorporated them into semiotic models applicable to all narrative. German scholars, on the other hand, Karl Eimermacher (1972) among them, saw in Propp's typology potential progress for a general theory of genre definition relevant to all literary works.

Propp died in 1970. Throughout most of his writing career, he was plagued by the political situation in Russia. He suffered from being associated with the Formalists although he did not belong to their circle, and was harassed because he was German. The publication of his second major book, *Historical Roots of the Wondertale*, completed in 1939, was delayed until 1946. The eventual breaking of the political frost coincided with the publication of the English translation of *Morphology of the Folktale* (1958). It brought him belated international fame. Propp's genius lies in recognizing the importance of invariant structure for the definition of genre and in devising a method of analysing just one such structure. His limitations lie precisely in the restriction of his method to the needs of one subgenre which he then examines in isolation, that is, excluding social context or cultural conditions. But then, that was not his primary concern. Propp was a folklorist with a lifelong interest in history and typology. However, the field of application of his theoretical principles has lately been widened to include the areas of media and theatre amongst others.

Further reading

Greimas, Algirdas Julien, *Sémantique structurale*, 1966 [Structural Semantics, 1976; Lincoln and London: Nebraska University Press, 1983].

Lévi-Strauss, Claude, 'La structure et la forme. Réflexions sur un ouvrage de Vladimir Propp' [Structure and Form: Reflections on a Work by Vladimir Propp] (*Cahiers de l'Institut de science économique appliquée*, 1960).

Maranda, Pierre (ed.), *Soviet Structural Folklorists* (The Hague: Mouton, 1974).

Propp, Vladimir, *Morphology of the Folktale* (Austin: University of Texas Press, 1968).

Ferdinand de Saussure

1857–1913

Born in 1857 in Geneva, Saussure is rightly considered the founder of modern linguistics. Having studied physics and chemistry as well as linguistics, he taught at the universities of Leipzig and Paris before taking up a university chair specially created for him (Sanskrit and Indian-European languages) at Geneva University, where he stayed for the rest of his life. Saussure is said to have been an austere scholar, totally devoted to intellectual research. It is true that the influence of his work is widely regarded as seminal not only with regard to the study of language but also in its effect on French thought in general. In fact it was his scientific approach that brought about the development of the intellectual movement known as French structuralism. His theory of language introduced a sign model to describe the nature of the linguistic sign; and, finally, relating his science to other social sign systems, it was Saussure who outlined a project supposed to link linguistics to social psychology which he termed *sémiologie* [semiology] and which eventually led to modern semiotics. Saussure published little during his lifetime. His major work, the *Cours de linguistique générale* [Course in General Linguistics], 1916, was compiled posthumously from notes taken by students during his lectures (1907–1911).

Saussure's great contribution to the study of language was that meaning does not reside in individual words but in a complex system of relationships or structures. His motto was *Il n'y a de sens que dans la différence* [There can be no meaning without difference]. He pointed out that language structures could be explored by describing them in their current form as well as in a historical perspective. His most revolutionary discoveries, however, relate to applying the structure principle to the individual sign or word and to language as a sign system.

A word, according to Saussure, is not a symbol corresponding to an object, i.e. its referent. It is in fact a sign made up of two components: the 'sound-image' or material substance which he named *signifiant* [signifier] and its 'concept' or *signifié* [signified]. Things themselves therefore play no part in Saussure's language system. Signifier and signified represent the two fundamental levels of language. The first term, signifier, refers principally to the concrete sensorial world while the second term, signified, relates to the idea or concept expressed by the sound or icon. The relationship between the two sides of the sign has been described by Saussure as comparable to that between the front and the back of a piece of paper. In other words, the two levels of language are in a relationship of presupposition: form and content cannot be disassociated, their indissoluble unity being a precondition for the possibility of language itself. Moreover, according to his theory, the relations between signified and signifier are governed by two principles: the linguistic sign is *arbitrary* and it is *linear.* The relationship is arbitrary in that it is not motivated or governed by any outside constraint; and the sign is *linear* because its temporal and spatial characteristics present it as a line just as sentences form syntagmatic sequences with signs preceding and following each other. The whole approach to structural linguistics depends on these properties. Finally, the relationship between signifier and signified is entirely defined by the 'value' of the sign, that is to say by the different oppositions which its signifier and signified entertain with other signifiers and signifieds within the same language, both in a synchronic context where this value is unchanging, and in a diachronic perspective testifying to the evolution of language, in the course of which the link between the two may totally change.

Another major contribution to linguistic study is Saussure's theory of language as a signifying whole which he divided into *langue* (abstract language system, language as a structured system of signs) and *parole* (the individual utterance, speech or text, making use of the abstract system). He developed this idea further by introducing the dichotomy synchrony/diachrony for the description of language in a historical perspective (dealing with the transformation of language over a period of time) and a synchronic perspective (analysis of the language system at a given point in time, irrespective of its history).

Saussure's interest, however, did not stop with structural linguistics. He saw language as a social institution with signs expressing ideas. It therefore included other forms of sign systems, such as written signs or the sign language for the deaf or forms of politeness, symbolic rites, etc. He thus envisaged a more general science of signs which he called semiology and which would study the role of signs as part of social life. The precise purpose of this science was to investigate the nature of signs and the laws governing them. Saussure saw semiology as a branch of sociology and psychology; however, within it a special role was to be assigned to linguistics. For, according to Saussure, the laws of linguistics will be applicable to all sign systems. Nonetheless, Saussure did not consider semiology a general science to be applied to all sign systems. He seems to have excluded involuntary, 'natural' signs (storm clouds, blushing) or those deliberately controlled by the decisions of individuals. Rather, his interest focused on those public institutional signs where the relationship between signifier and signified was arbitrary.

After Saussure's death in 1913, the importance of his scientific discoveries did not become immediately apparent despite the publication of his *Cours de linguistique générale* in 1916. In fact, it took until the mid-1940s and the efforts of Claude Lévi-Strauss for Saussure's theories to be accepted as pioneering ideas in all the social sciences. His fame grew with the establishment of structuralism and there is no doubt that his findings have had a major influence on the development of European semiotics. In particular, Saussure's structuralist definition of verbal signs and sign systems has impacted on semiotic thought as well as the idea of linguistics as a blueprint for semiotic exploration. Nonetheless, whilst paying tribute to Saussure's contribution to the theory of meaning, the Greimassian School distinguishes clearly between the study of sign-systems (semiology) and the study of the process of the generation of meaning (semiotics).

Further reading

Culler, Jonathan, *Ferdinand de Saussure* (Ithaca, NY: Cornell University Press, 1986).

Harris, Roy, *Reading Saussure* (London: Duckworth, 1987).

Mounin, George, *Saussure ou le structuraliste sans le savoir* (Paris: Seghers, 1968).

Saussure, Ferdinand de, *Course in General Linguistics*, transl. R. Harris (London: Duckworth, 1983).

Key Texts in Semiotics

Arrivé, Michel and Coquet, Jean-Claude, *Sémiotique en jeu. A partir et autour de l'œuvre d'A. J. Greimas* (Paris/Amsterdam: Hadès-Benjamins, 1987).

Barthes, Roland, *Mythologies*, transl. Annette Lavers (St Albans: Paladin, 1973).

Barthes, Roland, *Camera Lucida: Reflections on Photography*, transl. Richard Howard (London: Vintage, 1993).

Bertin, Eric, 'Image et stratégie: la sémiotique au service des fabricants de sens', in Anne Hénault (dir.), *Questions de sémiotique* (Paris: Presses Universitaires de France, 2002), pp. 171–98.

Bertrand, Denis, *L'Espace et le sens. Germinal d'Emile Zola* (Paris/Amsterdam: Hadès-Benjamins, 1985).

Bertrand, Denis, 'Le Corps émouvant. L'absence. Proposition pour une sémiotique de l'émotion', *La Chouette* (Birkbeck College), 20 (1988), 46–54.

Bertrand, Denis, *Narrativity and Discursivity*, Paris School of Semiotics, vol.1, transl. P. Perron and F. Collins (Amsterdam/Philadelphia: Benjamins, 1989).

Bertrand, Denis, *Précis de sémiotique littéraire* (Paris: Nathan, 2000).

Bordron, Jean-François, 'Perception et énonciation dans l'expérience gustative. L'exemple de la dégustation du vin', in Anne Hénault (dir.), *Questions de sémiotique* (Paris: Presses Universitaires de France, 2002), pp. 640–65.

Broden, Thomas F., 'A. J. Greimas: Commemorative Essay', in *Semiotica* 105–3/4 (1995), 207–42.

Chomsky, Noam, *New Horizons in the Study of Language and Mind* (Cambridge: Cambridge University Press, 2000).

Cook, Guy, *The Discourse of Advertising* (London: Routledge, 1992).

Coquet, Jean-Claude, *Le Discours et son sujet*, vol I, *Essai de grammaire modale* (Paris: Klincksieck, 1984).

Coquet, Jean-Claude, *Le Discours et son sujet*, vol II, *Pratique de la grammaire modale* (Paris: Klincksieck, 1985).

Coquet, Jean-Claude, *La Quête du sens: le langage en question* (Paris: Presses Universitaires de France, 1997).

Costantini, Michel and Darrault-Harris, Ivan (eds), *Sémiotique, phénoménologie, discours: Du corps présent au sujet énonçant* (Paris: L'Harmattan, 1999).

Courtés, Joseph, *Introduction à la sémiotique narrative et discursive* (Paris: Hachette, 1976).

Courtés, Joseph, *Sémantique de l'énoncé: applications pratiques* (Paris: Hachette, 1989).

Courtés, Joseph, *Analyse sémiotique du discours: de l'énoncé à l'énonciation* (Paris: Hachette, 1991).

Courtés, Joseph, *Du lisible au visible* (Brussels: De Boeck Université, 1995).

Darrault-Harris, Ivan, 'L'éthosémiotique, la psychosémiotique', in Anne Hénault (dir.), *Questions de sémiotique* (Paris: Presses Universitaires de France, 2002), pp. 299–425.

Eco, Umberto, *The Role of the Reader: Explorations in the Semiotics of Texts* (London: Hutchinson, 1981).

Eco, Umberto, *Mouse or Rat: Translation as Negotiation* (London: Weidenfeld & Nicolson, 2003).

Everaert-Desmedt, Nicole, *Sémiotique du récit* (Bruxelles: De Boeck-Wesmael, 1989).

Fairclough, Norman, *Language and Power* (London: Longman, 1989).

Fanon, Frantz, *The Wretched of the Earth*, transl. Constance Farrington (Harmondsworth: Penguin, 1967).

Fanon, Frantz, *Black Skin, White Masks*, transl. Charles Lam Markmann (London: Pluto, 1986).

Floch, Jean-Marie, *Petites Mythologies de l'æil et de l'esprit. Pour une sémiotique plastique* (Paris/Amsterdam: Hadès-Benjamins, 1985).

Floch, Jean-Marie, *Sémiotique, marketing et communication* (Paris: Presses Universitaires de France, 1990).

Floch, Jean-Marie, *Identités visuelles* (Paris: Presses Universitaires de France, 1995).

Floch, Jean-Marie, *Une Lecture de Tintin au Tibet* (Paris: Presses Universitaires de France, 1997).

Fontanille, Jacques, *Le Savoir partagé* (Paris/Amsterdam: Hadès-Benjamins, 1987).

Fontanille, Jacques, *Les Espaces subjectifs* (Paris: Hachette, 1989).

Fontanille, Jacques, *Sémiotique du visible* (Paris: Presses Universitaires de France, 1995).

Fontanille, Jacques, *Sémiotique du discours* (Limoges: Presses Universitaires de Limoges, 1998).

Fontanille, Jacques, *Sémiotique et littérature: essais de méthode* (Paris: Presses Universitaires de France, 1999).

Fontanille, Jacques, 'Modes du sensible et syntaxe figurative', *Nouveaux Actes sémiotiques* 61–62–63, (1999).

Fontanille, Jacques and Zilberberg, Claude, *Tension et signification* (Liège: Mardaga, 1998).

Fowler, Roger, *Language in the News: Discourse and Ideology in the Press* (London: Routledge, 1991).

Genette, Gérard, *Figures II* (Paris: Seuil, 1969).
Genette, Gérard, *Palimpsestes* (Paris: Seuil, 1982).
Genette, Gérard, *Seuils* (Paris: Seuil, 1987).
Geninasca, Jacques, *La Parole littéraire* (Paris: Presses Universitaires de France, 1997).
Greimas, Algirdas J., *Sémantique structurale* (Paris: Larousse, 1966).
Greimas, Algirdas J., *Du Sens: Essais sémiotiques* (Paris: Seuil, 1970).
Greimas, Algirdas J., *Maupassant, la sémiotique du texte: exercices pratiques* (Paris: Seuil, 1976).
Greimas, Algirdas J., *Sémiotique et sciences sociales* (Paris: Seuil, 1976).
Greimas, Algirdas J., *Du Sens II: Essais sémiotiques* (Paris: Seuil, 1983).
Greimas, Algirdas J., *De l'imperfection* (Périgueux: Fanlac, 1987).
Greimas, Algirdas J., 'On Meaning', *New Literary History*, 20 (1989), 539–50.
Greimas, Algirdas J. and Courtés, Joseph, *Sémiotique, dictionnaire raisonné de la théorie du langage*, 2 vols (Paris: Hachette, 1979 and 1986).
Greimas, Algirdas J. and Fontanille, Jacques, *Sémiotique des passions: des états de choses aux états d'âme* (Paris: Seuil, 1991).
Greimas, Algirdas J. and Landowski, Eric, *Sémiotique et sciences sociales* (Paris: Seuil, 1976).
Grivel, Charles, *Production de l'interêt romanesque* (The Hague-Paris: Mouton, 1973).
Halliday, Michael and Hasan, Ruqaiaya, *Cohesion in English* (London: Longman, 1976).
Hallward, Peter, *Absolutely Postcolonial: Writing between the Singular and the Specific* (Manchester: Manchester University Press, 2001).
Hammad, Manar, 'L'architecture du thé', *Actes sémiotiques*, IX (1987).
Hamon, Philippe, *Introduction à l'analyse du descriptif* (Paris: Hachette, 1981).
Hamon, Philippe, 'Un discours contraint', in *Littérature et réalité*, eds Gérard Genette and Tzvetan Todorov (Paris: Seuil, 1982).
Hatten, Robert S., 'Théorie de la musique et sémiotique générale: une intéraction créative', in Anne Hénault (dir.), *Questions de sémiotique* (Paris: Presses Universitaires de France, 2002), pp. 563–83.
Hawkes, Terence, *Structuralism and Semiotics* (London: Methuen, 1977).
Hénault, Anne, *Les Enjeux de la sémiotique* (Paris: Presses Universitaires de France, 1979).
Hénault, Anne, *Narratologie, sémiotique générale: les enjeux de la sémiotique 2* (Paris: Presses Universitaires de France, 1983).
Hénault, Anne, *Histoire de la sémiotique* (Paris: Presses Universitaires de France, 1992).
Hénault, Anne, *Le Pouvoir comme passion* (Paris: Presses Universitaires de France, 1995).

Hénault, Anne (dir.), *Questions de sémiotique* (Paris: Presses Universitaires de France, 2002).

Hénault, Anne and Beyaert, Anne (dir.), *Ateliers de sémiotique visuelle* (Paris: Presses Universitaires de France, 2004).

Hodge, Robert and Kress, Günther, *Language as Ideology* (London: Routledge, 1979).

Hodge, Robert and Kress, Günther, *Social Semiotics* (Cambridge: Polity Press, 1988).

'Hommages à A. J. Greimas', *Nouveaux Actes sémiotiques*, 25 (1993).

Jakobson, Roman, *Fundamentals of Language* (The Hague-Paris: Mouton, 1975).

Jakobson, Roman, *Language in Literature*, eds K. Pomorska and S. Rudy (Cambridge, MA: Belknap Press, 1987).

Kristeva, Julia, *La Révolution du langage politique* (Paris: Seuil, 1974).

Kristeva, Julia, *Le Temps sensible: Proust et l'expérience littéraire* (Paris: Gallimard, 1994).

Kristeva, Julia, *La Révolte intime: discours direct* (Paris: Fayard, 2000).

Landowski, Eric, *La Société réfléchie: Essais de socio-sémiotique* (Paris: Seuil, 1989).

Landowski, Eric, 'Pour une problématique socio-sémiotique de la littérature', in *La Littérature*, eds Louise Milot and Fernand Roy (Sainte-Foy: Presses de l'Université de Laval, 1991), pp. 95–119.

Landowski, Eric (ed.), *Lire Greimas* (Limoges: Presses Universitaires de Limoges, 1997).

Landowski, Eric, *Présences de l'autre. Essais de socio-sémiotique II* (Paris: Presses Universitaires de France, 1997).

Landowski, Eric, 'Sémiotique gourmande. Du goût entre esthésie et socialité', *Nouveaux Actes sémiotiques*, 55–56 (1998).

Landowski, Eric, *Passions sans nom. Essais de socio-sémiotique III* (Paris: Presses Universitaires de France, 2004).

Larsen, Erik, 'Sémiotique urbaine, Prospect Park à Brooklyn', in Anne Hénault (dir.), *Questions de sémiotique* (Paris: Presses Universitaires de France, 2002), pp. 441–66.

Lévi-Strauss, Claude, *Structural Anthropology*, transl. C. Jacobson and G. Grundfest Schoepf (London: Allen Lane, 1968).

Lyotard, Jean-François, *The Postmodern Condition: A Report on Knowledge*, transl. Geoffrey Bennington and Brian Massumi (Minneapolis: University of Minnesota Press, 1984).

Martin, Bronwen, *The Search for Gold: Space and Meaning in J. M. G. Le Clézio* (Dublin: Philomel Productions, 1995).

Martin, Bronwen, 'Introduction to Semiotic Analysis', *La Chouette* (Birkbeck College), 27 (1996), 7–18.

Martin, Bronwen, *Semiotics and Storytelling* (Dublin: Philomel Productions, 1997).

Martin, Bronwen, 'Spatial Figurativity in Marguerite Duras', in *Marguerite Duras: lectures plurielles*, eds C. Rodgers and R. Udris (Amsterdam: Rodopi, 1998).

Martin, Bronwen and Ringham, Felizitas (eds), *Sense and Scent: An Exploration of Olfactory Meaning* (Dublin: Philomel Productions, 2003).

Merleau-Ponty, Maurice, *Phenomenology of Perception*, transl. Colin Smith (London: Routledge, 1962).

Parret, Herman, *Le Sublime du quotidien* (Paris/Amsterdam/Philadelphia: Hadès-Benjamins, 1998).

Perron, P. and Collins, F. (eds), *Paris School Semiotics*, 2 vols (Amsterdam-Philadelphia: Benjamins, 1988).

Propp, Vladimir, *Morphology of the Folktale* (Austin: University of Texas Press, 1968).

Ringham, Felizitas, *Reader-Related Truth: A Semiotics of Genre and Paratext in Early Eighteenth Century Prose Fiction in France* (doctoral thesis, University of London, 1994).

Ringham, Felizitas, 'Seduction and Commitment in the Paratext', *La Chouette* (Birkbeck College), 27 (1996), 29–39.

Ringham, Felizitas, 'Riquet à la houppe: conteur, conteuse', *French Studies*, vol. 52 No. 3 (July 1998), 291–302.

Ringham, Felizitas, 'Le corps textuel: forme ou substance?', *La Chouette* (Birkbeck College), 29 (1998), 9–14.

Saint-Martin, Fernande, 'A case of intersemiotics: The reception of a visual advertisement', *Semiotica*, 91 (1–2), 1992, 79–92.

Saint-Martin, Fernande (dir.), 'Approches sémiotiques sur Rothko', *Nouveaux Actes sémiotiques*, 34–35–36 (1994).

Saussure, Ferdinand de, *Course in General Linguistics*, transl. R. Harris (London: Duckworth, 1983).

Scholes, Robert, *Structuralism in Literature: An Introduction* (New Haven and London: Yale University Press, 1974).

Sebeok, Thomas A., *The Sign and Its Masters* (Austin: University of Texas Press, 1979).

Sebeok, Thomas A., *Essays in Zoosemiotics* (Toronto: Toronto Semiotic Circle, 1990).

Sebeok, Thomas A., *Signs: An Introduction to Semiotics* (Toronto: University of Toronto Press, 1994).

Sebeok, Thomas A. and Umiker-Sebeok, J. (eds), *Biosemiotics* (Berlin: Mouton de Gruyter, 1991).

Urbain, Jean-Didier, 'Idéologues et polylogues: Pour une sémiotique de l'énonciation', *Nouveaux Actes sémiotiques*, 14 (1991), 1–51.

Zilberberg, Claude, *Raison et poétique du sens* (Paris: Presses Universitaires de France, 1988).

Appendix

A Semiotic Analysis of *Sleeping Beauty*[1]

There once lived a King and Queen who were very unhappy because they had no children. They had been married a long time and had almost given up hope when, to the Queen's great joy, she found she was going to have a baby.

Not long after the baby, a beautiful daughter, was born, the King and Queen arranged a huge Christening party. All the fairies in the kingdom were invited, for the King and Queen knew that they would each give a wonderful gift to the new princess. All that is, except one, whom nobody liked because she was so bad-tempered.

After a magnificent feast, the fairies began to offer their gifts. The first fairy gave the gift of Beauty, the second gave Happiness, the others gave Goodness, Health, Gracefulness and Kindness. The seventh fairy was just stepping forward when the door burst open. In rushed the bad-tempered fairy, furious that she had not been invited to the Christening. Everyone shrank back as she rushed up to the cradle.

'On your sixteenth birthday you will prick your finger with a spindle and die,' she hissed spitefully at the baby princess, before disappearing in a puff of smoke. Everyone shivered with horror, but at that moment the seventh fairy, who was also the youngest, stepped forward.

'Take heart,' she said to the King and Queen. 'Your daughter will not die. My magic isn't strong enough to break the wicked spell but I can weaken the evil. Instead of dying, the princess will fall asleep for a hundred years.'

The King, hoping to save his daughter, immediately ordered every spinning wheel and spindle in the land to be burned.

For fifteen years, everything went well. The princess grew into the most beautiful, the kindest, the most graceful child anyone had ever seen.

At last, the day of her sixteenth birthday arrived. The King and Queen held a magnificent party for her in their castle. They thought that this would stop her from finding a spindle on that day and so protect her from the wicked fairy's curse. After the feast, the princess asked if they could all play hide-and-seek.

When it was her turn to hide, the princess ran to the far corner of the castle and found a small doorway she had never seen before. She climbed a spiral staircase to a high tower thinking that this would be a wonderful place to hide. When she reached the top, she found a little room. Inside was an old woman sitting at a spinning wheel.

'What are you doing?' asked the princess, fascinated by the twirling wheel and the whirling spindle, for, of course, she had never seen anything like it.

'I am spinning,' replied the old lady cunningly, for she was the wicked fairy in disguise. 'Would you like to try?'

The princess sat down and took the spindle. No sooner had she picked it up than the point of the spindle pricked her finger. At once she fell to the ground as if she were dead. The wicked fairy's curse had come true.

But the good fairy's spell came true, too, for the princess was not dead, only sleeping. Immediately everyone else in the castle fell asleep as well. The King and Queen nodded off on their thrones. The guests dozed off as they looked for the princess. The cook started snoring in front of her oven. All over the castle, nothing could be heard but the gentle sounds of hundreds of people sleeping.

As the years passed by, a great hedge of thorns grew up around the castle. Nearly everyone forgot about the King and Queen and their beautiful daughter.

But one day, a hundred years later, a young prince rode by and saw the great hedge of thorns. He stopped and asked an old man what was behind it. The old man told the prince about the castle. The prince was excited by the story and, impatient to find out whether it was true, he drew his sword and started to hack at the briars.

To his surprise, the thorns seemed to part in front of him and in a very short time he had reached the castle. He went through the open door and was amazed to see all the people inside fast asleep. Every single thing was covered in dust and there were huge cobwebs hanging from the ceiling. He explored all the rooms in turn and finally climbed a spiral staircase to the top of a high tower. There, in a small room, lying on the floor, was the most beautiful girl he had ever seen. She was so lovely that, without thinking, he leaned forward and kissed her.

Immediately his lips touched hers, the spell was broken and the princess opened her eyes. The first thing she saw was the handsome prince. As the prince and princess gazed at each other, they fell in love on the spot.

The prince led the princess gently down the spiral staircase. All around them they could hear the sound of the castle coming to life. The prince asked the King and Queen for permission to marry their beautiful daughter. They agreed, and soon plans were being made for the wedding.

The seven good fairies were invited to the wedding feast. They wished the princess and her prince a long and happy life together.

As for the wicked fairy, nobody knew what happened to her, but she was never heard of again!

A semiotic analysis of the fairy-tale *Sleeping Beauty*: an example of the Greimassian approach

The semiotic method presented below has been used for several years now in the teaching of literature to university and other students. The approach has yielded outstanding results, proving itself to be particularly effective in the uncovering of the multiplicity of meanings within – and beyond – the text. When applied to opening paragraphs, the method has also provided a means of access to difficult and challenging works (Calvino, Sartre, etc.). The intention of the present authors, however, is not to be prescriptive: semiotic analysis is open-ended and flexible and can be adopted to meet specific requirements. For instance, a student may wish to concentrate on a particular aspect of a novel such as the treatment of place or time. In this case the analysis – especially of the discursive level – will restrict itself to these components and it will not be necessary to list all the figurative isotopies. Similarly, depending on the nature of the text, a student may wish to concentrate more time and energy on one level of meaning (see below) than another. S/he may even feel it necessary to omit a particular methodological device (e.g. the semiotic square) if its application to the text yields little of interest or relevance.

Our semiotic analysis of *Sleeping Beauty*, then, will start with a reminder that, in contrast to more traditional literary approaches, semiotics postulates the existence of different levels of meaning. Any analysis of a story will begin, therefore, with what is known as the discursive level, that is, with an examination of the specific words – grammatical items/structures – that are visible on the surface of the text. It will then proceed through a process of decoding to uncover ever deeper and more abstract layers of meaning until we arrive at what Greimas terms the elementary structure of meaning. For precise details on the models used in the analysis of the different textual levels, please turn to the Introduction (pp. 10–15). We will now begin with an examination of the discursive level and focus in the first place on the figurative component of the text.

The discursive level

The figurative component

Figurative elements are those elements in a text that correspond to the concrete physical world and that can be apprehended by the five senses. They are essential ingredients in the construction of a reality effect or illusion of a real world. In other words, their primary function is to create an impression of time, of place and of character.

Let us begin by exploring the vocabulary of *Sleeping Beauty* and grouping together notations relating to place (including objects), time and actors (characters). These groupings of words with similar meanings (i.e. with at least one meaning in common) are known as lexical fields, or, in more strictly semiotic terms, figurative isotopies. The words 'house', 'shop', 'street', for instance, have the meaning 'city' in common ('city' is the common denominator): we say, therefore, that these lexical items belong to the isotopy of the 'city'.

Figurative isotopies in *Sleeping Beauty*:

Place	Objects
kingdom	gift
land	spindle
cradle	spinning wheel
castle	thrones
door/doorway	oven
place to hide	dust
inside	cobwebs
top	sword
room	every single thing
spiral staircase	thorns
floor	briars
ceiling	
ground	
high tower	

Time

once
a long time
at that moment
sixteenth birthday
for fifteen years
a hundred years
immediately
on that day
after the feast
no sooner
at once
in a very short time
finally
as the years passed
but one day

Actors (characters)

King
Queen
children
baby
daughter
princess
the fairies
seven good fairies
bad-tempered fairy
wicked fairy
seventh fairy
everyone
nobody
guests
cook
hundreds of people
prince
old man
all
all the people
old woman/lady
girl

The following isotopies also contribute to the construction of a reality effect:

States of being

born
will fall asleep
only sleeping
fell asleep
sound of hundreds of people sleeping
opened her eyes
and die
as if she were dead
fast asleep
nodded off
snoring

Social events/celebrations

Christening
feast
party
marry
wedding

Looking back at these lists of figurative isotopies, the reader may be struck by the relatively sparse nature of the references to place and to objects. Indeed, in keeping with the timeless nature of fairy-tales, it is left to the reader's imagination to fill in the descriptive details – appearance of actors, etc. – and to locate the action within a more specific cultural and historical setting.

Having extracted and made lists of the principal isotopies, the next stage in our analysis will be to look for oppositions. These oppositions can be found a) either within the individual isotopies or b) between one isotopy and another.

Oppositions

Place: within this isotopy the following oppositions can be discerned:

1)	**high**	vs	**low**
	high tower		castle
	the top		ground
	ceiling		floor
	up		down
2)	**wild/natural**	vs	**cultivated/artificial**
	briars		castle
	hedge of thorns		door/doorway
	hacked		room/tower
			spiral staircase
3)	**outside**	vs	**inside**
	outside		inside
	hedge of thorns		castle
			door/doorway

With indications of time, there is an opposition between durativeness (a continual process) and punctuality (happening at one particular moment in time):

durativeness	vs	**punctuality**
a long time		on your sixteenth birthday
for fifteen years		the day . . . arrived
as the years passed by		at once
		one day . . . a hundred years later

For actors, the key oppositions that emerge are old versus young, fairies versus humans, male versus female:

old	vs	**young**
old woman/lady		baby
old man		daughter
		new princess
		baby princess
		young prince
		girl

fairies	vs	**humans**
all the fairies		King and Queen
seventh fairy		daughter/princess
bad-tempered/		old lady/guests/cook
wicked fairy		prince/old man

male	vs	**female**
King		Queen
prince		daughter/princess
old man		bad-tempered fairy
		old lady

Within this isotopy of the actors there is also an opposition between plural and singular. Notations such as 'all the fairies', 'everyone', 'all the people', 'all the rooms' are contrasted with references to individual people and places.

And finally, within the isotopy of states of being, notations of 'death' are contrasted with those of 'life'; notations of 'sleep' with those of 'awake'.

We must now ask ourselves: What do these oppositions signify? With what values are they being invested by the narrator? As Denis Bertrand has commented,[2] the figurative level makes no sense on its own, it only acquires meaning in relationship to a subject – the narrator – and to the feelings and judgements of this narrator. It is at this point in our analysis, therefore, that we bring to bear what is known as the thymic category – the category related to the world of emotions/feelings and situated at the deep level of the utterance. This category is articulated in the opposition euphoria versus dysphoria (pleasant versus unpleasant) and gives rise to a basic positive/negative evaluation.

In *Sleeping Beauty* the opposition euphoria versus dysphoria is of particular significance in the construction of the actors. As is customary in the fairy-tale, divisions between pleasant and unpleasant, happy and sad, positive and negative are very clear-cut and unambiguous. The reader is left in no doubt as to where her/his sympathies should lie.

Bearing this in mind, we can extract the following isotopies and oppositions:

1) The isotopy of the emotions with the opposition euphoria versus dyphoria:

euphoria	vs	**dysphoria**
joy		unhappy
happiness		bad-tempered
excited		furious
surprise		spitefully
amazed		hissed
fell in love		with horror
happy life		

Here positive emotions are associated with one group of actors – the King, Queen, princess, prince and seven fairies – whereas the negative are linked (with one exception at the beginning) with the wicked fairy. A process of evaluation is clearly taking place, producing a second grouping:

2) The isotopy of evaluative terms (physical and moral) with the opposition positive versus negative:

	positive	vs	**negative**
physical	beautiful		
	beauty		
	lovely		
	wonderful		
	magnificent		
	graceful		
	gentle		
	handsome		
	health		

moral	goodness	evil
	kindness	wicked
	kindest	curse
	good	cunningly

Positive physical terms are associated with the princess – beauty, grace, health. These are coupled with positive moral terms: goodness, kindness. The prince is described as handsome but he is not invested explicitly with any moral attributes. Implicitly, however, he could be linked to curiosity ('impatient to find out whether it was true') and determination. The other actors in the story are devoid of any physical attributes. The fairies, for example, are evoked in exclusively moral terms: the seven good fairies and the one wicked one.

Figurativity and grammatical/syntactical features

The illusion of the real may be strengthened through the use of linguistic devices such as repetition, ellipsis, active/passive, nominalization and cohesive markers. In our particular version of *Sleeping Beauty*, adapted for very young children, the sentence structure is very simple. What is striking is the frequent use of temporal connectors particularly at the beginning of sentences, for instance: 'there once', 'not long after', 'after a magnificent feast', 'on your sixteenth birthday', 'for fifteen years', 'at last', 'no sooner', 'at once', 'immediately', 'as the years passed by', etc. The effect is to heighten the drama and pace of a narrative in which the passage of time is itself an important theme.

Another interesting device is the use of repetition – a characteristic feature of children's writing. Nouns are frequently employed to refer to people where it would be more customary to use a pronoun. For instance, the terms 'the wicked fairy', 'the good fairy' are repeated in close proximity. The effect once more is to heighten the drama by foregrounding the opposition between good and evil. A sense of symmetry is conveyed, of a universe that is highly ordered. The almost incantatory repetition of these two sets of terms in the last paragraph has the effect of reassuring the child that the threat has been lifted, and that the good is restored.

Further linguistic devices worthy of attention include the use of lists (e.g. The King and Queen ..., The guests ..., The cook ...'), the frequent positioning of the subject (human) at the beginning of a sentence and finally, the marked preference for the active voice.

The enunciative component

The enunciative strategies are clearly those of traditional story-telling. The narrator is third-person and extradiegetic (i.e. not an actor in the story). This hidden narrator is also omniscient in that the reader has access to the thoughts and emotions of all the actors. The story is told in the past, we are kept at a distance from the events recounted; indeed, telling itself becomes a narrative motif: it is the old man's account of what happened in the castle that prompts the prince to embark on his quest.

Looking at the use of modality – the degree of the speaker's adherence to a statement – the utterances are of a categorical nature. They express certainty on the part of the narrator, there are no tentative utterances suggesting probability or possibility. An impression of narratorial distance and of complete objectivity is thereby conveyed.

At the same time, however, the presence of a narrator – of a subjectivity – can be discerned indirectly in the abundant use of evaluative terms. The sharp divisions between positive and negative, good and evil that we analysed above suggest a particular interpretation of reality or vision of the world.

The enunciative strategies employed in *Sleeping Beauty* thus contribute to a strong sense of reality and to a fictive world whose authenticity is never open to doubt or to questioning. The explicit and clearly delineated categorization – whether in terms of space, time or the actors – serves to reassure the reader, and the child in particular, suggesting a world that is stable and inherently meaningful.

The narrative level

The next stage in our analysis will be an examination of what is known as the narrative level. More abstract than the figurative, this is the level of story-structure proper, that is, the level at which underlying universal narrative models operate (see Introduction).

These models can be applied globally to a whole story and/or they can be applied to smaller units or episodes. In order to decide on our approach, it may be helpful to answer the following question: What is (are) the principal event(s)? In other words, what is (are) the principal transformation(s)? If we are having difficulty in selecting key transformations, it may be useful to try to summarize the plot in one or two sentences. It may also help to look at the end of the story – the final event – and compare it with the beginning.

In *Sleeping Beauty* two principal transformations are apparent:

1) the princess pricks her finger and falls to sleep for a hundred years
2) after a hundred years a prince arrives, wakes her (breaks the spell) and marries her.

These transformations are also marked on the surface level by actorial and temporal disjunctions: after the feast (her birthday party), the princess meets an apparently new actor (an old woman) who gives her the spindle with which she pricks her finger; another new actor (the prince) arrives on the scene 'one day, a hundred years later'. The story thus falls neatly into two parts or two major episodes (narrative programmes). Our analysis will therefore mirror this pattern. The divisions will be: Part 1: from the beginning to 'Nearly everyone forgot about the King and Queen and their beautiful daughter'; Part 2: from 'But one day, a hundred years later' to the end.

We begin by examining the distribution in each of the two parts of the text of the six/seven key narrative roles outlined in the **actantial narrative schema** (see Introduction):

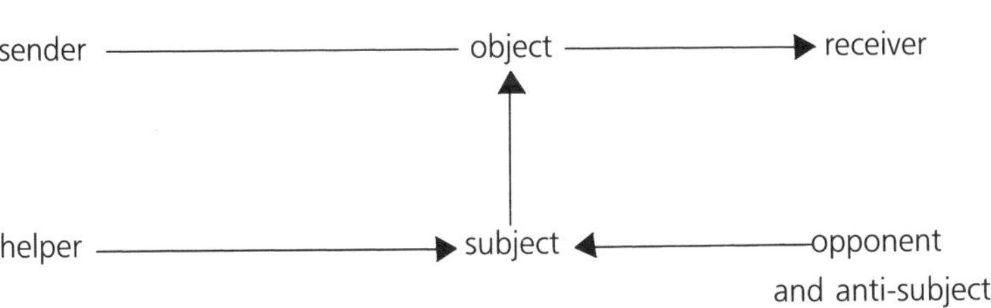

The following questions should be asked of the text:

1) Who (person or persons) is the subject of the quest? The subject is usually the main protagonist but the role can also be enacted by a group of people such as the miners in Emile Zola's *Germinal*.
2) Who or what is the object of the quest? Is there more than one object? The object may be concrete such as money or abstract such as knowledge.
3) Does the subject have helpers and/or opponents? If so, who or what are they?
4) Who is the anti-subject and what is the goal of the anti-subject's quest? An anti-subject, unlike an opponent, possesses its own goal or quest which is in opposition to that of the subject.

5) Who or what is the sender? In other words: what motivates the quest of the subject?

In Part 1 of *Sleeping Beauty* the distribution of narrative roles can be envisaged as follows:

Subject: the subject of a quest is the collective actor, the King and Queen.
Object: the quest has two objects, one concrete (or pragmatic) and one abstract (or cognitive). Concrete: to preserve the life of their daughter and to prevent the wicked fairy's spell from coming true. Abstract: to protect their daughter from all evil and to preserve the gifts/values of Beauty, Happiness, Goodness, Health, Gracefulness and Kindness that she embodies. To see the triumph of good over evil.
Helper: an implied helper are the subjects of the King and Queen who try to burn all the spinning wheels in the land. The magnificent party on the princess' sixteenth birthday is also designed as a helper: 'they thought that this would stop her from finding a spindle on that day'.
Opponent: the princess' desire to play hide-and-seek as well as her curiosity concerning the spinning wheel function as opponents.
Sender: the sender of the parents' quest to preserve the life of their daughter is the wicked fairy's curse that the good fairy can only weaken.
Anti-subject: the principal anti-subject is the wicked fairy herself who, in the guise of an old woman, lures the princess into touching the spinning wheel. The object of her quest is the destruction of the princess' life, that is, her goal is in conflict with that of the King and Queen. Her own sender is her desire for revenge.

The quest of the King and Queen fails: they do not succeed in protecting their daughter from evil. The quest of the wicked fairy succeeds (partially) in that the princess pricks her finger and falls to the ground 'as if she were dead'. The quest of the good fairy also succeeds, however, in that the princess sleeps rather than dies. To put it more abstractly, the values of Beauty, Happiness, Goodness, Heath, Gracefulness and Kindness lie dormant rather than being destroyed altogether.

Having examined the distribution of narrative roles in Part 1 of *Sleeping Beauty*, we go on to divide the quest into a number of logical stages in accordance with the **canonical narrative schema** (see Introduction). These stages are:

The contract

The contract is enacted in two episodes in the text: 1) the wicked fairy's curse and 2) the good fairy's desire to weaken the curse by changing death to sleep. By pronouncing the curse whose effect the good fairy can only mitigate, the wicked fairy incites in the King and Queen the desire and necessity to protect their daughter (both from death and falling asleep) – 'hoping to save his daughter' and implicitly to preserve the gifts she embodies. The King and Queen, now in possession of the modality of wanting-to-do and of having-to-do, become virtual subjects of a global narrative programme or quest.

The qualifying test

Hoping to acquire the ability to carry out his quest (a being-able-to-do), the King orders every spindle in the land to be burnt. However, his efforts meet only with partial success: we learn later that not all the spindles are destroyed. His competence is undermined by an anti-subject, the wicked fairy. Her intention is to harm the princess and, being in possession of supernatural, magic powers, she is stronger than the King.

The decisive test

The arrival and celebration of the princess' sixteenth birthday is the principal event (transformation) towards which the whole story has been moving; it is also the moment of confrontation between two opposing parties or forces. In this confrontation it is the wicked fairy – with her lure – who prevails over the father's attempts to protect his daughter.

The glorifying test

It is at this stage in the quest that the reader learns of the outcome of the decisive test, whether, for example, it has failed or succeeded. In other words, it is at this point that the decisive action is being evaluated. The princess falls asleep: it can be said, therefore, that the parents have failed in their quest to protect their daughter from the effects of evil. The narrator interprets the action of falling asleep as follows: 'At once she fell to the ground as if she were dead. The wicked fairy's curse had come true.' And the next paragraph adds: 'But the good fairy's spell came true, too, for the princess was not dead, only sleeping.'

This global narrative programme of the quest in the first part of the story is preceded by a couple of significant episodes (smaller narrative programmes). We recall here that a narrative programme designates a narrative unit expressing a transformation in the relationship between a subject and an object.

At the very beginning of the tale, the King and Queen are introduced as disjoined from their objects of value: a child and happiness. At the end of the paragraph, they are presented as conjoined with these objects: a baby and joy. This is followed by an episode conveying a similar narrative programme. The subject, the seven fairies, give to the princess a number of gifts which she thus acquires through a process of attribution. It is these objects (Beauty, Health, etc.) that, as we have seen, are at stake when the wicked fairy triggers the quest.

Let us now look at the second half of *Sleeping Beauty*, Part 2, commencing with the arrival of the prince and continuing to the end.

In the distribution of narrative roles in this section, the following pattern emerges:

Subject: the prince.
Object(s) of the quest: he wishes to discover if the old man's story about the princess is true. His aim, therefore, is to see the princess and implicitly (by reference to other familiar versions of the tale) to be the one who awakens her with a kiss. The object of his quest, again implicitly, may also be the pursuit of the values of Beauty, Kindness, etc., that is, the values represented by the gifts of the fairies, as well as that of love.
Helper(s): the prince's own impatience and impetuosity – 'impatient to find out whether it was true' together with his sword are helpers.
Opponent(s): the thorns and briars are initially his opponents – he 'started to hack at the briars', only to be transformed into helpers – 'the thorns seemed to part in front of him'.
Sender: with his story of the princess, the old man implants in the prince the desire to go on this quest.
Anti-subject: the prince meets with no resistance. A potential anti-subject, the wicked fairy, does not appear on the scene.

Let us now divide the prince's quest into the logical stages of the **canonical narrative schema**.

Contract

The old man arouses in the prince the desire to go on a quest. The prince accepts the contract and decides to act on his desire.

The qualifying test

The prince chops down the briars and thorns: by overcoming this obstacle he acquires the ability (a being-able-to-do) to attain his goal. In other words, he possesses the necessary competence enabling him to reach the castle and the princess.

The decisive test

The arrival in the small room in the high tower of the castle and kissing the princess constitute the decisive test or principal performance.

The glorifying test

We learn that the decisive test has been successful: the princess wakes up, the spell is broken, prince and princess fall in love. The marriage, a further episode in the glorifying test, can be considered a reward for the prince and a confirmation of the triumph of good – love and happiness – over evil. The wicked fairy's curse no longer has any power: 'nobody knew what happened to her, but she was never heard of again'.

Finally, a global view of the whole story – Part 1 plus Part 2 – still defines the King and Queen as the subject of a quest to protect their daughter from evil and death. In this perspective, however, the prince and his actions function as helper and the overall quest can be deemed successful.

The deep level

After analysing the discursive and narrative levels of meaning, we go on to examine the deep level, known also as the thematic level. This is the level of the abstract or conceptual: it relates to the inner world of the mind as opposed to the outer physical world of the figurative level. Most importantly, it is the level at which the fundamental values of the text are articulated. But how do we arrive at these values?

Let us begin by looking for the fundamental opposition(s) or transformation(s) underlying the text. To facilitate this task, it may be helpful to ask the following questions:

- Can we reduce all the oppositions found on the figurative and narrative levels to one or two basic umbrella oppositions that can function as a common denominator for the text?
- What are the two most abstract poles of meaning between which the text moves?
- What fundamental transformation of values is at stake? Here it might help to bear in might the object of the quest(s).

In *Sleeping Beauty*, a key opposition is that between evil and good. This opposition can be seen as an umbrella term encompassing on the figurative level the passage from high to low, sleep to awake, individual isolation to community.

The fundamental transformation between two poles of abstract meaning can be mapped out on a **semiotic square** (see Introduction). With regard to evil and good, the diagram illustrates relationships of contrariety and of contradiction (evil and non-evil). It also allows for the transformation in the story to be plotted.

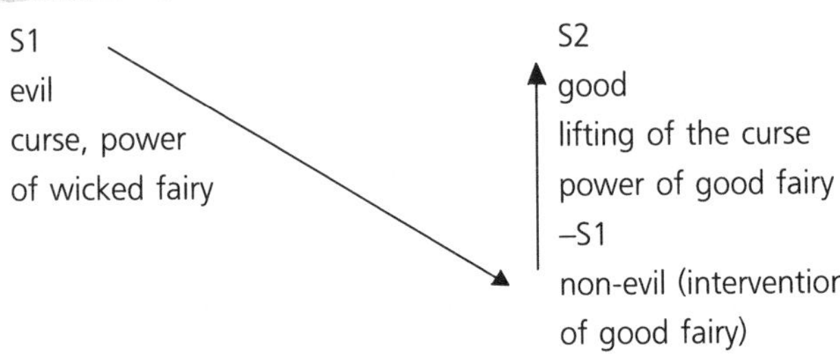

This transformation between evil and good parallels that between death and life:

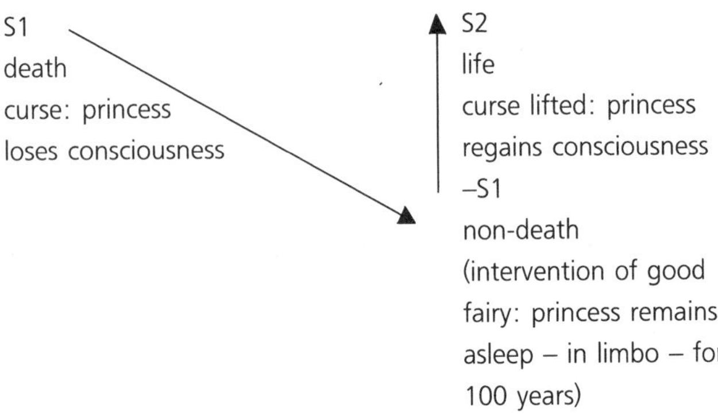

A third semiotic square could express these transformations in terms of the more specific values represented by the princess:

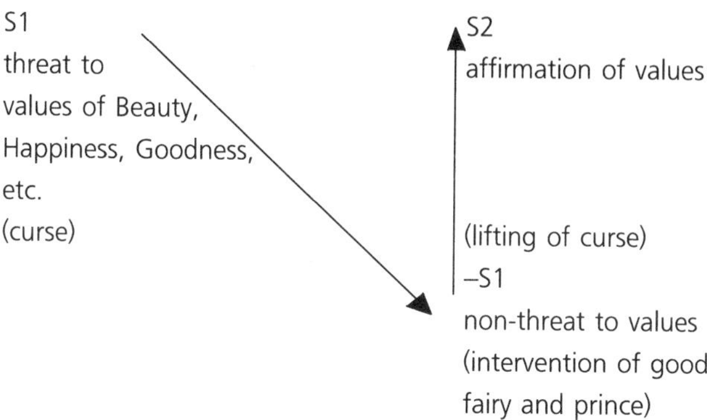

Text and context

Having ascertained the universal values underlying the text, we then open up the analysis to broader considerations of sociopolitical and cultural context. What additional values can be brought to bear on the text by the contemporary reader? How relevant is *Sleeping Beauty* to us today? Does the story, like many fairy-tales, lend itself to a multiplicity of levels of interpretation?

We would like to suggest, by way of introduction to this wider canvas of meaning, the following readings which are, of course, by no means exclusive[3]:

A) *Sleeping Beauty* can be envisaged as the embodiment of stereotypical attitudes

As such the story becomes a vehicle for strengthening social prejudice and social inequality in contemporary society. These attitudes – those generally associated with the traditional fairy-tale and with nineteenth-century romantic fiction – are prevalent in today's media and entertainment literature:

1) Men are active and women are passive. A woman needs the love of a man in order to truly exist, to bring out qualities that lie dormant. It is of course the prince who brings about the key transformation in *Sleeping Beauty*. He also possesses two important actantial roles, that of subject

of a quest and of helper. This contrasts with the princess who appears uniquely in the role of object of someone else's quest (be it that of the parents, the wicked fairy or the prince). In her versions of well-known fairy-tales, Angela Carter challenges this traditional distribution of gender roles: in Bluebeard's *The Bloody Chamber*, for example, it is the mother, arriving on her gallant steed, who finally rescues the heroine from the clutches of her husband.[4]

2) The story attaches great importance to the value of physical beauty – we noted the recurrence of this term in our examination of the figurative component. Implicitly, therefore, it is the beautiful people (the princess and the prince) who are successful in life and who attain their heart's desire. The text thereby legitimizes certain current practices: the tendency, for example, to offer the best jobs to the best looking. It thus ignores any contemporary concern with the notion of human/civil rights (rights of the disabled, etc.). As the concept of beauty is itself largely culturally determined, its overvaluation could fuel feelings of racism and xenophobia.

3) The story also links moral worth with physical beauty. As a baby, the princess is given the gifts of Beauty, Goodness and Kindness (in addition to those of Happiness, etc.). The handsome prince is implicitly associated with bravery: he has the courage and temerity to hack down the thorns around the castle. This linking of beauty with moral value is itself, of course, challenged by some conventional fairy-tales such as *Beauty and the Beast* (although the Beast eventually turns back into a handsome prince). It is further subverted by Angela Carter in, for example, her story *The Tiger's Bride*: here Beauty, far from being presented as good, is clearly attracted by acts of violence, sado-masochism and sexual perversion.[5]

4) *Sleeping Beauty* also associates beauty with, on the one hand, youth and, on the other, sexual love. From this point of view, too, the text can be said to reinforce a dominant ideology in Western society: it encourages an overestimation of youth and an accompanying devaluation of the later equally important stages in human life. Such attitudes lead to the dismissal and disparagement of older people in particular. These assumptions are forcefully challenged by, *inter alia*, G. Marquez in *Love in the Time of Cholera*, where old age sees the blossoming of physical love, beauty and passion.[6]

5) The text can furthermore be said to enact a number of fantasies. Most significant perhaps is the desire for eternal youth, recalling the Faust story. This desire in turn reflects an underlying and all-too-human fear of growing old, of change and of death.
6) In its focus on 'love at first sight', the story finally reinforces a number of stereotyped assumptions concerning the nature of love. The outcome of events – marriage followed by a long and happy life – rests on the supposition that love (together with physical beauty) will endure the test of time.

As a reflection of stereotypical attitudes and fantasies, *Sleeping Beauty* – and similar stories – have an important function within the contemporary debate concerning human/civil rights and how to foster in the younger generation the notion of world citizenship.[7] The story is not a text for passive consumption but demands a critical reading on the part of the reader – be it an adult or a child. As we have seen, this critical reading will necessarily go beyond the confines of the text itself. It should stimulate active discussion encompassing the wider canvas of contemporary social and philosophical issues.

B) The impact of *Sleeping Beauty* on the reader is not, however, entirely negative

Indeed, certain aspects of the text call for a positive, more 'liberatory' interpretation, one that is not without its own contemporary relevance. The story presents a self-contained meaningful universe in which the boundaries of good and evil are clearly delineated. In his seminal work *Language and Silence*, G. Steiner relates the increasing tendencies in our language usage to blur ethical frontiers to the growth of widespread political inhumanity in the twentieth century (e.g. the Holocaust).[8] In his novel *Le Chercheur d'or* [The Seeker for Gold] the contemporary French writer J. M. G. Le Clézio links the survival of being human, and of meaning itself, to a memory of this vital distinction between good and evil – a memory that is perpetuated in myth and in the fairy-tale.[9]

Not only, however, is the distinction between good and evil clear-cut and unambiguous. As we would also expect from a traditional fairy-story, the unfolding of events heralds the triumph of good over evil, the possibility that our goals may be achieved, that our dreams may come true. It thus foregrounds the value of hope – for many the mainspring of all human action – offering a healthy antidote to current tendencies to cynicism. Moreover, this triumph of positive values, be they aesthetic (Beauty), spiritual (Goodness, Kindness) or personal/psychological, takes place against all odds – the power of the wicked fairy is stronger than that of the good one – that is, it takes place against a backdrop of a realistic acceptance of the power of destructive forces within contemporary society. But, however strong these forces, positive qualities and creative energy can never be entirely destroyed. These values remain in a virtual state, in limbo (dormant) awaiting to be activated through the initiative of the individual. We may note here the theme of memory in *Sleeping Beauty* and its role in preserving these values from eventual oblivion and death: it is the recounting of the past by the old man that awakens the prince's curiosity to embark on the quest.

In addition to these predominantly moral and sociopolitical readings of the text, a more strictly mythical/religious interpretation is possible. Our analysis of the figurative component noted the division of space into 'high' and 'low'. This configuration (division) possesses symbolic and, according to Bachelard, archetypal connotations.[10] The 'high' is linked with semes of myth and magic (the princess pricks her finger and falls asleep). It also represents the spiritual dimension of eternal and universal values – those of Kindness, Goodness, etc. – that cannot be altered or destroyed by time. In contrast, the 'low' is associated with the historic space of social ceremony (christening, marriage, etc.). The princess, herself, inhabits both these dimensions.

Sleeping Beauty presents, therefore, a mythical non-Cartesian view of the world. Like many fairy-tales, it challenges the hegemony of reason, suggesting the workings of powerful unseen and irrational forces. Its insights – meanings – are clearly of relevance to contemporary debates on the nature of the human subject. Indeed, present-day psychologists and philosophers, in their attempt to elaborate ever more complex models of the self, increasingly draw upon folk-tales and myth for their source of inspiration.

Notes

1. Taken from: Tim and Jenny Wood, *Favourite Fairy Tales* (London: Conran Octopus, 1988), pp. 4–7.
2. *Narrativity and Discursivity*, Paris School Semiotics, vol.1, transl. P. Perron and F. Collins (Amsterdam/Philadelphia: Benjamins, 1989).

3. *Sleeping Beauty* lends itself, for example, to psychological readings. See, *inter alia*, Bruno Bettleheim, *The Uses of Enchantment: The Power and Importance of Fairy Tales* (London: Thames and Hudson, 1976).
4. Angela Carter, *The Bloody Chamber and Other Stories* (Penguin, 1979).
5. *The Bloody Chamber and Other Stories*, pp. 51–67.
6. Penguin, 1985 (translated by Edith Grossman).
7. The philosopher Habermas, for example, links the concept of world citizenship to an agreed acceptance amongst all nations of a number of key moral values/codes.
8. *Language and Silence* (Pelican Books, 1969).
9. Paris: Gallimard, 1985.
10. For Bachelard the enclosed space of the attic is also linked to the semes of intimacy and of refuge. See *La Poétique de l'espace* (Paris: Presses Universitaires de France, 1957).